CHAUCER

CHAUCER

by

G. K. CHESTERTON

GREENWOOD PRESS, PUBLISHERS
NEW YORK

Originally published in 1956 by Pellegrini & Cudahy

Reprinted by permission of Dorothy Collins

First Greenwood Reprinting 1969

SBN 8371-2237-6

PRINTED IN UNITED STATES OF AMERICA

Contents

5

Introduction

If I were writing this in French, as I should be if Chaucer had not chosen to write in English, I might be able to head this preliminary note with something like *Avis Au Lecteur*; which, with a French fine shade, would suggest without exaggeration the note of warning. As it is, I feel tempted to write, 'Beware!' or some such melodramatic phrase, in large letters across the frontispiece. For I do really desire to warn the reader, or the critic, of some possible mistakes in or about this book: touching its real purpose and its inevitable pitfalls.

It were perhaps too sanguine a simplicity to say that this book is intended to be popular; but at least it is intended to be simple. It describes only the effect of a particular poet on a particular person; but it also expresses a personal conviction that the poet could be an extremely popular poet; that is, could produce the same effect on many other normal or unpretentious persons. It makes no claim to specialism of any sort in the field of Chaucerian scholarship. It is written for people who know even less about Chaucer than I do. It does not in any of the disputed details, dictate to those who know much more about Chaucer than I do. It is primarily concerned with the fact that Chaucer was a poet. Or, in other words, that it is possible to know him, without knowing anything about him. A distinguished French critic said of my sketch of an English novelist that it might well bear the simple

Introduction

title, 'The Praise of Dickens'; and I should be quite content if this tribute only bore the title of 'The Praise of Chaucer'. The whole point, so far as I am concerned, is that it is as easy for an ordinary Englishman to enjoy Chaucer as to enjoy Dickens. Dickensians always quote Dickens; from which it follows that they often misquote Dickens. Having long depended on memory, I might be quite capable of misquotation; but I fear I have fallen into something that may seem even more shocking: a sort of irregular popular translation. I do incline to think that it is necessary to take some such liberties, when first bringing Chaucer to the attention of fresh and casual readers. However that may be, all this part of the explanation is relatively easy; and the intention of the book is tolerably obvious.

Unfortunately this plan of simplification and popularity is interrupted by two problems, which can hardly be prevented from presenting a greater complexity. In the second chapter, I plunged rather rashly into the wider historical elements of Chaucer's age; and soon found myself among deep tides that might well have carried me far out of my course. And yet I cannot altogether regret the course that I actually followed; for there grew upon me, while writing this chapter, a very vivid realization which the chapter itself does not very clearly explain. I fear that the reader will only pause to wonder, with not unjust irritation, why I sometimes seem to be writing about modern politics instead of about medieval history. I can only say that the actual experience, of trying to tell such truths as I know about the matter, left me with an overwhelming conviction that it is because we miss the point of the medieval history that we make a mess of the modern politics. I felt suddenly the fierce and glaring *relevancy* of all the walking social symbols of the Chaucerian scene to the dissolving views of our own social doubts and

Introduction

speculations to-day. There came upon me a conviction I can hardly explain, in these few lines, that the great Types, the heroic or humorous figures that make the pageant of past literature, are now fading into something formless; because we do not understand the old civilized order which gave them form, and can hardly even construct any alternative form. The presence of the Guilds or the grades of Chivalry, the presence of the particular details of that day, are not of course necessary to all human beings. But the absence of the Guilds and the grades of Chivalry, and the absence of any positive substitute for them, is now a great gap that is none the less a fact because it is a negative fact. Feeling this so strongly, at the moment, I simply could not force myself to the usual stiff official attitude of dealing with all such things as dead; of talking of Heraldry as if it were Hieroglyphics or dealing with the friars as if they had disappeared like the Druids. But I apologize for the disproportion of the second chapter, which spoils the simplicity of the opening and the general intention. Perhaps I might put up my notice of warning, and warn the reader not to read the second chapter. Now I come to think of it, I might warn him not to read the book at all; but in this, perhaps, there would be a tinge of inconsistency. Nevertheless, the book would have served its purpose if anyone had learned, even by getting as far as this page, that what matters is not books on Chaucer, but Chaucer.

Lastly, it would be affectation on my part to deny that the very subject forces me to face (or as ostentatiously to avoid) a subject on which I am in a sense expected to be controversial; on which I could not really be expected to be non-controversial. But this problem is all the more practical, because of the particular summary, or main truth about Chaucer, which is most borne in upon my mind, on rereading and reconsidering his work. Chaucer

9

Introduction

was a poet who came at the end of the medieval age and order; which certainly contained fanaticism, ferocity, wild asceticism and the rest. There are some who really suggest that it contained only fanaticism, ferocity and the rest. Anyhow, I was faced with the fact that Chaucer was the final fruit and inheritor of that order. And I was also confronted with the fact, which seems to me quite as certain a fact, that he was much *more* sane and cheerful and normal than most of the later writers. He was less delirious than Shakespeare, less harsh than Milton, less fanatical than Bunyan, less embittered than Swift. I had in any case to construct some sort of theory in connexion with this practical problem and this practical fact. Therefore in this book I advance the general thesis; that, in spite of everything, there was a balanced philosophy in medieval times; and some very unbalanced philosophies in later times.

I am sorry; I could easily have ended differently; it would be much more simple and sociable to treat Chaucer only as a charming companion and sit down with him at the Tabard without further questioning about whence he came. But something is due to conviction; my book was bound to make some attempt to explain Chaucer; and this is the only way I can explain him.

G. K. C.

Chapter I

THE GREATNESS OF CHAUCER

It is beginning to be realized that the English are the eccentrics of the earth. They have produced an unusually large proportion of what they used to call Humorists and would now perhaps rather call Characters. And nothing is more curious about them than the contradiction of their consciousness and unconsciousness of their own merits. It is nonsense, I regret to say, to claim that they are incapable of boasting. Sometimes they boast most magnificently of their weaknesses and deficiencies. Sometimes they boast of the more striking and outstanding virtues they do not possess. Sometimes (I say it with groans and grovellings before the just wrath of heaven) they sink so low as to boast of not boasting. But it is perfectly true that they seem to be entirely unaware of the very existence of some of their most extraordinary claims to glory and distinction. One example among many is the fact that they have never realized the nature, let alone the scale, of the genius of Geoffrey Chaucer.

I say advisedly the scale; for what seems to me altogether missed is the *greatness* of Chaucer. Men say the obvious things about him; they call him the Father of English Poetry, but only in the sense in which the same title has been given to an obscure Anglo-Saxon like Cædmon. He also has been called the Father of English Poetry, though what he wrote is not in that sense poetry and not in any sense English. They say that Chaucer marks

The Greatness of Chaucer

the moment when our language began to be formed out of French and Saxon elements; but they see nothing elemental about the man who did so much to form it. They say (probably falsely) that Chaucer borrowed from Boccaccio the notion of a framework of stories; and they admit that he brightened it a little by giving more personality to the tellers of the Canterbury Tales. They admit (sometimes with a faint air of surprise) that this fourteenth-century man was acquainted with the nature of a joke; they concede a certain courtesy and urbanity, and then generally turn with relief to digging up the old original dull stories which Chaucer made interesting. In short, there has been perceptible, in greater or less degree, an indescribable disposition to *patronize* Chaucer. Sometimes he is patted on the head like a child, because all our other poets are his children. Sometimes he is treated as the Oldest Inhabitant, partially demented and practically dead, because he was alive before anybody else in Europe to certain revolutions of the European mind. Sometimes he is treated as entirely dead; a bag of dry bones to be dissected by antiquarians, interested only in matters of detail. But in no common English ears, as yet, does his name actually sound as a thunderclap or a trumpet-peal, like the name of Dante or of Shakespeare. It may seem fanciful to say so, but the name of Chaucer has not yet completely achieved the sound of a *serious* thing. It is partly the popular sense that Early English is a sort of Pidgin English. It is partly the penanic prejudice that medieval civilization was not civilized. It is partly a sheer incapacity to thank those who have given us everything, because we cannot imagine anything else.

The medieval word for a Poet was a Maker, which indeed is the original meaning of a Poet. It is one of the points, more numerous than some suppose, in which Greek and medieval simplicity nearly touch. There was

The Greatness of Chaucer

never a man who was more of a Maker than Chaucer. He made a national language; he came very near to making a nation. At least without him it would probably never have been either so fine a language or so great a nation. Shakespeare and Milton were the greatest sons of their country; but Chaucer was the Father of his Country, rather in the style of George Washington. And apart from that, he made something that has altered all Europe more than the Newspaper: the Novel. He was a novelist when there were no novels. I mean by the novel the narrative that is not primarily an anecdote or an allegory, but is valued because of the almost accidental variety of actual human characters. The Prologue of *The Canterbury Tales* is the Prologue of Modern Fiction. It is the preface to *Don Quixote* and the preface to *Gil Blas*. The astonishing thing is not so much that an Englishman did this as that Englishmen hardly ever brag about it. Nobody waves a Union Jack and cries, 'England made jolly stories for the whole earth'. It is not too much to say that Chaucer made not only a new nation but a new world; and was none the less its real maker because it is an unreal world. And he did it in a language that was hardly usable until he used it; and to the glory of a nation that had hardly existed till he made it glorious.

I know not why the people who are so silent about this go about glorying in the fact of having painted Tasmania red in an atlas or introduced the golf of Tooting to the upper classes of Turkey. But it is certain that, while some of them have (if it were possible) overrated the greatness of Shakespeare, most of them have unaccountably underrated the greatness of Chaucer. Yet most of the things that are hinted in depreciation of Chaucer could be said as easily in depreciation of Shakespeare. If Chaucer borrowed from Boccaccio and other writers, Shakespeare borrowed from anybody or anything, and often from the same

13

The Greatness of Chaucer

French or Italian sources as his forerunner. The answer indeed is obvious and tremendous; that if Shakespeare borrowed, he jolly well paid back. But so did Chaucer, as in that very central instance I have named; when he turned the decorative picture-frame of the Decameron into the moving portrait-gallery of the ride to Canterbury.

It is worth noting, touching that patronizing tone towards the childishness of Chaucer, that there is very much the same patronizing tone in many of the earlier compliments to Shakespeare. In the case of Shakespeare, as of Chaucer, his contemporaries and immediate successors seem to have been struck by something sweet or kindly about him, which they felt as too natural to be great in the grand style. He is chiefly praised, and occasionally rebuked, for freshness and spontaneity. Is it unfair to find a touch of that patronizing spirit even in the greatest among those who were less great?

> *Or sweetest Shakespeare, fancy's child,*
> *Warble his native wood-notes wild.*

I suspect Milton of meaning that his own organ-notes would be of a deeper and grander sort than wood-notes so innocently warbling. Yet somehow, as a summary of Shakespeare, the description does not strike one as comprehensive. Hung be the heavens with black . . . have lighted fools the way to dusty death . . . the multitudinous seas incarnadine . . . let the high gods, who keep this dreadful pother o'er our heads, find out their enemies now—these do not strike us exclusively as warblings. But neither, it may respectfully be submitted, are all the wood-notes of Chaucer to be regarded as warblings. There are things in Chaucer that are both austere and exalted, such as certain lines in his religious poems, especially his addresses to the Blessed Virgin; there are things in Chaucer that are both grim and violent, such as the description of

The Greatness of Chaucer

the death-blow that broke the neck of the accuser of Constance. And if he only occasionally rises to the grand or descends to the grotesque, it is not obvious that he is the less like life for that.

These examples, I may say in passing, afford an opportunity to say a word of explanation, even at this stage, about the spelling and diction of Chaucer and how I have decided to deal with it. In this also Chaucer suffers from a somewhat unfair disadvantage as compared with Shakespeare. Much of Shakespeare, as a matter of fact, was actually printed in an old spelling which would make many familiar lines look fantastic or awkward. Shakespeare's old English was near enough to be easily modernized; Chaucer's old English was just remote enough to make it hard to do so while preserving the accent and melody. Nobody can read it, indeed, without wishing that some of its antiquated words were in modern use. The wretched scribe, starving for descriptive terms, will find many which he will envy the scribe of the fourteenth century. Indeed, the two examples I have given themselves illustrate the point. There is no nobler image of the ideal, in the ideal sense of that vulgarized term, than that single glimpse in Chaucer:

> *Virgin, that art so noble of apparail*
> *That leadest us unto the highë tower*
> *Of Paradise . . .*

nor can I ever read it without a sort of vision, of a garden tilted on a remote turret and a woman in trailing raiment, splendiferous like a comet, going up a winding stair. But, incidentally, what a pity that we cannot say 'apparail', instead of being dismally reduced to saying 'apparel'. And, oddly enough, there is a similar detail in the other instance I took at random; for when the slanderer of Constance was 'strook' so as to break his neck-bone, we have the pleasing

15

The Greatness of Chaucer

further fact that his eyes 'brast out of his head'; which is going about as far as grotesque violence will go. But will not the envious man of letters think pensively and tenderly about the possibilities of the word 'brast'? When the sensational novelist makes the hero burst the bonds knotted by the atrocious Chinaman, how much better if he brast them! When the comic novelist says that Mr. Pobbles burst his collar, how much more forcible if he brast his collar! For this reason there is every argument for leaving Chaucer's language as it stands, and even admitting its superiority for some of Chaucer's purposes. Nevertheless, for reasons which I shall explain more fully elsewhere, I propose in many cases boldly to modernize the Chaucerian language, and especially for the purpose that is immediate here: that of showing that Chaucer was great in the sense in which Matthew Arnold connected greatness with what he called 'high seriousness' and the grand style.

Let anyone knowing only the popular and patronizing impression of a merry gossip or warbling court minstrel, suppose that he has presented to him without context or criticism merely such a verse as this, printed as I have printed it:

> *Such end hath, lo, this Troilus for love:*
> *Such end hath all his greatë worthiness,*
> *Such end hath all his royal estate above,*
> *Such end his lust, such end his nobleness,*
> *Such end hath all the false world's brittleness:*
> *And thus began his loving of Creseid*
> *As I have told; and in this wise he died.*

Nobody who knows what English is will say that that verse is not dignified. Nobody who knows what tragedy is will say it is unworthy of a tragic poet. The words and spelling are not exactly as Chaucer wrote them, but they

The Greatness of Chaucer

represent with some reasonable worthiness what Chaucer meant us to read. Now if anybody is so excruciatingly fond of the expression 'swich fin' that he desires to mingle it with his daily talk, as I have desired to use 'brast' and 'apparail', it will be easy for him (by the laborious literary research involved in looking at the book) to discover that 'swich fin' is Chaucerian for 'such end' and to convict me of having poisoned the well of English undefiled. But I will modestly yet obstinately repeat that it does not give the modern reader an idea of the dignity, that was in Chaucer's mind and gesture, to repeat 'swich fin' five times; especially as we do not know how Chaucer pronounced it and are almost certainly pronouncing it wrong.

Here, however, I have introduced this quotation in a quotable form, in order to emphasize the fact that Chaucer was capable of greatness even in the sense of gravity. We all know that Matthew Arnold denied that the medieval poet possessed this 'high seriousness'; but Matthew Arnold's version of high seriousness was often only high and dry solemnity. That Chaucer was, in that passage about Troilus, speaking with complete conviction and a sense of the greatness of the subject (which seem to me the only essentials of the real grand style) nobody can doubt who reads the following verses, in which he turns with terrible and realistic scorn on the Pagan gods with whom he had so often played. I have mentioned these matters first to show that Chaucer was capable of high seriousness, even in the sense of those who feel that only what is serious can be high. But for my part I dispute the identification. I think there are other things that can be high as well as high seriousness. I think, for instance, that there can be such things as high spirits; and that these also can be spiritual.

Now even if we consider Chaucer only as a humorist, he was in this very exact sense a great humorist. And by

The Greatness of Chaucer

this I do not only mean a very good humorist. I mean a humorist in the grand style; a humorist whose broad outlook embraced the world as a whole, and saw even great humanity against a background of greater things. This quality of grandeur in a joke is one which I can only explain by an example. The example also illustrates that clinging curse of all the criticism of Chaucer; the fact that while the poet is always large and humorous, the critics are often small and serious. They not only get hold of the wrong end of the stick, but of the diminishing end of the telescope; and take in a detail when they should be taking in a design. The Chaucerian irony is sometimes so large that it is too large to be seen. I know no more striking example than the business of his own contribution to the tales of the Canterbury Pilgrims. A thousand times have I heard men tell (as Chaucer himself would put it) that the poet wrote *The Rime of Sir Topas* as a parody of certain bad romantic verse of his own time. And the learned would be willing to fill their notes with examples of this bad poetry, with the addition of not a little bad prose. It is all very scholarly, and it is all perfectly true; but it entirely misses the point. The joke is not that Chaucer is joking at bad ballad-mongers; the joke is much larger than that. To see the scope of this gigantic jest we must take in the whole position of the poet and the whole conception of the poem.

The Poet is the Maker; he is the creator of a cosmos; and Chaucer is the creator of the whole world of his creatures. He made the pilgrimage; he made the pilgrims. He made all the tales that are told by the pilgrims. Out of him is all the golden pageantry and chivalry of the Knight's Tale; all the rank and rowdy farce of the Miller's; he told through the mouth of the Prioress the pathetic legend of the Child Martyr and through the mouth of the Squire the wild, almost Arabian romance of Cambus-

18

can. And he told them all in sustained melodious verse, seldom so continuously prolonged in literature; in a style that sings from start to finish. Then in due course, as the poet is also a pilgrim among the other pilgrims, he is asked for his contribution. He is at first struck dumb with embarrassment; and then suddenly starts a gabble of the worst doggerel in the book. It is so bad that, after a page. or two of it, the tolerant innkeeper breaks in with the desperate protest of one who can bear no more, in words that could be best translated as 'Gorlumme!' or 'This is a bit too thick!' The poet is shouted down by a righteous revolt of his hearers, and can only defend himself by saying sadly that this is the only poem he knows. Then, by way of a final climax or anticlimax of the same satire, he solemnly proceeds to tell a rather dull story *in prose*.

Now a joke of that scale goes a great deal beyond the particular point, or pointlessness, of *The Rime of Sir Topas*. Chaucer is mocking not merely bad poets but good poets; the best poet he knows; 'the best in this kind are but shadows'. Chaucer, having to represent himself as reciting bad verse, did very probably take the opportunity of parodying somebody else's bad verse. But the parody is not the point. The point is in the admirable irony of the whole conception of the dumb or doggerel rhymer who is nevertheless the author of all the other rhymes; nay, even the author of their authors. Among all the types and trades, the coarse miller, the hard-fisted reeve, the clerk, the cook, the shipman, the poet is the only man who knows no poetry. But the irony is wider and even deeper than that. There is in it some hint of those huge and abysmal ideas of which the poets are half-conscious when they write; the primal and elemental ideas connected with the very nature of creation and reality. It has in it something of the philosophy of a phenomenal world, and all that was meant by those sages, by no means pessimists, who have

The Greatness of Chaucer

said that we are in a world of shadows. Chaucer has made a world of his own shadows, and, when he is on a certain plane, finds himself equally shadowy. It has in it all the mystery of the relation of the maker with things made. There falls on it from afar even some dark ray of the irony of God, who was mocked when He entered His own world, and killed when He came among His creatures.

That is laughter in the grand style, *pace* Matthew Arnold; and Arnold, with all his merits, did not laugh but only smiled—not to say smirked. It is the presence of such things, behind the seeming simplicity of the fourteenth-century poet, which constitutes what I mean here by the greatness of Chaucer. He was a man much less commonplace than he appeared; I think that he deliberately appeared. He had so great a faith in common sense that he seems to have accepted with a smile the suggestion of the commonplace. But he was not commonplace. He was not superficial. His judgments are sufficient to show that he was not superficial. There is perhaps no better example of it than his journey to Italy and probable friendship with Petrarch, who was crowned with universal acclamation in the Eternal City as the one and only supreme and universal poet of the age; nor indeed was the admiration of the age undeserved. Petrarch was a poet, a prophet, a patriot, almost everything except what he was called, the greatest genius alive. It is typical of the neglected side of Chaucer that he admired Dante more than Petrarch.

It may be questioned, in passing, whether this understanding is understood. Dante was very different from Chaucer; but he was not so utterly different as the sound of the two names would now generally imply. It must be remembered that people began to talk patronizingly of a cheerful or almost chirpy Chaucer, at the very time when they talked about a merely Byronic or melodramatic Dante. Those who see Dante as something to be illus-

The Greatness of Chaucer

trated by Doré might well be content that Chaucer should be illustrated by Stothard. But there was another Chaucer who was illustrated by Blake. There was an element in Chaucer that was symbolic to the eye of a serious mystic. A medieval writer actually said that Chaucer's *House of Fame* had put Dante into English. And though this is an extravagant exaggeration, it is not (as some would think) an extravagant contrast. There is much more of Dante in the description of Chaucer, as he is whirled aloft by the golden eagle of the gods, feeling that Thought can lift us to the last heaven with 'the feathers of philosophy', than there is in the ordinary nineteenth-century notion that Dante was a dark and lowering Dago who was really only at home in Hell. Chaucer caught sight of the eagle; his tale is not always 'of a cock'. Yet he is greatest perhaps with the cock and not the eagle. He is not a great Latin epic poet; he is a great English humorist and humanist; but he is great. The very case of the cock in the Nun's Priest's Tale is concerned with richer and deeper things than a mere fable about animals. It is not enough to talk, as some critics do, about Reynard the Fox or the Babrian origins. Just as they mainly insist that 'Sir Topas' is a parody, so they are chiefly struck by the fact that the fable is a fable. Curiously enough, in actual fact, it is either much more or much less than a fable. The interpretation is full of that curious rich native humour, which is at once riotous and secretive. It is extraordinarily English, especially in this, that it does not aim at being neat, as wit and logic are neat. It rather delights in being clumsy; as if clumsiness were part of the fun. Chaucer is not accepting a convention; he is enjoying a contradiction. Hundreds of years afterwards, a French poet was struck by the strutting parody of humanity in the poultry yard, and elaborated the same medieval jest, giving the cock the same medieval name. But the Chantecler of Rostand, with its many beautiful

21

The Greatness of Chaucer

and rational epigrams in the French manner, has about it a sort of exact coincidence of mimicry, which fits it to the province of an actor. Rostand is pleased, as a stage manager, with the aptness of making a man act like a cock. Chaucer is pleased with the absurdity of making a cock act like a man. These are aesthetic and psychological impressions, about which nobody can prove anything; but I am pretty certain that Chaucer revelled, I might say wallowed, in the wild disproportion of making his little farmyard fowl talk like a philosopher and even a scholar. The chicken in question is hatched from the works of Aristotle and Virgil; the Song of Roland, or at least the Carolingian legend; and was also (it is reassuring to know) very properly instructed in the Gospels. In a speech of great eloquence, the fox is compared to Ganelon and Judas Iscariot and to the Greek who betrayed Troy to its downfall. The cock's oration involves a deep dissertation on the reliability of Dreams, and their relation to the problem of freewill, fate and the foreknowledge of heaven; all considered with a sensitive profundity of which any chicken-run may well be proud. In other words, in one sense the very sense of all this is its nonsense; at least its aptitude is its ineptitude. It is always difficult to make the fable, or even the four-footed animal, go on all fours. In this case Chaucer does not care if his two-footed animal has a leg to stand on. It has to limp as well as strut; the whole fun of the fable is in its being lop-sided; and he only partially disguises his biped in feathers. Then, when the imposture is quite obvious, he delights in asserting it again, allowing, as it were, his cock to hide hurriedly behind the one feather it has left. I can imagine nothing more English, or more amusing, than this exasperating evasion. He launches a denunciation of Woman as the destroyer of Paradise, and then explains to the ladies, as with a bow and a beaming smile:

The Greatness of Chaucer

If I the counsel of woman woldë blame
Pass over, for I said it in my game . . .
These be the cockë's wordës and not mine,
I can none harm of no woman divine.

There is something intensely individual in this playing
in and out of the curtain, and putting on and off of the
feathered mask. It is all the more subtle because nobody
who reads Chaucer as a whole will doubt that, despite
his occasional and probably personal grumblings against
some faithless or scornful woman, he did really have a respect for women, which was not merely a bow to ladies.
But if there is something here of subtlety, there is also
something here of scope or scale. There is a largeness and
liberty in the humorist who gets such huge enjoyment out
of the metaphysical chicken, and expands so large a world
of fancy out of the little opportunity of the fable. That is
the quality in Chaucer which I would here emphasize first,
because it should be realized before we go on to the
secondary matters of origins and parallels and interpreta-
tions of particular points. The mind of Chaucer was
capacious; there was room for ideas to play about in it.
He could see the connexion, and still more the discon-
nexion, of different parts of his own scheme, or of any
scheme. In the first example of 'Sir Topas', he com-
pletes his own scheme with his own incompleteness. In
the second example we find him taking the tiny opening
of a trivial farmyard fable, to expand it into an almost
cosmic comedy. He seems to see himself as a small
featherless fowl talking about the riddle of Destiny and
Deity. Both have the same quality, not very easy to describe, the quality by which a very great artist sometimes
allows his art to become semi-transparent, and a light to
shine through the shadow pantomime which makes it confess itself a shadowy thing. So Shakespeare, at the highest

23

moment or two of his happiest comedies, utters those deep and not unhappy sayings, that the best in this kind are but shadows, and that we are such stuff as dreams are made on, and our little life is rounded with a sleep. I say that this deeper note does exist in Chaucer, for those who will start with sufficient sympathy to listen for it, and not be content with some crabbed inquisition into whether he stole something from Petrarch or wrote something to please John of Gaunt. For one thing is quite certain; nobody who takes Chaucer quite so literally, I might say quite so seriously, will ever understand him. There is a sort of penumbra of playfulness round everything he ever said or sang; a halo of humour. Much of his work is marked by what can only be called a quiet exaggeration, even a quiet extravagance. It is said, in the description of him, that there was something elvish about his face; and there was something elvish about his mind. He did not object to playing a kind of delicate practical joke on the reader, or on the plan of the book; and all this may be summed up here, for convenience, under the example I have given. He did not mind making his fable something more than fabulous. He enjoyed giving a touch or two to the story of a cock and hen; that made it look like the story of a cock and bull.

We shall see more of this double outlook when we come to the conjectures about his private life, and especially about his personal religion. For the moment the matter to be established is a matter of scale or size; the fact that we are not here dealing with a mind to be merely patronized for its simplicity, but with a mind that has already baffled many commentators with its complexity. In one sense he is taken too seriously and in the other sense not seriously enough. But in both senses, almost as many men have lost themselves in Chaucer's mind as have lost themselves in Shakespeare's. But in the latter case they are like children wondering what their father means; in the

24

The Greatness of Chaucer

former, like beaming uncles, wondering what the child means.

I mean that in the popular attitude towards Chaucer, and to some extent even in the more cultured criticism of him, there is a curious and rather comic suggestion of 'drawing him out'. I have said elsewhere that to many modern Englishmen a fourteenth-century Englishman would be like a foreigner. These modern Englishmen do really treat Geoffrey Chaucer as a foreigner. Some of them treat him very much as Mr. Podsnap treated the foreign gentleman. It will be remembered that that worthy merchant not only talked to the alien as if he must necessarily be slightly deaf, but as if he was in every other way defective, and had to have things put very plainly to him in words of one syllable. Yet Mr. Podsnap was really encouraging the foreign gentleman; he was drawing him out. Only there was a general feeling of pleased surprise that there was anything there to be drawn out. Chaucer is treated as a child, just as the foreign gentleman was treated as a child; but I am sure that Chaucer was quite sufficiently subtle to be as much amused at it as the foreign gentleman. Hence it will be generally found, even now, that anything like a problem or puzzle in Chaucer is approached quite differently from a problem or puzzle in Shakespeare. When somebody finds one of the Sonnets as dark as the Dark Lady, he admits that it is just possible that Shakespeare's mind may have been slightly superior to his own. But he has made up his mind that Chaucer's mind must have been more simple than his own, merely because Chaucer lived at the most complicated and entangled transitional time in European history, and drew on the traditions of about four European literatures instead of one. We shall get no further till we allow for this central and civilized character in the medieval poet; for the fact that he knew his philosophy; that he thought

25

about his theology; and for the still more surprising fact that he saw the joke of the jokes he made, and made a good many more jokes than his critics have ever seen.

There is indeed one character, which Chaucer shares with all the great ancient poets, which may in some quarters weaken his position as a great modern poet. There are many moderns who say that a man is not a thinker, when they mean he is not a freethinker. Or they say he is not a freethinker, when they mean that his thinking is not tied tight and fast to some special system of materialism. But the point I mean is much deeper than these mere quarrels about secularism and sectarianism. The greatest poets of the world have a certain serenity, because they have not bothered to invent a small philosophy, but have rather inherited a large philosophy. It is, nine times out of ten, a philosophy which very great men share with very ordinary men. It is therefore not a theory which attracts attention as a theory. In these days, when Mr. Bernard Shaw is becoming gradually, amid general applause, the Grand Old Man of English letters, it is perhaps ungracious to record that he did once say there was nobody, with the possible exception of Homer, whose intellect he despised so much as Shakespeare's. He has since said almost enough sensible things to outweigh even anything so silly as that. But I quote it because it exactly embodies the nineteenth-century notion of which I speak. Mr. Shaw had probably never read Homer; and there were passages in his Shakespearean criticism that might well raise a doubt about whether he ever read Shakespeare. But the point was that he could not, in all sincerity, see what the world saw in Homer and Shakespeare, because what the world saw was not what G. B. S. was then looking for. He was looking for that ghastly thing which Nonconformists call a Message, and continue to call a Message, even when they have become atheists and do not know

The Greatness of Chaucer

who the Message is from. He was looking for a system, one of the very little systems that do very truly have their day. The system of Kant; the system of Hegel; the system of Schopenhauer and Nietzsche and Marx and all the rest. In each of these examples a man sprang up and pretended to have a thought that nobody had ever had. But the great poet only professes to express the thought that everybody has always had. The greatness of Homer does not consist in proving, by the death of Hector, that the Will to Live is a delusion and a snare; because it is not a delusion and a snare. It does not consist in proving, by the victory of Achilles, that the Will to Power must express itself in a Superman; for Achilles is not a Superman, but, on the contrary, a hero. The greatness of Homer consists in the fact that he could make men feel, what they were already quite ready to think, that life is a strange mystery in which a hero may err and another hero may fail. The poet makes men realize how great are the great emotions which they, in a smaller way, have already experienced. Every man who has tried to keep any good thing going, though it were a little club or paper or political protest, sounds the depths of his own soul when he hears that rolling line, which can only be rendered so feebly: 'For truly in my heart and soul I know that Troy will fall.' Every man who looks back on old days, for himself and others, and realizes the changes that vex something within us that is unchangeable, realizes better the immensity of his own meaning in the mere sound of the Greek words, which only mean, 'For, as we have heard, you too, old man, were at one time happy.' These words are in poetry, and therefore they have never been translated. But there are perhaps some people to whom even the words of Shakespeare need to be translated. Anyhow, what a man learns from *Romeo and Juliet* is not a new theory of Sex; it is the mystery of something much more

27

than what sensualists call Sex, and what cads call Sex Appeal. What he learns from *Romeo and Juliet* is not to call first love 'calf-love'; not to call even fleeting love a flirtation; but to understand that these things, which a million vulgarians have vulgarized, are not vulgar. The great poet exists to show the small man how great he is. A man does not learn from Hamlet a new method of Psycho-analysis, or the proper treatment of lunatics. What he learns is not to despise the soul as small; even when rather feminine critics say that the will is weak. As if the will were ever strong enough for the tasks that confront it in this world! The great poet is alone strong enough to measure that broken strength we call the weakness of man.

It has only been for a short time, a recent and disturbed time of transition, that each writer has been expected to write a new theory of all things, or draw a new wild map of the world. The old writers were content to write of the old world, but to write of it with an imaginative freshness which made it in each case look like a new world. Before the time of Shakespeare, men had grown used to the Ptolemaic astronomy, and since the time of Shakespeare men have grown used to the Copernican astronomy. But poets have never grown used to stars; and it is their business to prevent anybody else ever growing used to them. And any man who reads for the first time the words, 'Night's candles are burnt out,' catches his breath and almost curses himself for having neglected to look rightly, or sufficiently frequently, at the grand and mysterious revolutions of night and day. Theories soon grow stale; but things continue to be fresh. And, according to the ancient conception of his function, the poet was concerned with things; with the tears of things, as in the great lament of Virgil; with the delight in the number of things, as in the light-hearted rhyme of Stevenson; with thanks for things, as in

The Greatness of Chaucer

the Franciscan Canticle of the Sun or the *Benedicite Omnia Opera*. That behind these things there are certain great truths is true; and those so unhappy as not to believe in these truths may of course call them theories. But the old poets did not consider that they had to compete and bid against each other in the production of counter-theories. The coming of the Christian cosmic conception made a vast difference; the Christian poet had a more vivid hope than the Pagan poet. Even when he was sometimes more stern, he was always less sad. But, allowing for that more than human change, the poets taught in a continuous tradition, and were not in the least ashamed of being traditional. Each taught in an individual way; 'with a perpetual slight novelty,' as Aristotle said; but they were not a series of separate lunatics looking at separate worlds. One poet did not provide a pair of spectacles by which it appeared that the grass was blue; or another poet lecture on optics to teach people to say that the grass was orange; they both had the far harder and more heroic task of teaching people to feel that the grass is green. And because they continue their heroic task, the world, after every epoch of doubt and despair, always grows green again.

Now Chaucer is a particularly easy mark for the morbid intellectual or the mere innovator. He is very easily pelted by the pedants, who demand that every eternal poet should be an ephemeral philosopher. For there is no nonsense about Chaucer; there is no deception, as the conjurers say. There is no pretence of being a prophet instead of a poet. There is no shadow of shame in being a traditionalist or, as some would say, a plagiarist. One of the most attractive elements in the curiously attractive personality of Chaucer is exactly that; that he is not only negatively without pretentiousness, but he is positively full of warm acknowledgement and admiration of his models. He is as awakening as a cool wind on a hot day, because he breathes forth

29

The Greatness of Chaucer

something that has fallen into great neglect in our time, something that very seldom stirs the stuffy atmosphere of self-satisfaction or self-worship. And that is gratitude, or the theory of thanks. He was a great poet of gratitude; he was grateful to God; but he was also grateful to Gower. He was grateful to the everlasting Romance of the Rose; he was still more grateful to Ovid and grateful to Virgil and grateful to Petrarch and Boccaccio. He is always eager to show us over his little library and to tell us where all his tales come from. He is prouder of having read the books than of having written the poems. This easy and natural traditionalism had become a little more constrained and doubtful even by the time of the Renaissance. There is no question of Shakespeare concealing or disguising his borrowed plots; but we do feel that he dealt with them as mere dead material, of no interest until he made it interesting. He did in a sense destroy the originals by making the infinitely more mighty and magnificent parodies. Even great originals sink under him; he comes to bury Plutarch not to praise him. But Chaucer would want to praise him; he always confesses a literary pleasure which may well conceal his literary power. He seems the less original, because he is concerned to praise and not merely to parody. There is nothing he likes better than telling the reader to read books that are not his own books; as when the Nun's Priest expansively refers the company to the numerous works dealing with the subject of Woman, which excuse him from justifying the sentiments of a cock or further analysing the defects of a hen. Perhaps, by the way, there is a Chaucerian joke, of the sort that is called sly, in making the Confessor of the Nuns (of all men) say that he, for his part, knows no harm about any woman. It is the same in any number of passages, as in that admirably cheerful passage that begins:

The Greatness of Chaucer

A thousand timës have I heard men tell
That there is joy in heaven and pain in hell,
And I accord right well that it is so,
And yet indeed full well myself I know
That there is not a man in this countrie
That either has in heaven or hell y'be,

and which goes on to explain that these things rest on Authority; and that we must depend on Authority for many things, especially the things of which we can only read in books. It is typical of the obtusity of some partisans that this passage has been quoted as evidence of scepticism, when it is in perfectly plain words a justification of faith. But the point is that Chaucer talks in that cheerful voice, or writes in that almost jaunty style, because he is not in the least ashamed of depending on 'oldë bookës', but exceedingly proud of it, and, above all, exceedingly pleased to testify to his own pleasure. This is a temper which will always seem 'unoriginal' to the sensational sectarian; or the quack with a new nostrum; or the monomaniac with one idea. Yet, as a fact of literary history, Chaucer was one of the most original men who ever lived. There had never been anything like the lively realism of the ride to Canterbury done or dreamed of in our literature before. He is not only the father of all our poets, but the grandfather of all our hundred million novelists. It is rather a responsibility for him. But anyhow, nothing càn be more original than an origin.

When we have this actual originality, and then added to it this graceful tone of gratitude and even humility, we have the presence of something which I will venture to call great. There is in the medieval poet something that can only be conveyed by the medieval word Largesse; that he is too hearty and expansive to conceal the connexion between himself and his masters or models. He would not stoop to ignore a book in order to borrow from it; and it does not occur to him to be always trying to secure the copyright of a copy. This is the sort of cool and contented character that looks much less original than it is. A man must have a balance of rather extraordinary talents, and even rather extraordinary virtues, in order to seem so ordinary. As they say of St. Peter's at Rome, it is so well proportioned that it looks almost small. To the eyes of sensational innovators, with their skyscraper religions toppling and tumbling, and conspicuous by their crazy disproportion, it does look very small. But it is in fact very large; and there is nothing larger in its way than the spirit of Chaucer, with its confession of pleasure and its unconsciousness of power.

May I be pardoned if I insert a sort of personal parenthesis here? All this does not mean, what I should be the last man in the world to mean, that revolutionists should be ashamed of being revolutionists or (still more disgusting thought) that artists should be content with being artists. I have been mixed up more or less all my life in such mild revolutions as my country could provide; and have been rather more extreme, for instance, in my criticism of Capitalism than many who are accused of Communism. That, I think, is being a good citizen; but it is not being a great poet; and I should never set up to be a great poet on any ground, but least of all on that ground. A great poet, as such, deals with eternal things; and it would indeed be a filthy notion to suppose that the present industrial and economic system is an eternal thing. Nor, on the other hand, should the idea of the poet dealing with things more permanent than politics be confounded with the dirty talk of the 'nineties, about the poet being indifferent to morals. Morals are eternal things, though the particular political immorality of the moment is not eternal. Here again I can modestly claim to have cleared my-

The Greatness of Chaucer

self long ago of the horrid charge of being a True Artist.
I have been mixed up in politics, but never in aesthetics;
and I was an enthusiast for the Wearing of the Green, but
never for the Wearing of the Green Carnation. In those
days I even had something like a prejudice against pure
Beauty; there seemed to be very much the wrong sort of
betrothal between Beauty and the Beast. But, for all that,
it is true that the true poet is ultimately dedicated to
Beauty, in a world where it is cleansed of beastliness, and
it is not either a new scheme or theory on the one hand,
nor a narrow taste or technique on the other. It is concerned with ideas; but with ideas that are never new in the
sense of neat, as they are never old in the sense of exhausted. They lie a little too deep to find perfect expression in any age; and great poets can give great hints of
them in any. I would say no more of Chaucer than that
the hints that he gave were great.

There is at the back of all our lives an abyss of light,
more blinding and unfathomable than any abyss of darkness; and it is the abyss of actuality, of existence, of the
fact that things truly are, and that we ourselves are incredibly and sometimes almost incredulously real. It is
the fundamental fact of being, as against not being; it is
unthinkable, yet we cannot unthink it, though we may
sometimes be unthinking about it; unthinking and especially unthanking. For he who has realized this reality
knows that it does outweigh, literally to infinity, all lesser
regrets or arguments for negation, and that under all our
grumblings there is a subconscious substance of gratitude.
That light of the positive is the business of the poets, because they see all things in the light of it more than do
other men. Chaucer was a child of light and not merely
of twilight, the mere red twilight of one passing dawn of
revolution, or the grey twilight of one dying day of social
decline. He was the immediate heir of something like

33

The Greatness of Chaucer

what Catholics call the Primitive Revelation; that glimpse
that was given of the world when God saw that it was
good; and so long as the artist gives us glimpses of that,
it matters nothing that they are fragmentary or even
trivial; whether it be in the mere fact that a medieval
Court poet could appreciate a daisy, or that he could write,
in a sort of flash of blinding moonshine, of the lover who
'slept no more than does the nightingale'. These things
belong to the same world of wonder as the primary wonder
at the very existence of the world; higher than any common pros and cons, or likes and dislikes, however legiti-
mate. Creation was the greatest of all Revolutions. It was
for that, as the ancient poet said, that the morning stars
sang together; and the most modern poets, like the medieval poets, may descend very far from that height of realization and stray and stumble and seem distraught; but we
shall know them for the Sons of God, when they are still
shouting for joy. This is something much more mystical
and absolute than any modern thing that is called opti-
mism; for it is only rarely that we realize, like a vision of
the heavens filled with a chorus of giants, the primeval
duty of Praise.

Chapter II

THE AGE OF CHAUCER

One of the most necessary and most neglected points, about the story called history, is the fact that the story is not finished. Generally speaking, we do not realize a problem of the past till we realize it as a problem of the present, and even of the future. This is what was really the matter with the 'liberal' historians of the nineteenth century. No men talked more about the future, as something different from the past. No men thought less about the future, as something different from the present. The Victorians are somewhat excessively derided to-day, because their notion of a novel was a story that ended well. The real vice of the Victorians was that they regarded history as a story that ended well—because it ended with the Victorians. They turned all human records into one three-volume novel; and were quite sure that they themselves were the third volume. History had come to an end; if not to a cessation, at least to a consummation. Therefore their doubts about the past were easily resolved, because they were not really troubled by doubts about the future. Whatever had obviously led to their own Constitutionalism or Commercialism was good. They did not really ask to what their Constitutionalism and Commercialism would lead. We, on the other hand, know where they have already led. They have led us to where we are at present; and where that is, the Lord only knows.

There are four facts about Chaucer, which are the four

The Age of Chaucer

corners of the world he lived in; the four conditions of Christendom at the end of the fourteenth century. In themselves they can be stated very simply. Chaucer was English; at a time when the full national identity was still near its beginning. Chaucer was Catholic; at a time when the full Catholic unity of Europe was near the beginning of its end. Chaucer was chivalric, in the sense that he belonged, if only by adoption, to the world of chivalry and armorial blazonry, broadly French, when that world was in its gorgeous autumn, glorious with decay. Finally, Chaucer was none the less *bourgeois*, as our dear comrades say, in the sense that he himself was born and bred of burgesses, of tradesmen working under the old Guild system, also already rather too grand for its own good, but fresher and stronger than the fading feudal system. His figure bestrides the gap between these two last systems. It is as if he had the Trade Guild for a mother and the Order of Knighthood for a father.

Now we cannot understand any of these things by dismissing them as dead things, as the nineteenth century did, and never thinking of their application to our own present or future. We cannot, like the Victorians, talk about them as if they were stone hatchets or wattle houses; things obviously left behind in the past. They are no longer only in the past but also in the future; if not as possibilities at least as comparisons. Take the first two together; for they were parts of one problem. If we think (and rightly) that Rome did not adequately realize the growth of national life in the north, we must still follow the idea further; at least as far as the time when patriotism turned into Prussianism. Quite apart from religion, we must realize that there was a case, and may again be a case, for Europe having a centre. And we must anticipate, in the future, many pathetic attempts of Europe to be centralized without a centre. It is the same with the two last as with the two first of the four conditions. We may reasonably or even rightly think that society was fettered by feudal heraldry; but we must understand exactly what we lost by losing it. Similarly, we may think that trade was fettered by Guilds; but our own trade is not so happy just now that we can forget the Guild, without understanding exactly what we lost by losing it. Touching all these things, we must try to imagine, not so much merely what is to be said for them, as what is to be said against the absence of them.

I have therefore decided, after some doubt and reflexion, to dwell a little further on each of these four conditions; to dwell at what some may think disproportionate length on the real reason for their presence in those days, and the real problem of their absence in these days. All are subject to one formula. We have not seen the last of any of them, but if they are really lost in the future, it may yet turn out to be through losing the forms they had in the past. I will preface these four brief sketches by two generalizations. The great medieval civilization had already been wounded, perhaps mortally wounded, by two great griefs; the first material and the other moral. The first was the Black Death, which turned Christendom into a house of mourning, and had dreadful results of every kind; the worst being that priests became so few, and bad priests had so easily become priests, that the whole great Christian philosophy and morality was brought into contempt. The second fatality, I think, was the failure of the Crusades, which remained as a sort of hopeless taunt or challenge never accepted. Half the men of Chaucer's time were haunted by a Crusade that never happened. His friend Froissart tells how Bruce sent his heart to Palestine, whither he had failed to go; his patron Henry of Bolingbroke consoled himself by dying in the Jerusalem Chamber after his failure to go to Jerusalem.

37

The Age of Chaucer

As will be seen in a moment, in more ways than one, the Crusade was a sort of dark background of judgment to all the bright and brittle triumphs and scandals of that day.

First, the special spirit of Chaucer as an Englishman I have dealt with at length in the chapter under that name. It is only necessary to note here one fact that was really peculiar to England, which, unlike the Church and the Chivalric Orders and the Guilds, was not common to all Europe. This was the particular break in the history of the Plantagenets. By this time England had ceased to be a King and his people, and had become a group of gentlemen and their servants. It is but a bitter consolation to call them the best gentlemen and the best servants. Everywhere else, whatever was lost by the Pope was gained by the King. Sometimes it happened even though the King were a Catholic King. The French King had already made a monopoly of the Papacy; the Spanish King was later to attempt to make a sort of monopoly of the Church; and even the English King did, for a brief and brazen hour of triumph, become Head of the Church. But whatever happened to the English King, this was not what happened to the English nation. There another and special force was already at work, which was destined to make the triumph of the King as brief as it was brazen. That fact was the evolution of the Aristocratic State, which begins far back in Chaucer's time and before; chiefly by an alliance between the Barons and the great merchants of the City of London. It thus touches the life of Chaucer at two points, since his people were London traders and his patrons were, at least partly, of the baronial party. It was also mixed up with the problem of the peasants, or those who regarded themselves as peasant proprietors, while the lawyers still regarded them as serfs. They therefore rose in the famous Peasant Rising and killed the lawyers; a comprehensible and (relatively) even commendable course;

though they also showed some disposition to hang anybody who could read or write; which is perhaps carrying the distrust of professionalism too far. But with all this Chaucer had less to do, being a Londoner and, on his more popular side, a son of the Guilds and not the peasantry. Nevertheless, it was at the Court, where he counted for a good deal, that the whole quarrel of kings, barons, merchants and peasants came to a crisis and a crash.

The life and death of Richard the Second constitute a tragedy which was perhaps the tragedy of English history, and was certainly the tragedy of English monarchy. It is seldom seen with any clearness; because of two prejudices that prevent men letting in on it the disinterested daylight of their minds. The first is the fact that, though it happened more than five hundred years ago, it is still dimly felt to be a Party Question. Shakespeare, in the time of the Tudors, saw it as an opportunity for exalting a sort of Divine Right; later writers, in the time of the Georges, have seen in it an opportunity for depreciating Divine Right. What is much more curious is the fact that neither ever noticed that the unfortunate Richard did not by any means merely stand for Divine Right; that in his earliest days he stood for what we are accustomed to consider much later rights, and for some which were, at least relatively speaking, the rights of democracy. The origin of this oblivion is in the second of the two modern prejudices. It is the extraordinary prejudice, sometimes identified with progress, to the effect that the world has always been growing more and more liberal, and that therefore there could be no popular ideals present in earlier times and forgotten in later times. The case of Richard the Second might have been specially staged in order to destroy this delusion. He was very far from being a faultless sovereign; he did various things which permit modern

39

The Age of Chaucer

Parliamentarians to represent him as a despotic sovereign; but he was, by comparison with many contemporaries and most successors, a democratic sovereign. He did definitely attempt to help the democratic movement of his day, and he was definitely restrained from doing so. Shakespeare is full of sympathy for him, but Shakespeare was not full of sympathy for what most modern people would find sympathetic. He does not even mention the fact that the prince, whom he represents as bewailing the insult to his crown, and appealing to the sacred immunity of his chrism, had in his youth faced a rabble of roaring insurgent serfs, had declared that he himself would be their leader, the true demagogue of their new democracy, had promised to grant their demands, had disputed desperately with his nobles to get those demands granted, and had finally been overruled and forced to abandon the popular cause by that very baronial insolence which soon forced him to abandon the throne. If we ask why the greatest of dramatists was blind to the most dramatic of historic scenes, the young king claiming the leadership of the oppressed people, the explanation is perfectly simple. The explanation is that the whole theory, that 'the thoughts of men are widen'd with the process of the suns', is all ignorant rubbish.

How could the suns widen anybody's thoughts? The explanation is that the men of Shakespeare's time understood far less of the democratic ideal than the men of Chaucer's time. The Tudors were occupied in their own time, as Shakespeare is occupied in his great play, with the sixteenth-century mystical worship of The Prince. There was much more chance in the fourteenth century of having a mystical feeling about The People. Shakespeare's Richard is religious, to the extent of always calling himself The Lord's Anointed. The real Richard would also, very probably, have referred to the people as God's Flock.

The Age of Chaucer

Ideas were mixed and misused in both periods, as in all periods; but in the time of Chaucer and Langland there was much more vague and general moral pressure upon the mind of the presence of problems of mere wealth and poverty, of the status of a peasant or the standards of a Christian, than there was in the time of Shakespeare and Spenser; of the splendour of Gloriana and the Imperial Votaress in the West. Therefore Shakespeare, great and human as he was, sees in Richard only the insulted king; and seems to think almost as little about the subjects of Richard as about the subjects of Lear.

But Richard had thought about the subjects of Richard. He had, in his early days and in his own way, tried to be a popular king in the sense of a popular leader. And though the popular ideas failed, and in some cases were bound to fail, they would have been much more present to the mind of a great writer of that time, than they were to the mind of one of the Queen's Servants under the last of the Tudors. In other words, even when there really is progress, as there certainly is growth, the progress is not a progress in everything, perfectly simple and universal and all of a piece. Civilizations go forward in some things, while they go backward in others. Men had better looms and steam hammers in 1850 than in 1750, but not handsomer hats and breeches or more dignified manners and oratory. And in the same way a man in the position of Shakespeare had more subtle and many-coloured arts, but not more simple and popular sympathies, than a man in the position of Langland. The Renaissance exalted the Poet, but even more it exalted the Prince; it was not primarily thinking about the Peasant. Therefore the greatest of all the great sons of the Renaissance, rolling out thousands of thunderous and intoxicant lines upon the single subject of the reign of King Richard the Second, does not trouble himself about The Peasants' War.

41

The Age of Chaucer

The real stories of this world are not melodramas or fables with a moral, and we seldom see simple retribution for a simple crime or even simple martyrdom for a simple idea. Nobody maintains that Richard was dethroned on the direct issue of the frustrated popular sympathies of his youth; he was dethroned for the somewhat simpler reason that he had an unscrupulous relative who wanted his throne. Nor need anyone maintain that there were no other excuses for the dethronement; though almost certainly there was no other motive. But the fact remains that there did disappear, with the last true Plantagenet, the last true attempt of the monarch to take the side of the mob against the governing class; and it is certain that since that day, and for centuries increasingly, the mob in England has been impotent and the governing class has governed. A profound instinct told our modern historians that with the quarrel of Richard and Bolingbroke the true Party System had begun. They might be more or less indifferent to York and Lancaster, and admit that the tangle and thicket of the Wars of the Roses mostly consisted of thorns. But the long quarrel of English history was not between the Lancastrians and the Yorkists, but between the Lords and the King. Long before we were born the Lords had completely conquered; and the historian could at least see that the first blow was struck at Pomfret, three hundred years before the last blow was struck at Whitehall.

Here is the first typical instance; showing that medieval history is useless unless it is modern history. The problem has remained; anyhow it has returned. The general view of government by a gentry, even in its best sense, must be affected by the present problem of whether it ought to continue; whether it can continue; whether a thing so undefined and atmospheric can be restored. It is not at all impossible that the age following Maurras and

The Age of Chaucer

Mussolini may want Monarchy restored. It is one thing to tolerate the rich because they are gentlemen; and another to tolerate the bounders because they are rich. The latest phase of the thing may be seen in what is called the Public School tradition; the final outcome of the fact that medieval schools dedicated to poverty or pure learning were turned, after the Reformation, into the fenced training-camps of a governing class. The paradox of such a system, at this moment, is that it might really be easier to revive it as a medieval Public School than as a modern Public School. Anyhow, anybody can see that such associations are at the very instant of transition. The finest of Public School songs unconsciously confesses that even gazing at the past involves gazing at the future; and few will claim to know what will happen to that tradition, twenty or thirty or forty years on.

Next, as to the religious position: put these four facts together. Chaucer was a perfectly orthodox Catholic, and the English had hitherto been little interested in the old medieval heresies. But to them the Pope had begun to seem faintly foreign; *not* on the theory that he was an Italian priest in Rome, but, on the contrary, on the theory that he was a French priest at Avignon. The French King had carried the Papacy there; challenging the Schism and almost dragging it into the French Wars. The Papacy stood, of course, for the international ideal; but it stood for two other things, good or bad. First, for the Friars and such international movements which depended *only* on the Papacy. Second, for more dubious 'drives' of the Charity Bazaar sort; not always producing (or receiving) perfect charity. Lastly, there was a general discontent with the *practical* Christianity of the time; producing Lollards, the most practical (and therefore the most stupid) of heretics. But most men were Reformers without being Lollards.

43

The Age of Chaucer

Most wanted what was called 'a reform of the Head and Members'. Unfortunately too many, even at the later reforming councils of Basle and Constance, confined themselves rather to reforming the Head; because of the special horror of the two-headed monster of the Schism. It is by no means certain, however, that the Head was worse than the Members.

It is the paradox of history that the Pope was really more important after the Reformation than before it. He was always important to Catholics, of course, as the tribunal of truth in disputed matters; but as a political and social figure, he really bulks bigger in the modern world than he did in the medieval world; at least in the later medieval world. The reason for this is really very reasonable. His personal position had been diminished by division and rivalry. But his doctrinal position was rather more clearly defined after it had been defied. In the scandal of the Schism there had been two or even three Popes; whom various nations accepted. But in the supreme struggle of the Reformation there was only one Pope; even if he was one whom nations renounced. The proceedings of the Protestant nations who renounced him made it quite clear, for the first time, why the earlier nations had accepted him. Whoever was right or wrong in the quarrel, it became perfectly clear that those who quarrelled with the Pope began to quarrel with the Creed. There had been no hint of that sort of thing in the rather squalid squabble of the rival Popes of the Middle Ages. The Popes might make each other look foolish, or denounce each other as fools; but they did not denounce the Faith as folly. Nobody who attacked the Pope attacked the Papacy. Still less did anybody attack the Papacy in the sense of attacking the Church. Thousands of Christians were shocked and pained at the mere fact that a false Pope could put himself up against a real Pope. But.

44

they would not have been shocked, but startled out of their wits, if one of the Popes had stood up and said there was no such thing as Purgatory. They would not have felt pain, they would have felt mortal terror at a world gone mad, if a Pope had told another Pope to leave off talking nonsense about prayers for the dead or praise of the Blessed Virgin. When the nations that had broken away from the Papacy did begin to say things like this, an entirely new sort of importance began to attach to the Papacy from which they had broken away. Even the people who said these things could see that fact. They could see that the Pope was now the power who held a whole moral and metaphysical system together; as they themselves had proved, by parting with him in order to found a new moral and metaphysical system. But in the later Middle Ages, before the break had come in actual ecclesiastical government, the whole situation was much more vague and dim. People knew that the Pope was a part of the system; but the system was so solid and universal that they hardly thought that anything was needed to be the protector of the system. We must not look therefore to men in the age of Chaucer for any of that sharp partisanship, any more than that sharp antagonism, which afterwards came to clash over the position of the Roman Pontiff. A man like Chaucer would most certainly have been a furious Papist, if he had thought that the alternative was to be a Puritan. But he lived in a world which had not yet even seen a real Puritan. In that world, in that sense, and in that sense alone, we may say that such a man felt himself rather as a Catholic than as a Papist. He had no notion of what results would follow a real split in Christendom; for since the beginnings of such a split had been stopped by St. Dominic, in the Albigensian affair, there had never been anything to suggest such a catastrophe to such a Catholic layman. But the Catholic layman, especially the good Catholic layman, was very far from happy. He knew that things were going wrong; he knew that the Church ought to put them right; but he did not look at the Pope to put them right precisely as a Catholic would look to-day: and that all the less, in Chaucer's case, because the Pope was a prisoner of the French King—as Chaucer had been; the prisoner of an enemy.

Meanwhile, however, the Pope had long appeared to Europe in another aspect that had nothing to do with his theological 'authority, but which was destined more than any other accident to precipitate the disaster. He wanted to collect money for various objects; many of them normal, some of them rather of the Renaissance type of ambition; like that which was destined later on to bring about the break in Germany: the building of St. Peter's. The trouble was not so much what he was doing as the way in which the thing was done. The shortest way of describing it is to say, in modern language, that the Papacy condescended to employ up-to-date methods of Advertisement. It put its trust in people who professed to be a sort of Publicity Experts. In the religious atmosphere of the time, it took the form of going about delivering ranting sermons about the Indulgences attached to works of piety and charity; and then sending round the hat in the usual rather vulgar' fashion. But the trouble with these men, as with many Publicity Experts, was that there was nothing pious or charitable about *them*. They were only expert—and vulgar. It constantly happens, even now, when good people are so silly as to trust merely capable people. These hustling advertising agents dragged religion in the mire; but they got the money. But the root of the whole evil was there. It was that they had not been chosen as priests or preachers, not even as fanatical priests or preachers, but as what the Americans would call

The Age of Chaucer

live wires and go-getters. These in turn doubtless produced a rabble of imitators of yet more ragged reputation,
touts and cheapjacks entirely irresponsible, but familiar-
izing everybody with the idea of making the Faith a
stunt or (worse still) a business proposition. The contempt that normal Catholics felt for all this is written in
red-hot letters in Chaucer's account of the Pardoner.

When Chaucer says, in his vivid way, that the Pardoner
had pardon 'brought from Rome all hot', he means what
moderns call Hustle. But during part of this period, there
was another problem. Rome was not always situated in
Rome. The Pope of Avignon was rather unfairly regarded as a Frenchman because he was a prisoner of the
French. Often, of course, he was a Frenchman—for the
same reason. Chaucer's great contemporary Petrarch felt
the scandal, though not from the English standpoint, like
Chaucer. Petrarch also had his quarrel with the 'French'
Popes. He was perhaps most famous, after his love for
Laura, for his lamentations over Babylon; which was his
polite name for the city of Avignon, the French exile of
the Roman Pontiffs. Critics are beginning to be rather
more reasonable in discriminating, if not discrediting,
the religious denunciations of particular partisans in the
Middle Ages. We should allow for the fact that Petrarch
was a little partial to Laura; and we may well allow that
he was not entirely impartial about Avignon. The time
has gone by when any poet denouncing any Pope was
assumed to have the gift of Infallibility. Something may
be discounted in the invectives of Dante; more in the invectives of Petrarch; and something (which concerns us
more closely here) in the invectives of Chaucer, not indeed against any Pope or Anti-Pope, but against certain
religious groups or parties which were really, though only
relatively, connected with the Papacy.

It is a commonplace that Chaucer makes fun of the

47

The Age of Chaucer

Friar. Chaucer makes fun of so many people, that I always doubted whether we could lean so heavily as the learned do on the political or partisan significance of his satire. Still it may well be that, like Langland, he was of the party opposed to the Friars, probably because his sympathies were with the ordinary village priests. What is not so fully understood is that this question also was indirectly connected with the undercurrent of quarrel about the Popes. Men criticized the Roman officialism in many matters in which it was really wrong. But it is typical of its history that it was even then criticized, more severely, for an attitude in which it was right. It is impracticable to discuss fully here the merits of the quarrel about the Friars. There is a merely traditional anecdote that Chaucer, in early youth, was fined for fighting with a friar and knocking him about in Fleet Street. There is no historical proof of it; but, if it were true, it would be possible that his aversion to the friar in the story was as personal and accidental as his aversion to the friar in the street. Shakespeare is admitted to have been very fond of friars, even by those who regard him as an emancipated Englishman of the Elizabethan settlement. Chaucer is recognized as having uttered very violent and outspoken criticism of friars, even by those who regard him as the slave of a superstition that silences every criticism. It is perfectly possible that there were merely personal affections or aversions in both cases; and it is as likely that Chaucer was wrong as that Shakespeare was right. But many of the learned have thrown themselves into the quarrel with all the fury of Chaucer attacking the friar in Fleet Street; and have done their best to reproduce the edifying quarrel of the Frere and the Sompnour, in the interests of England or of Rome. As I say, these large historical matters cannot be adequately considered here. But in so far as we do consider them, it had better be upon principles that are really historical and really large.

48

The Age of Chaucer

The Sompnour, or Summoner, is an official of the ecclesiastical court, and he stands in this story for the ecclesiastical authorities actually ruling England, from the Archbishop of Canterbury downwards. The Frere, or Friar, stands for the Dominican and Franciscan Orders, of preaching and begging brethren, who claimed freedom from local jurisdictions and appealed direct to the Pope. It is always assumed that Chaucer was entirely on the side of the former, mainly because he makes a more or less amusing figure of the Friar. The argument might well be turned the other way; for he makes a most horrifying and revolting figure of the Summoner. Many a man would prefer to be satirized as the Friar, with his popularity and athletic prowess, his strong white neck and eyes twinkling like frosty stars, rather than to be championed in the person of the Summoner with his red eruptive visage, and pimples and rank onion-laden breath. If Chaucer really was championing the Church authorities of England against foreign friars, he seems to have chosen a queer sort of champion. But I have myself a dark suspicion that Chaucer was writing a poem, and especially telling a story; and that to him as an artist the vivid and coloured figures of the Summoner and the Friar were of much more importance than the interests they represented in ecclesiastical law. Nevertheless, as I have said, it is well to see the ecclesiastical and social situation in the large, if we see it at all. There were two sides to the dispute between the Friars and the national or parochial clergy, and there is one side that is almost entirely neglected and never certainly emphasized.

It will be found again and again, in ecclesiastical history, that the new departure, the daring innovation, the progressive party, depended directly on the Pope. It was naturally more or less negatively resisted by the bishops, the canons, the clergy in possession under political and

49

patriotic settlements. Official oligarchies of that sort generally do resist reform and experiment, either rightly or wrongly. It is no more peculiar to Catholics than to an Anglican Archdeacon talking about Bolshevism or a Baptist in Tennessee talking about Negro Education. But whenever there appeared, in Catholic history, a new and promising experiment, bolder or broader or more enlightened than existing routine, that movement always came to be identified with the Papacy; because the Papacy alone upheld it against the resisting social medium which it rent asunder. So, in the present case, it was really the Pope who upheld St. Francis and the popular movement of the Friars. So, in the sixteenth century, it was really the Pope who upheld St. Ignatius Loyola and the great educational movement of the Jesuits. The Pope, being the ultimate court of appeal, cannot for shame be a mere expression of any local prejudice; this may easily be strong among local ecclesiastics, without any evil intention; but the remote arbiter at Rome must make some attempt to keep himself clear of it. Thus arises the situation of which Chaucer very possibly complained, of which many in Chaucer's time certainly complained; that a particular set of men, more recent or less rooted than the parish clergy, talked as if they were the Pope's pet children, and need take no notice of anybody but him. Anybody can see that this could be an irritating attitude; but there were two sides to the question. The Friars or the Jesuits were partly irritating because they were innovating, and in many matters, especially at the beginning, improving. And the Pope often supported the improvement, because he alone was independent and strong enough to do so. The Pope was often very much in advance of the Church, as the Encyclical on Labour of Pope Leo XIII would have been very much in advance of many reactionary bishops and priests of his time. Protestants will not damage their Protestantism by understanding that for Catholics, in history, the Pope is a *leader* as well as a ruler.

By the time of Chaucer, indeed, it is likely enough that the movement of Dominic and Francis had passed its best period; and that the popular Friars were sometimes unpopular, with the people as well as the priests. It is quite probable; but the poet's personal jokes against friars do not prove it. Chaucer was no more certainly justified in abusing the friars in poetry than in belabouring the friar in Fleet Street; in both cases we should need to know a little more of the facts; a little more about the friars—and the friar. But it is worth while to note that Rome had originally supported an innovation in supporting the Friar; as later a less worthy innovation in supporting the Pardoner. Both came from Rome being in the centre of civilization and readier for new notions than the provinces were. If this was so about ideas that really were new, like those of St. Francis, it is the more obvious about ideas like the unity of nations, that never were new— except to very new people.

The international ideal, which seems so very modern to the moderns, was of course very ancient to the Popes. They had originally risen in a cosmopolitan community, covering the civilized world, and their real mistake was that they thought the world was more international than it was. But this is not a mistake of barbaric bigotry; it rather amounted to thinking the world more enlightened than it was. Anyhow, the misunderstanding between the national and international ideas had begun long before; even in the time of the English discontent about Peter's Pence. France, the first of the entirely national nations, had been responsible for the prolonged insult of Avignon. The monstrous progeny of Anti-Popes had been born largely out of the readiness of rival kingdoms to back rival Pontiffs. The nations, for good or evil, were be-

The Age of Chaucer

coming themselves; and it would doubtless have been better if the Popes had understood the process. But it is far from self-evident that the process was entirely what we now call a progress.

In any case, we have seen that the Church was heavily weakened by these three calamities. The Black Death which decimated the priesthood, leaving hardly enough priests to go round and admitting a good many who had much better not have gone round. The captivity of the Pope, who seemed to be in the pocket of the French King, and was defied by other Popes supported by other kings. And the uneasy conscience and general depression following on the failure of the Crusade. In this spiritual desert it was natural that there should appear prophets, whether we call them fanatics or reformers; and to some extent at least they were supported by a general discontent. It is very difficult to be fair to them to-day; because their ghosts have been set to lead armies that they never led, and would probably have refused to lead. Anybody who was born within three hundred years either way, of the one great crack or explosion of the sixteenth century, is dragged out of his grave to demonstrate as a Protestant or Papist, and carry a banner in a triumph of St. Bartholomew or the Boyne. Men like Wycliffe, living in Chaucer's time, had no notion of such things. They probably began by feeling a quite comprehensible sympathy with the hard-worked village priests, as against the monks, whose life should mean contemplation, and often did mean contemplation, but obviously might mean idleness. Whenever it really meant contemplation, it meant incessant activity. Generations before, the Friars had thus rebelled against the Monks; now a new school of Simple Preachers was rebelling against the Friars. But for events utterly different in origin, the Simple Preachers might have been absorbed by Christendom like the Friars—

and later had the honour of being denounced as decadent like the Friars. But there was another difference: and it did arise partly from the operation of a very ordinary human weakness.

Some historical critics seem to express a faint surprise that a number of people were sympathetic with Wycliffe up to a certain point, and then lost their sympathy with him. There is supposed to be a vague savour of this in a whole group, which included a gentleman named Chaucer (with whom we are more immediately concerned); another literary man like Langland; a great lord like John of Gaunt; possibly even a King like Richard the Second. Various explanations have been offered to this change or chill in their relations to the reformers. John of Gaunt was one of those rather dangerous aristocrats who have too much activity for their intelligence; and, being rather stupid, probably prided himself on being broadminded. It is said that he felt a faint coolness creeping over his sympathy with the New Movement, when the peasants in revolt took particular care to burn down his own palace. Reasons far less reasonable have been alleged for the fine distinction which others drew between Wycliffe the reformer and Wycliffe the theologian. Many explanations are indeed possible; but I would timidly suggest this possibility; that men like Chaucer and Langland may have supported Wycliffe to some extent in practice, and then repudiated him more completely in theory, for a particular reason of their own. The reason was (odd as it will sound in modern ears) that they supported him when he was right and repudiated him when he was wrong.

Wycliffe was only one example of a man who yields to a temptation, which few reformers have been sufficiently clear-headed to resist. He became so irritated with the fact that the Idea was badly carried out in practice, that at last he was weak enough to turn and attack the Idea

53

in theory. The idea that God gives Himself to mankind in the Blessed Sacrament has nothing to do with the fact that some particular priests are fools or knaves, or ignorant or incompetent for their office. Wycliffe began by objecting to the latter condition, to which Chaucer and Langland, and probably John of Gaunt, equally and rightly objected. But there is here some haunting temptation which perpetually betrays reformers. It betrays the reformers of modern as of medieval times. It is as applicable to the idea of property as to the idea of priesthood; to the Married State as to the Mass. In a dark hour, poor Wycliffe seems to have tried, though very vaguely, to apply it to the Mass. Therefore we find him splitting hairs about Transubstantiation, which was much less logical than splitting heads with bills and axes, like the sane though savage peasants. The logical, or rather illogical, process is perfectly simple and perfectly familiar. A man sets out to distribute Milk to mothers or families or the whole community. He very soon discovers that distribution is not so easy as it looks. Before long he is perfectly familiar with the fact of people intercepting milk, stealing milk, making a corner in milk, adulterating milk, poisoning milk. He is very naturally in a rage, which verges on a revolutionary rage; nor is he wrong in proposing even precipitate and violent action against those who swindle about milk or poison milk. But there always comes a time when he is tempted to turn, in a towering passion, and say, 'There shall be no Milk.' That is what happened at the Reformation. That is what happens in nearly every revolution. That is why modern revolutionists want to destroy the household because of the housing shortage; or abolish private property because most people have not got enough of it.

There is therefore nothing to be deduced from the fact, if it be a fact, that Chaucer sympathized with the

The Age of Chaucer

Wycliffites in matters of discipline, but abjured them in matters of doctrine, except the fact (otherwise already familiar) that Chaucer had a clear head. But it has some relation to the general thesis of this book; that he also had a clear philosophy. That philosophy was a Christian philosophy, and all the more so because it had been mixed in the original Christian fashion with many Pagan influences. What is not sufficiently realized is that this Christian philosophy, even in the Middle Ages, could be, and was, a cool and well-balanced philosophy. The true meaning of the importance of Boethius has not been seen. There is a truth, perhaps unconscious, in Chaucer's use of the phrase about the 'feathers of philosophy'. His own touch was as light as a feather; but the feather came truly from an angel's wing.

It is the same with Chivalry: the long shadow falling on the fourteenth century from the Crusade. What we call militarism was almost unknown to medievalism. But that is partly because what we call militarism depends on most people being unmilitary. Medieval kings seldom possessed what was afterwards called a standing army; in the sense of a professional specialist army. Nevertheless, away at the back of all that was medieval was a sort of half-forgotten foundation which was military. This arose from two facts, far back in the beginning; first, that when Rome itself collapsed it left a number of garrisons and military outposts, to be the nuclei of national and local recovery; and second, that this world, when it began to recover, was suddenly invaded and almost vanquished by Islam; so that it could think of nothing but swords and spears for nearly a thousand years. One result was that the social *formation* remained military. The standing army soon became a very standing-at-ease army, and later, so to speak, a sitting army or even a sleeping army. But the system of subordination and obedience had been origin-

The Age of Chaucer

ally military. European aristocracy was a military hierarchy; just as Indian aristocracy was a religious hierarchy. The Duke is the Commander-in-Chief; the Marquis is the Warden of the Marches; the Knight is the Cavalry soldier; the Squire is the shield-bearer, and so on. These local commands, mixed with the Pagan legacy of slavery and modified by the family sentiment of Christianity, had produced what we call the feudal system. As a whole, these local commands tended to gather round certain central commands, some eight or ten of them in Western Europe, which were called monarchies. But even in France, where the monarchy was most centralized, there had been a time when the great Dukes had been too strong for it; and in England the great Dukes overthrew it. Apart from this, however, a change had passed over all that chivalry and aristocracy; a change vividly visible in Chaucer's time, as compared with the time of its original beginnings in the Roman Camp or the early medieval Crusade.

The crucial phrase 'bearing arms' had begun to shift its emphasis from the notion of carrying weapons to the notion of carrying coats of arms. This is far from meaning that men did not fight. They fought in the wars between England and France in Chaucer's time. They fought even more in the wars between England and England just after Chaucer's time. But it might fairly be said that, where the first medieval men had fought for a cross or a creed, the later medieval men actually fought for a coat of arms. The French Wars were heraldic wars; fought upon a point of pedigree; ending in the quartering of the Leopards and the Lilies. The Wars of the Roses were heraldic wars; also fought upon a point of pedigree; ending characteristically in the Tudor Rose parti-coloured, parti-per-pale. But there was a collateral effect of all this, of which a word must be said, if we are to realize the

The Age of Chaucer

peculiar rich autumnal atmosphere of the Chaucerian epoch. There went side by side with the exaggeration of heraldry, an exaggeration of costume; a fantasy in coats as well as in coats of arms. The figures of the lords standing round the long sunset of the splendour of Edward the Third, the lords who were to rebel against his heir, have indeed something of the burning but decaying colour of the sunset clouds. There is doubtless something ominous and unnatural, especially in the lurid light of later disasters, about those toppling headdresses, those sleeves slashed into points like plumes, those crazily curling shoes; like the outlines of prehistoric birds or fabulous beasts rather than men. Nevertheless, there was another side to the matter, and if we are to understand Chaucer, we must try to sympathize with something that is behind such heraldry, and even such fantasy; something that was universally taken for granted in the fourteenth century; something that has been almost entirely forgotten by the twentieth.

I have remarked elsewhere on a common saying; supposed to be shrewd and realistic and rational; actually shallow and ignorant and totally false. I mean the statement that modern people think modern dress ugly, only because all people have always thought contemporary dress ugly. If I find less than perfect loveliness in a billycock hat, it is insisted that Garrick thought the same about a three-cornered hat; that Van Dyck thought the same about a Van Dyck hat; and Chaucer the same about a hood. It is enough to answer that Garrick did not think it odd to act Roman or Romantic heroes in his own clothes; that Van Dyck *did* think the Van Dyck costume beautiful, as anybody can tell to whom paint is plain like print; and that there is not a line or a word to suggest that Chaucer as a poet thought that there was anything particularly unpoetical about his own clothes. The truth

57

The Age of Chaucer

is (as I have shown in another place) that nobody until the nineteenth century, and the ugly industrial revolution, ever *did* think that there was anything particularly unpoetical about his own clothes. All of them, without exception, would paint the Twelve Apostles, or even the Greek gods, in what were for them modern clothes. We have thought our modern clothes ugly, simply because our modern clothes have been ugly; and it does credit to our taste. But the real point to grasp about the costume of another period, such as that of the later Middle Ages, is not so much aesthetic as moral. The ultimate justification of heraldry, even in its extravagant decline, lay in the fact that it was a sort of pattern or standard of significance, by which even slighter and more trivial things tended to be significant. And this fact was not a little helpful, to a humane and humorous writer, in the matter of really enjoying the costumes and customs of his own time.

This truth runs like an ornamental design through the whole of the Canterbury Pilgrimage, and especially the Prologue to the Pilgrimage. Sir Walter Scott was accused of antiquarian antics, when he dwelt on the details of badge or baldrick worn by the minor vassals of Marmion. He was accused of being pompously poetical about trifles, merely because they were the trifles of a previous age. But Chaucer has just as much pomp and poetry about the trifles of his own age. He has no difficulty in making poetry out of them, but it is only fair to say that they really are poetical. Everybody who has seen medieval pictures knows how beautiful and balanced a colour scheme can depend on those stiff attitudes or flat perspectives; and the Prologue is, among other things, a medieval picture of exactly that type. We can all see, as clearly as a child sees the figures in a toy theatre, the Yeoman in his green coat and hood and his great silver clasp of St. Christopher, and his quiver of arrows plumed with

58

The Age of Chaucer

peacock-feathers; the Wife of Bath with her scarlet stockings and hat as large as a target; the Squire with his long sleeves powdered with a pattern of red and white flowers like a meadow, and hair curled close as in a press; the Shipman with his brown sunburnt face and his dagger hanging round his neck and armpit on a string, whose beard had been shaken in tempests from Hull to Carthage; the Franklin with his sanguine complexion and beard white as a daisy, with his white silk pouch and prosperous philosophy of Epicurus; the Summoner with the gigantic garland on his head, which seems to give an additional frightfulness to his 'fire-red cherubim's face', of which children were frightened. All this description is in the true sense imaginative. But Chaucer was doing what a great poet does; he was imagining what he saw. Certainly there is no artistic suggestion of his despising what he saw. I mean that, in the moral sense, he despised many of the vices of many of the characters; but he did not in an artistic sense despise their emblems and externals, as unsuited to serious art. Above all, he enjoyed them even more as emblems than as externals. And with that we encounter a medieval idea which students of Chaucer must consider with some sympathy, but which is seldom considered with even reasonable justice.

I for one should be the last to wish to see such things as Sumptuary Laws restraining the liberty of the citizen. It is true that the men who suffered the old Sumptuary Laws would have thought their King had gone raving mad, if he had suddenly risen up and forbidden anybody to drink ale, as does the President of the modern American democracy. It is far more of an interference with liberty to veto a man's drink, which he consumes in his private house, than to limit the choice of his dress, in which he walks down the public street. Nevertheless, I should rejoice in being free alike from the medieval rules about dress and the modern rules about drink. Yet I doubt if there is any free-minded and imaginative man, looking at the modern world, who has not sometimes wished that there were some way of ordering the externals of life, so as to make them appropriate; and, above all, so as to make them expressive. The garments and attributes of the Canterbury Pilgrims are expressive. They express what the people are; they express what the poet means. It may be very dreadful that a Knight should bear arms (and we have the assurance of Mrs. Wiffle that this is the case); it may be very luxurious of the young Squire to have flowers embroidered all over his coat; and Chaucer is obviously chaffing him, to some extent, upon his foppishness. But the arms do express the Knight and the flowers do express the Squire. When such flowers were dotted all over the flowered waistcoat of a fat stockbroker in 1860, who read *The Times* and talked about the danger of Puseyites in the Protestant Church of England, the flowers did not express anything at all. They did not make us think that the the stockbroker was like a flower; or even, in Chaucer's phrase, that he was like a meadow.

In short, if we ever did want Sumptuary Laws, it would not be so much against waste of money as against waste of work; waste of art, waste of effect, waste of colour and design. It is not that we dislike colour, but that we should rather like a language of colours; not that we dislike design, but that we should like designs to appear by design, and not by accident. I confess, though I am as fond of the colour of life as another, I have sometimes had a weird complex of thoughts on seeing a dull dumpy woman, with an expressionless face, approaching me in a hat or coat of flaming crimson like a tremendous Turner sunset. I feel inclined to ask her, as if she were at a masquerade ball, what she is meant to *be*. Perhaps I do her a wrong. Perhaps she glows within with so glorious a charity, that she

The Age of Chaucer

has a right to robe herself as the Rose of the World. Perhaps she has merely brooded on burning wrongs till she is ready to set fire to London and burn it to ashes. That would be quite a reasonable explanation. But short of that, I have a sort of Sumptuary feeling, that it is a waste of red; a waste of blood and fire; a waste of the most glorious colour God has given to our eyes. Now when those red robes are hung on a Cardinal, or even on a soldier or a judge, they do have this extra glow or intensity of having a meaning. And that is because the custom which clothes such figures is inherited from the old system of symbolism; and that system of symbolism ran through the whole system of medievalism. Chaucer's coloured figures are all the more coloured, because their colours mean something, as do the colours of heraldry. But that system, of which heraldry was the stamp, is so remote from us that it is necessary to go through all this explanation and argument in order to begin to see what it meant to medieval men. There are different sorts of freedom and even of comfort. And there is such a thing as a coat that fits because it is fitting. A Friar feels freer in a Friar's gown; as a man feels freer in a man's body.

When once we realize that heraldry was not a mummery or even a mystery; but a meaning part of a passion for significance which made all colours, stones, planets, beasts and flowers emblematic to the medieval mind, we may go on to agree that heraldry badly wanted pruning by the time of Edward the Third. If the twelfth century was the medieval spring, and the thirteenth the medieval summer, the fourteenth was a sort of rank and overgrown autumn that was already menaced by the crooked and cruel fifteenth century; in the north at least, very truly, the 'winter of our discontent'. The costumes of the rich, which had already become fanciful, became utterly fantastic; and that with something that was already sinis-

61

The Age of Chaucer

ter as well as fantastic. Chaucer's Parson denounces the motley figures of contemporary fops, striped and cut up into patterns, by saying that they look as if they were blasted white or yellòw or red by leprosies and loathsome plagues. It was not for nothing that the popular preachers denounced the horned and towering headdresses of great ladies as toppling travesties of the horns of Satan. It is true that the Court looked gay, and also true that there was already something ghastly about its gaiety. Its fine French dances had already something of the Dance of Death, and indeed the Black Death had already led the world a dance. It was in this world, in which the chivalric civilization of the fourteenth century was already passing into the cynicism of the fifteenth, that Geoffrey Chaucer had to live his life, in frequent contact with the Court and complete familiarity with the systems of heraldry and precedence. These things were, in the eyes of many of his contemporaries, by far the chief affairs of his time. They were to that age what Aviation, Breaking the World Record, Swimming the Atlantic, or any use of science for the purpose of speed, are to ours. Some followed them with an excitement quite superficial; others saw them as more or less significant; but they filled the landscape, as Push and Publicity now fill the land and sea and sky. It is only fair to remember that to this period belong many really graceful and worthy stories of dignity and delicacy of behaviour, like that of the Black Prince, when he acted as a servant to his royal captive. It is quite a mistake to suppose that such things were insincere; but it is quite valid to say they were not inconsistent, for instance, with the Black Prince sacking a city in the blind rage of a sick man. What is much more to the point, it may be noted that courtesy and conquest were alike shown in a purely dynastic, that is, a purely family war; a family quarrel dividing the great family of Christendom.

The Age of Chaucer

There is one very strange fact, which a few have noticed, about the figure of the Knight in *The Canterbury Tales*. It may be an accident; but, like some other accidents, it is as awful as an omen. The obvious point to be made about the Knight is that he has won great glory in battle; and the poet makes the point quite clear. The obvious example of winning glory in battle, in the poet's own period, was winning glory in the French campaign, on the fields of Crécy and Poictiers. But the poet seems actually to take a detour in order to avoid the fields of Crécy and Poictiers. The poet himself had been distinguished in the contemporary foreign fuss; the tourney between St. Denis and St. George. But the Knight has had nothing to do with pitting St. Denis against St. George. Chaucer goes out of his way to say that his hero has fought for the Cross and not the Crown. He has fought against the heathen in Prussia (which some might indeed call an omen), but anyhow he has only fought against the heathen; and to such a company Prussia was as remote as Palestine. Indeed, it is all very remote; and apparently deliberately remote. The last great war had been between the English and the French. The next great war was to be between the English and the English. But the noblest Pilgrim of the great Pilgrimage has only heard of a war between the Crescent and the Cross. He comes from the ends of the earth; from those ultimate enmities in which Christianity is in collision with the things really outside itself. He is the ghost of a grander Europe; of that first De Montfort, with the fixed fanatical eyes, who rode away from the Fourth Crusade because he would not war with Christian men; of that last of the Nine Worthies, who declared that no man must wear a crown of gold, where God had worn a crown of thorns.

Therefore the Knight is of a larger make or framework than the rest; and throws a sort of giant shadow on the

63

The Age of Chaucer

coloured crowd; a shadow almost of shame. But the shadow lies on us and on our children. It is a problem of the present and even more of the future, whether we can make even so large a commonwealth of nations as combined in the Crusade. But if this is true of the significance of the Knights, it is even truer of the Guildsmen or the Burgesses. The point is that, looking into the fog of the future, we may see figures losing their *identity*; as ·the eventual result of having lost the Crest and the Trade Mark. Here indeed is the vital example of this long and difficult preface; on the need of seeing medieval things as living (or dying) modern things. Blake said that Chaucer numbered the types of men as Linnaeus numbered the plants. But he was a mystic and not a prophet. Most normal men suppose these types to be normal. But in truth the Types are Trades; and the Trades are Guilds. Destroy the Guild and you destroy the natural classification of men. This appears vividly in the great Chaucerian characters. For Chaucer himself was a child of the old Craft and Mystery. And to men to-day the Mystery is a Mystery indeed.

There exists a misunderstanding rather than a quarrel about medieval and modern ideas; because the two do not meet on the same plane. The medieval world, with all its crimes and crudities, was intensely concerned with ideas as ideas; and not in the least concerned with them as medieval ideas. But the moderns, and especially the modernists, are intensely concerned with the fact that modern ideas are modern. They are sometimes so much excited about it that they neglect to make them anything like ideas. I know some very learned writers on the Middle Ages, whose heads are so constructed as not to permit the entrance even of the idea of an idea. The modern world has immeasurably surpassed the medieval world in organization and the application of such ideas as it has; so that the general improvement in certain kinds of humanity, certain kinds of instruction, and certain kinds of arbitration and order, is not merely an idea, but a material fact. But that does not alter the moral fact; that when we compare medieval ideas with modern ideas, we often find that the modern ideas are comparatively hasty, superficial or unbalanced; or else that the ideas, as ideas, really do not exist at all. There could not be a better example than the comparison between the *idea* of Guilds with the *fact* of Capitalism. The idea of Guilds was worked out very narrowly and imperfectly; and the fact of Capitalism may work out, at least in the opinion of some, more practically and prosperously. But there *was* an idea of Guilds; and there is not and never was any idea in Capitalism. Nobody knew where it came from; nobody especially wanted it to come. Nobody knew where it was going to; and at this moment it appears to be going straight to sheer strangling Monopoly and then to bankruptcy.

Nobody understands the modern world who does not realize this primary truth. The modern world began with the problem of the grocer and the grocer's assistant. It is in fact ending with a vast growth of grocers' assistants and no grocer. It must still be emphasized, obvious as it is, that the grocers' assistants have not *grown* into grocers. They have all remained assistants; only, instead of assisting a humble human grocer, with a soul to be saved, they are assisting the International Stores or the Universal Provision Department. In other words, the servants have not become masters, and will never have the faintest chance of becoming masters. They remain servants; only they are like those slaves that were held to public service in pagan antiquity; they have personal servants over them, but only an impersonal master over all. Now, very broadly, one idea in the Guild is that the grocer's assistant should grow into a grocer. For that purpose, it is obviously necessary to

65

preserve a large number of equal and independent grocers. It is necesary to prevent these grocers from being bought out or sold up by the Stores or the Super-Grocer. With this object the Guild deliberately checked certain forms of competition, protected the weaker brethren; and, preserved the Types that seem eternal in Chaucer's Tales.

Now to anybody who knows an idea when he sees it, it is relatively irrelevant whether the application of this idea be patchy or imperfect, at any particular period. It is not patchy and imperfect, but very nearly non-existent, in our own period. But the point is in the clear comprehension of the idea. If there had been only one Guild, instead of scores and hundreds, it would still have stood for one medieval idea and not for the other modern idea. If its benefits had only been extended to two Guildsmen, they would still have been benefited in a particular way, and according to an idea other than the idea of modern competition or modern monopoly. Chaucer mentions several Master Craftsmen, evidently attached to a Guild, as going on his Canterbury Pilgrimage; he mentions, for instance, a Dyer and a worker in tapestry. If we compare the first with the huge development of the modern Dye Industry, we shall recognize at once the main distinction I mean. More and more people may have come to work in dye factories; more and more processes may have been invented; more marvellous as a matter of science, though often much less marvellous as a matter of art. And although for some time the logic of Capitalism produced worse and worse conditions, the wisdom of Capitalists (following on the courage of Trades Unionists) may now produce (or pretend to produce) better and better conditions. But they produce better and better conditions for servants; they do not attempt to produce a Guild, which is a fraternity of masters. And if we wish to consider the idea itself, clear of all these muddled bickerings about 'medievalism', we cannot do better than take the example of a trade which does still exist to-day, in something resembling the guise and function which it had in the days of Chaucer.

There rode in the cavalcade to Canterbury, along with the Dyer, the more conspicuous figure of the Doctor. He is conspicuous even in a literary sense; for he is picked out in colours that are still clear and fresh; a striking and almost startling example of Chaucer's power of describing a complete and even complex personality in a few lines. His combination of rich and impressive dress with cautious and hygienic diet is a calculation from two angles finding the exact point of a personality. He was particular that his food should be nourishing and digestible, but took it in small quantities; and though he did not talk about proteids and vitamins, he probably talked in some similar terms from the same learned language. The moment we know this, we know that it is true that he was irreligious; sceptical and anti-clerical in a rather negative way. He was dignified; but not averse from fees. That sort of man still exists; and his general sense of status, his social position and his professional etiquette, are still very much the same. The Doctor, in short, still exists as a roughly recognizable figure. The Dyer has totally disappeared; his hand is not subdued to what it works in, but his whole body and soul dissolved in his own dyevat. He has become a liquid; a flowing stream of tendency; an impersonal element in the economics of the dyeworks. He is not a Master-Dyer; he is at the most a Master of Dyers. But, in plain truth, he is not really a master, but only a paymaster. With every day that passes there is less importance in the mastery and more importance in the pay. The reason why the Doctor is recognizable, and the Dyer is unrecognizable, is perfectly simple,

67

The Age of Chaucer

It is that the Doctors not only were, but still are, organized on the *idea* of a Medieval Guild.

In the modern doctor we can see and study the medieval idea. We shall not, even if we are medievalists, think it an infallible or impeccable idea. The Guild is capable of pedantry; it is sometimes capable of tyranny. The British Medical Council, which is the council of a Guild, sometimes condemns men harshly for very pardonable breaches of professional law; it sometimes excludes outsiders from membership who might well have been members. But it does do what a Guild was supposed to do. It keeps the doctors going; it keeps the doctors alive; and it does prevent one popular quack from eating all his brethren out of house and home. It sets limits to competition; it prevents the growth of monopoly. It does not allow a fashionable physician in Harley Street to destroy the livelihood of four general practitioners in Hoxton. It does not permit one professional man to buy up all the practices, as one grocer can buy up all the grocers' shops. And it does permit us to study, in a clear modern example, outside all the medieval controversies, religious and other, what is really to be said for and against this system of economic combination, and what it is that can really be criticized, and can really be valued, in the idea of a Guild.

The Physician of Chaucer has changed, it may be said, in every other character except his economic relation to the Guild, which is still founded on medieval economics. As a matter of fact, the story is more comic than the common story of evolution. He has changed so often that he has very nearly changed back to what he was before. It is true that he no longer regards the art of healing as founded on Astrology; though he sometimes founds it on the yet more ancient superstition of Divination by Dreams. But though we have not yet gone far enough for eager young scientists to be dealing in Astrology, there is something curious and

68

The Age of Chaucer

almost creepy about their dealings with Alchemy. Many of the most modern speculations are a great deal nearer to the medieval notion of the transmutation of metals, than they are to the intervening materialist's dogmas of elemental and indestructible fixity. We may yet see the chemist turn into an alchemist, even if there is no immediate prospect of the astronomer turning into an astrologer. There is a typical piece of Chaucerian irony in the passage referring to the Doctor's purely scientific interest in gold:

For gold in physic is a cordial
Therefore he loved gold in special.

But nobody will say that this very special love of economic values is merely medieval, and cannot be admitted as modern. If avarice counted for something in alchemy, it has not been entirely absent from the services which modern science has offered to chemical combines and the discovery of mines. It is an amusing fact, by the way, that the quaint old legend, which Protestant prejudice set afloat some sixty years ago, to the effect that the Pope once condemned the study of Chemistry, really referred to this very fact; the fact that medieval religion did attempt to restrain medieval avarice. What the Pope did condemn was the practice of certain quack astrologers and alchemists, who used to go round to the houses of poor people and take away all their pots and pans with a promise of turning them all into gold. Against this great step in scientific progress the Pope did indeed set his face with ferocious medieval bigotry. If any modern moral authority were to condemn the somewhat similar students of the Art of Salesmanship, who go round tempting poor people to run into debt for all sorts of furniture and appliances for which they cannot ultimately pay, I for one should welcome such an outburst of Papal persecution. But I have no doubt that the progressive historian would give a simple sum-

69

mary of the incident; by saying that it was made a mortal sin to have any chairs and tables.

Anyhow, the Guild principle has in fact saved the Doctor; and left him standing as a separate social figure in any crowd going to Wembley or Wimbledon, as he did in the crowd going to Canterbury. But it is the tendency of all the separate social figures, falling into modern monopolist and impersonal tendencies, to disappear altogether. Standardization lowers the standard of personality and independence in all the types and trades. Under that tendency, we no longer see the Ploughman but the new methods of the Steam-Plough; we no longer recognize the Miller but only a particular machinery of mills; and the current tendency, even of gossip, is to discuss not so much cooks as cookery and not so much clerks as clerking. A certain decline in the Comic Characters, conceived in relation to common trades, once so typical of English literature, is probably due to the decline in the idea of men who were Masters of their trade; and the substitution of numberless servants who had less pride in their professions. And this is relevant; for it may be the end of that long procession of English figures of fun, which undoubtedly began with Chaucer.

True, this is masked by the fact that the moderns can find phrases which they call quite modern, when they mean that they are quite human. Chaucer's unsleeping eye on human nature did indeed spot any number of small but amusing facts, that were true in his time and are true in ours. This could be illustrated even in the examples which I have mentioned and contrasted; the examples of the Doctor and the Dyer. A modern reader gives something like a start of amusement, when he reads of the relation between the Doctor and the Chemist; how 'each of them made other for to win', that is, the Apothecary recommended the Physician and the Physician ordered the drugs from the Apothecary. That is the sort of social relation that might go on for ever, and can certainly go on to-day. On the other hand, Chaucer does not tell us much about the Dyer or his friends, and it is possible that they were an afterthought, inserted for some special reason, as were (in all probability) the three Priests who appear and disappear after the mention of the Second Nun. But he does tell us one thing in connexion with these worthy Guildsmen or Livery Men of City Companies, which is an excellent example of what men say is quite modern, when they mean that it is very ancient. He says that the Dyer, and the other Masters of their respective Mysteries, were quite in the way of becoming Aldermen. He throws a delicate veil, in his own indescribable way, over the question of whether they deserved to be Aldermen, or even wanted to be Aldermen. But he adds that, anyhow, their wives were all in favour of it; and that it is very pleasant to be distinguished from other women by being called 'Madame'. That is a drawing-room comedy that is modern enough, in that sense, and has a present and practical relation to the Honours List and the Sale of Peerages. There is many a knighthood given to-day, not so much because Mr. Biggs wishes to be Sir Benjamin Biggs, as because a more astute person has calculated that when she is Lady Biggs, it will sound quite as good as Lady Beauchamp or Lady Salisbury. The whole of Chaucer's book is dotted with details of this lively and accurate sort, to such an extent that a man might easily suppose that society had hardly changed at all, between the fourteenth and the twentieth centuries. The historic process of change is partly covered by certain comic antics of human nature, which can indeed occur in any age and are instantly recognized across the ages.

But we must not allow this to mislead us to the extent of underrating the change there has really been. Even in the instances I have given, there is sufficient evidence of what has changed and what has not. It is so with the Doctor and the Chemist. The Doctor, who is still the member of a living and real Guild, remains the same. The Chemist, who is not the member of a real Guild, is already changing. It is no longer a case of the private physician calling on a private apothecary, living at the corner of the street. He has to deal already with vast commercial combines, with multiple and identical shops, in which all the chemists are servants and none of the chemists are masters. The name of one apothecary is now written in a hundred towns. And we owe it to the survival of a true medieval Guild, that the name of a single physician is not written on a hundred brass plates.

In the same way, while men have ambitions in every age, and women change from age to age even less than men, there really is a difference between the Alderman and Livery in Chaucer's time and in ours. The old Dyers' Company was still concerned only, or mainly, with the defence of Dyers; not only with defence of unsuccessful Dyers, but also, in the long run, with attack on successful Dyers. I know not if there is still a Dyers' Company; if there is, it is doubtless charitable in all manner of ways, but not in that way. It does not exist to bar and break the International Chemical Dyeworks Combine; it does not perceptibly try to do it, and it certainly does not do it. This may be partly explained by the fact that a considerable number of Dyers are aged colonels and clergymen, who have never dreamed of dyeing anything, except possibly their hair.

This example of the Dyer and the Doctor and the Guild is the supreme example of what was meant, at the beginning of this chapter, by saying that we cannot understand the past life of the fourteenth century, until we have begun to look a little even into the future of the twentieth. We

72

The Age of Chaucer

are now in the middle of movements that may distort or dissolve all those distinctive and independent types which Chaucer distinguished by trades. In short, we may yet find, in the long run, that the loss of Arms and Heraldry has killed the Gentleman: the loss of Guilds and Mysteries has killed the Citizen. We cannot strike a right balance of judgment about the medieval attempt to organize trades and traders, without considering, not merely that it is now lost, but where the loss of it may ultimately lead. We must not judge by that later but intermediary phase, in which England could be called a nation of shopkeepers, with the implication that each man must keep his shop. If a man wanted to keep his shop, he would have been wiser to keep his guild. Where we have lost the guild principle, we have collapsed into a totally different sort of collectivist plutocracy. For that is what it is; whether we put it in revolutionary terms, by saying that one man keeps a hundred shops, or put it in humanitarian terms, by saying that one shop keeps a hundred men. One vital distinction is that in such a system the organizer can only be an organizer; he must deal with the abstractions and not the materials of the trade; with pen and ink and not with dye-vats or wine-barrels.

Now Chaucer came of a line of men that did deal directly with wine-barrels. They dealt as masters and not as servants, at least in the last two generations. But they dealt with a wine-barrel and not with a wine-list; with facts and not merely with figures. For them was natural magic and the world's desire stored in positive pots; solid as those that poured for Christ the incredible wine. He came of people who had dealt with the stuff and substance of things, and in his case, with a highly appropriate sort of thing. If we were to look for an allegory about him who dealt so often in allegories, we could hardly find for his birthplace a more appropriate House of Fame. Forth from among those vats of more than purple dye, forth from among the mighty vats of the vine, brought by the Shipman from the lands of Froissart and Petrarch, he came to walk the world; who went singing all his days as if wine were in his very veins, and hidden in his northern blood, the very secret of the sun.

Chapter III

PUBLIC AND PRIVATE LIFE

The name of Chaucer seems to have been quite common in medieval times, and is practically unknown in modern times. This alone strikes me as rather curious and unique. Almost all other famous names reappear in some fashion; there storms across the stage of relatively recent history somebody with the remarkable name of Sir Julius Caesar. We have accepted unstartled a worthy dissenting minister as the Rev. Mr. Shakespeare, and admired a brilliant stage-player with the Puritan name of Milton. But we look in vain for Mr. Chaucer, in Bohemia or Belgravia or the suburbs; nor in 'the Street', nor up the Strand is he. The surname has not even appeared as a florid alias, or alternative title, among those who periodically alter their own pedigree and, like the wanton lapwing, get themselves another crest. Curiously enough, the latter course was actually adopted, in the reverse direction, in the original Chaucer family, if certain historians are correct. According to this theory, the son of Chaucer did really abandon his father's crest and coat-armour in favour of that of the De Roets, his maternal ancestors, supposing, heaven help us (such is the simplicity of snobs), that it would aggrandize Chaucer to be turned into Roet. But nowadays, when the Roets are forgotten, it does not even seem likely that Roet would be turned into Chaucer. Not even the most glittering-shifting and opalescent Opalstein, changing his name for the tenth time, ever seems to change it to Chaucer. I suspect that there is in this fact some faint shadow of something already noted here; something that is not exactly neglect, but is in a sense negligence. I mean that vague popular feeling that poor old Chaucer is a joke; that he is a funny, snuffy old man, like an antiquary or a small bookseller selling black-letter and broadsheets. An odd association of ideas about him, who sang in courts and had the confidence of kings: but I believe a very real one, among those who only know his name; and possibly a partial reason for their failure to claim or cling to his name. As I have said, somehow or other, it does not yet sound quite like a serious name: but, whatever be the reason, it is now at least a very rare name. And though it is very likely that a hundred Chaucers will leap out of dark corners or remote colonies, and write me long letters about this rash statement, it is a fact, at this actual moment by the clock, that I have never seen or heard of any living person bearing the once widespread name of the greatest Englishman of the Middle Ages.

Oddly enough, we may say that it was Chaucer who abolished the name of Chaucer. He did a number of rather remarkable things, including, for all practical purposes, tossing off a little trifle called The English Language. The name of Chaucer, or Chausseur, the maker of footwear, was once a common name because it described a common trade. A man was called Shoemaker as another man was called Tailor or Baker or Butler or Gardener; only he was called Shoemaker in French. For that matter, of course, the terms for tailoring and butlering and other things were of Norman and not Saxon origin; but that is another discussion, and a very tiresome one. The really important fact to be seized is this: that it was rather an unexpected, belated and almost reactionary accident, that the glorious English language came into existence at all.

76

Public and Private Life

It was one of those lucky· things that are not likely to happen and do happen; and often nearly happen too late. The whole trend of progress or organic growth was towards France and England growing together, under the common captaincy of a French-speaking nobility and chivalry. If a serious sociologist, mapping out the evolution of mankind, had existed in the earlier Middle Ages (and they had many other plagues and pestilences), that scientific prophet would most certainly have said that England was destir̃ed to become as French-speaking as France. The cultured class generally has an unfair advantage over the uncultured; and the whole culture had originally been a Latin culture. The Plantagenet attempts to make France a part of England were really a half-confession that England was a part of France. Then something happened at the last moment, of the sort that confounds scientific politics; something dimly resembling the combined instinctive movements of a populace and a poet. There was a faint trail of Anglo-Saxon traditions and various dialects like Middle English; but left to itself the trail would have led nowhere. Then a great genius saw that he could Frenchify it enough to make it English. That is about as nearly as we can define the process. Chaucer Europeanized English; he brought it into the current of culture, by setting it to foreign tunes and mixing it with foreign terms. But Chaucer destroyed the domination of pure French; he destroyed all sorts of incidental terms, titles and conventions that went along with it; and, while he was about it, he destroyed his own name.

It would seem that the poet's grandfather was a certain Robert le Chaucer, who had some post in the Customs connected with the imports of wine from Aquitaine; so the connexion with the wine trade can be traced at least as far as that. The creator of The Wife of Bath, the great professional widow of literature, seems to have come of a

77

household somewhat haunted by widows; to an extent to
alarm Mr. Tony Weller. His grandmother was married
at least twice; his mother was apparently married three
times; and, touching later developments, it would seem
that his sister-in-law was at least once a widow, before
she became the third wife of that determined and un-
tiring widower, John of Gaunt. It is a trivial coincidence, and yet not wholly uninforming; for many earnest
students have missed the point about medieval life by not
noticing that a thing was often derided as comic and yet
was very common; was derided as comic because it was
very common. Similarly, when we find medieval moralists indignantly denouncing something, we can generally
deduce that it was a very medieval thing. Widowhood
was really tragic, which is why kings and knights swore
specially to defend the widow and orphan; but remarriage
was none the less comic because it was obviously convenient. Anyhow, the way in which these rather entangled
relations affected Chaucer is roughly this. His grandmother, Mary le Chaucer, who was probably born a Stace
and previously married to a Heyroun, had a son named
John Chaucer. After the death of her husband, Robert le
Chaucer, she married a certain Richard le Chaucer; having apparently a taste in Chaucers. Richard was certainly a vintner and lived in London, in a part called Cord-
waners-strete. There is a curious episode about some people called Stace, probably kinsmen, trying to kidnap young
John Chaucer and marry him for monetary purposes; the
youth being rescued by his stepfather. The stepfather died
in 1349; and John himself went on vintnering with increasing success; as he deputized for the King's Butler in
Southampton and even seems to have gone abroad in the
train of the King. It seems likely that the Chaucers had
for some time been, so to speak, among the camp-follow-
ers of the Court; but first in lowlier and afterwards in

Public and Private Life

loftier stations or offices. John married Agnes, daughter of John Copton, of a family connected with the Mint, and lived in Thames Street. When he died, the widow was married again to another vintner, bearing the pleasing name of Bartholemew atte Chapel. So that a certain child named Geoffrey Chaucer, who is presumed to be her son, was provided with a stepfather, as his father had been; and may have received in childhood that impression of a transformation-scene of marrying and remarrying, which he extended into vistas of somewhat unscrupulous exaggeration in the career of The Wife of Bath. There are many other complicated controversies about the Chaucer family; but they may be left, first because they cannot be settled; and second because the Chaucer family is not so interesting as Chaucer.

The life of Chaucer, in the somewhat limited sense of the biography of Chaucer, consists of a very few facts and an incredible crowd of fancies. Perhaps it would be fairer to say a crowd of conjectures; for part of the difficulty lies in the plausibility or probability of some of the conjectures, which come near the ground but never quite settle on it. At the very outset, the writer of a sketch of this poet has to decide whether he will confine himself to what he knows to be true, or speculate at length on many things which he can see to be possible, or even probable, but which may, after all (especially in the light of later research), be entirely misleading. I have here decided to dwell definitely only on the definite facts, and to reserve speculation for what must in any case be speculative: the spiritual and philosophical and literary meaning of the story. My reason is that the ramifications of the mere conjectures of the learned have been so vast, and, in some cases, so vain. They are liable to be pursued patiently, or impatiently, through thousands and thousands of words, and then brought to a stop with a few words. In one case I remem-

Public and Private Life

ber, Chaucer went on the wildest adventures in connexion with the revolt of the citizens of London concerning John of Northampton; a story in which the poet fled to Holland, was flung into the Tower, was released by the personal intervention of Anne of Bohemia, was put to thrilling tests involving the betrayal of his fellow-conspirators, before he could reappear in the light of day. To the whole of which story a subsequent biographer put a full stop of scepticism, by saying it was rather odd that through all these changes Chaucer regularly received his pension with his own hands, quite quietly, in his home in London. I am not going to erect towers of tentative theory which can be so rapidly ruined. The romance called 'The Possible Life of Geoffrey Chaucer, Gentleman', would be a most fascinating and spirited work; 'The Black Prince's Treasure'; 'In the House of Wat Tyler'; 'The Rescue of Laura'; 'What Became of Dante's Beatrice?'; or the great mystery story: 'Why Was Chaucer Robbed Twice in One Day?'—as he really was. Doubtless it was mixed up with the Pope or Wycliffe or someone; for the time was picturesque almost to excess: and the great men he may have met would need a volume apiece. But this volume is only about Chaucer; and this chapter is only about the ascertained facts about Chaucer. The trouble is that they are not only few, but they are not even always the few facts that make up the most rudimentary biography.

A good example, to begin with, is the question about the date of his birth. It is largely calculated from the evidence which he gave in the affair of Scrope and Grosvenor; a lawsuit in which he is officially recorded as being 'forty and upwards, and armed twenty-seven years'. This lawsuit was certainly in 1386, so that presuming that Chaucer was then about forty-five, he was probably born about 1341. But it has always struck me as quaintly typical of the time, as well as of the oddity of the Chaucerian problem, that the Court records should be so very exact about the period during which he had borne arms and possessed armorial bearings, and so very vague about the period during which he had been alive. It is possible that Chaucer was himself rather vague, possibly out of natural vagueness, possibly out of natural vanity; but it seems clear that the legal authorities did not trouble to pin him down about his age, when once they were certain about his status of Armiger. That double information, certain on the smaller point and uncertain on the larger, is typical of all the information about Chaucer. There are rather interesting possibilities in such matters, to which I shall refer elsewhere; here I only note in passing that the very date of his birth is doubtful, though the date of his admission into the system of chivalry is clear. The problem of his parentage is in the same lopsided state. It has been traditionally, and apparently truly said (indeed it is substantially certain) that he was the son of a vintner of the City of London; but we do not know this even, so well as we know that he appears later in totally different positions: often the last positions where one would expect the vintner's son to be.

One disadvantage of seeing the same figure in a series of flashes of lightning is that we cannot always be quite certain that it is the same figure. The fact that we have only disjointed bits and snippets of the biography of Geoffrey Chaucer involves the occasional possibility that, in the words of the ancient jest about a more ancient poet, it is not the biography of Geoffrey Chaucer, but of somebody else of the same name. In this connexion we cannot forget what we have already noted: that it was then a fairly common name. Nevertheless, there is a series of such glimpses of what would appear to be a continuous historical personality; though some of them seem to me less certainly, and others quite certainly, the personality

81

of the poet. But whether they are certain or uncertain, they are none of them continuous; they are isolated impressions which can only be treated like separate pictures. The searchlight of criticism can only fall here and there, like a spotlight, upon a particular spot; and that so briefly that we cannot always be equally sure that the human figure which we see is part of the human story which we study.

Thus, the very first figure we see is that of a boy in a short cloak with a pair of black and red breeches, who is hanging about in some more or less menial capacity in the house of the Countess of Ulster, who married Lionel of Clarence, one of the sons of Edward the Third. There is also an entry showing that he received a small sum 'for necessaries at Christmas'; and we will hope that the Countess of Ulster had proper ideas about what a boy's necessaries at Christmas are. But the whole thing was on a small scale, and seems to be suited to quite a subordinate position, and we cannot be absolutely certain that the boy in black and red breeches was father to the man with whom we deal.

Next, we have a much brighter glimpse, in much broader daylight, of a very sharp-eyed and observant young man, probably clad as a *scutifer* or subordinate and assistant of some knight, walking about among the tents and painted palisades of a medieval camp, gay with heraldry; noticing especially the blazonry of one particular pavilion, and falling into talk with old soldiers or heralds' followers on the subject. The young man was about twenty years old; the time was the year 1359; and the place was the northern plains of France, stretching from the poplars of Picardy to the vines of Champagne, somewhere near the place where the road goes up to the holy towers of Rheims. There is no doubt whatever that this young man is that Galfridus Chaucer who filled up the chinks in his chivalric or bureaucratic duties with a few little literary exercises, admittedly not without merit. The military campaign, in which he was thus serving as a soldier, was one of the last efforts made by Edward the Third in his later years to repeat the success, or recover the crown of glory, which he had won at Crécy long before. About it, as about much of that dying medieval glory, there was an atmosphere of doom. It was probably felt by all that the first English triumphs could not be recovered; though John of Gaunt's grandson was to make yet another very gallant throw for it at Agincourt. Anyhow, it ended in defeat, and Chaucer, fighting in the defeated army, was taken prisoner.

Here, however, we have the first really important light on the level of life, so to speak, on which he was by this time living. He was not only ransomed, but ransomed by a pretty large sum personally advanced by the King. It is clear that he was already a person of some distinction; or at least a person of some promise; and it is most probable that he was connected with the King by the tie of some task or commission, in which his own personality counted. He was still only a young squire, at most; but the Government was certainly employing the young squire on some particular business. In fact, it was a matter of what may be called (in every sense) Intelligence. It was as important then as now to have in the Intelligence Department at least one person of Intelligence. Such a man is valued, and efforts will be made to rescue or to ransom him. It seems clear at least that about the year 1360 and onwards, Chaucer, young as he was, was acting as some sort of King's Messenger or bearer of dispatches between France and England.

In one of these foreign journeys, later on, he became a friend of Froissart; and Froissart is the type of that time and task in his life. Froissart is the historian who really did know everything about chivalry; except the most important thing: that what had turned into a Tournament had once been a Crusade. Courtesy was stooping to court-liness: chivalry was entangled in heraldry; but much of it was still worth learning; and anyhow these were the things the young poet had to learn. I have already said some-thing of that flamboyant background of heraldry against which he stands. It is the vividness of heraldry in those days, and its vagueness in these days, which gives its amusing moral to the little incident that has often been quoted; one of the few living incidents in which the figure of Chaucer can be seen for a moment walking alive in the daylight. It happened, as noted, much later in his life; but it recalls the romantic youth here in question. The fashionable world, as we should put it, was divided into enthusiastic factions over a quarrel which had arisen about the legitimacy of a coat of arms, which then seemed al-most as thrilling as the legitimacy of a child or a last will and testament. The arms borne by the great Border family of Scrope, in popular language a blue shield with a gold band across it (I can say 'azure a bend-or' quite as prettily as anybody else) was found to have been also adopted by a certain Sir Thomas Grosvenor, then presumably the newer name of the two. The trial was conducted with all the voluminous detail and seething excitement of a Society divorce case; reams and rolls of it, for all I know, remain, in the records of the heraldic office, for anybody to read if he likes; though I have my doubts even about Garter King-at-Arms. But somewhere in that pile of re-cords there is one little paragraph, for which alone, per-haps, the world would now turn them over at all. It merely states that among a long list of witnesses, one 'Geoffrey Chaucer, gentleman, armed twenty-seven years', had testified that he saw the Golden Bend, displayed before Scrope's tent in the battlefield of France; and that long afterwards, he had stopped some people in the streets of

84

Public and Private Life

London and pointed to the same escutcheon displayed as a tavern sign; whereon they had told him that it was not the coat of Scrope but of Grosvenor. This, he said, was the first time he had ever heard tell of the Grosvenors. Such small flashes of fact are so provocative, that I can almost fancy he smiled as he said the last words.

Perhaps the chief interest of the incident is the reversal of the relations between the witness and the trial; and indeed between the witness and the world. Chaucer at that moment was only of importance because he offered testimony about Scrope and Grosvenor. Scrope and Grosvenor at this moment are only of importance because they elicited testimony from Chaucer. It is an old moral, and obvious enough, that the fashion of this world passes away; yet we often find it hard to believe about the fashion of this age. All that world of the heraldic and the emblematic, full of many very noble meanings as well as many very idle mummeries, has long been rolled away like a scroll and vanished like a cloud; and we cannot conceive that the world once thought all that nonsense necessary. Yet we are not always eager to realize that all which we call necessary may some day be called nonsense. It is amusing to reflect that some day the apocalyptic newspaper files, with their huge headlines about The First Man Who Flew Round The World, or the American professor who thinks we can send wireless waves to Mars, will all seem to our descendants a dust of indescribably dreary triviality; and that nobody will ever look at the long-lost records, except to find a paragraph in a corner, in which Mr. Laurence Binyon or Mr. T. S. Eliot gave evidence about a motor-car collision.

In dealing with all such incidents in Chaucer's life, it is unavoidable that we should have a very little fact to a great deal of theory or hypothesis; because it is impossible to recover the details of his life, but not altogether im-

85

Public and Private Life

possible to recover a good many of the details of his time. His appearance at the great Scrope and Grosvenor inquiry is entirely typical of all we know about him; of his footing among the gentry, which was yet not quite that of a conventional hereditary gentleman; of the confidence that was undoubtedly placed in his word and wisdom, in more important matters than this; of the good sense and clearness which marked all his modes of expression, and would in any case have made him an excellent witness; and even of a certain cheerful curiosity about common things, which made him stop in the street to find out the truth about the new public-house sign. But, on the whole, the difficulty of dealing with the life of Chaucer is that there are so very few of these flashes of daylight, in which the man himself can be seen and snapshotted, moving about on his personal affairs. Almost all we know of him comes from legal documents and official actions; not, as is the case with so many later poets, from contemporary memoirs or personal letters. No man is more personal in his work and more impersonal in his biography. So that, while we can see through his own eyes, with almost startling clearness, the Miller, blind and bloated and roaring with drink, thrusting aside the Monk and making sure of the second place in the series, or the Canon's Yeoman overtaking the cavalcade at a rush, with the foam on his horse's bridle, there was no one present to snapshot the figure of Chaucer himself, as he stood, sharp and observant, outside the blazoned tent in France or the painted tavern in London.

But we do at least know that the rulers observed his observation, and were sharp enough to note his sharpness. He was trusted with diplomatic missions of great dignity, and with some which were, perhaps, too important to be dignified. In other words, it looks as if some of his foreign commissions had been of the nature of what

Public and Private Life

we call Secret Service; and anyhow there is no doubt that
he was deep in the secrets of two, if not three Kings.
What we know of him publicly through his offices is entirely consonant with what we know of him personally
through his poems. If there is one thing that we could
have guessed for ourselves, about the personality of the
poet, it is that he would have made a perfectly admirable
diplomatist. The diplomatist of fiction and drama,
especially the diplomatist of melodrama, seems extraordinarily unfitted for diplomacy. He is represented as a
rigid and sinister person, with a perpetual sneer, and a
background of assassins and the Third Degree. What is
wanted in diplomacy is the careful cultivation of the exact
contrary of all this; and the exact contrary of all this was
Chaucer. The unshaken good temper which was combined with his wide knowledge of the world, his ready
realization of the variety of human character, his perfectly genuine geniality towards most people, combined
with an equally genuine knowledge of the weaknesses of
most people, were exactly the qualities most wanted in
that time of tangled feudal claims and touchy semi-
dependent vassals. No man ever understood better that
it takes all sorts to make a world, or even to make a
pilgrimage. No man suffered fools more gladly, for he
did actually suffer them gladly; getting any amount of
gladness or gaiety out of his private observation of their
folly. He was a polished adept in the dangerous diplomatic art of really getting some fun out of funny people.

I shall deal on another page with the details of his
political fortunes, the later part of which is admittedly
covered with some obscurity. We are not certain of his
personal attitude to the palace revolution which replaced
the true Plantagenet by the ambitious son of John of
Gaunt. We know that John of Gaunt had been in a general sense a patron of Chaucer, as of others; but it is

Public and Private Life

difficult to deduce from this all his individual views about rather unforeseen changes in the next generation. For the purpose of the present problem, it is enough to say that he never ceased to receive a certain amount of reward and protection from the Court; though in his later years he was somewhat poorer and less frequently in public employment. He was not the kind of man to quarrel if he could help it, and, even in those quarrelsome days, none of the rulers seems to have finally or seriously quarrelled with him. The end of their own increasing quarrelsomeness he did not see, but carried with him to the last something of the calmer splendour of the victorious age of Edward. He died before the Wars of the Roses.

I have summarized this chapter under the title of public and private life; and the difficulty is that the poet had a public life that was very much of a private life. Nay, in one sense, it was more private than his private life. We are not in fact told very much about the personal affairs of Geoffrey Chaucer; but what we are told we are told quite frankly. The biography of Chaucer is lost; but it is not hidden. When he does happen to talk about himself, he describes himself quite as vividly as he describes everybody else. He makes fun of himself as he does of everybody else. The description is incomplete, merely because there is not very much of it; and, like most light descriptions of the sort, it does not deal with the most serious matters. But though there is not enough of it to describe a complete person, it does not shrink from being personal, in the sense in which we now speak (generally with grave disapproval) about personalities. Chaucer has told us that he was fat, that he was reluctant to get out of bed, that he was content on occasion to look very much of a fool, that he was thought to neglect his neighbours for his craze for books; and many other things that are

Public and Private Life

quite private and confidential as far as they go. But he has told us nothing of what was really private and confidential: and that was his work in the public service. He was practically by profession a diplomatist; and *his* diplomacy was a very secret diplomacy. In all his maze of multitudinous words, in all his wandering paths of narrative and meditation, in all the thousand things that he touches on as a poet, a philosopher, a moralist and a humorist, he has not left one single word, I think, which throws any light on those political missions which the King his master trusted him to conduct with the princes of France or the great merchants of Italy. His silence is entirely creditable to him; it was doubtless part of his code of honour as a public servant, especially as a feudal servant; but it is not very helpful to his biographers. A little is known, merely because it was generally known, about the object of some of his journeys abroad; but there are others that seem to me to have been of the Secret Service that is really secret. But this contrast between his ease and gaiety on the subject of himself, and his sobriety and silence on the subject of his business, is very characteristic of the man; and strikes that note of balance, or the power of keeping two different considerations in the mind, which will later be found a clue to deeper things. Chaucer (as has been said) was not so simple as he looked. It would be quite false to say, in modern English, that his simplicity was doubled by duplicity. But it would be quite true to say, in the older Latin, that he was duplex; that is, that he could think about two things at once. This sort of noble and honourable duplicity will later be found relevant to his philosophy and his religion.

But the practical matter, for the moment, is that even his public life was a private life. It is only recorded in a few official entries, and we have to depend upon these, or upon things equally meagre, for much of our speculation about all that was really more private, in the sense of more personal. Perhaps this is most notably the case in the matter of the dates of his poems; a difficult matter which is somewhat doubtfully tested by the foreign influences brought in by his foreign travels. Thus, his work was at one time divided into a French and an Italian period; just as his diplomatic career was divided into a French and an Italian plan of movements. Later discussion has shown a tendency rather to turn on a distinction between the two Italian visits; many believing that it was not until the second that he received anything like the full Italian influence. These matters will be dealt with later, not indeed in detail; for there is little that can be called detail; but with reference to the real differences between his French and English and Italian elements. Here it is sufficient to fix the main facts as they concern a biography, even if it be a literary biography. Chaucer began his career as an envoy in foreign parts with certain negotiations in France, referring probably to the peace after the disastrous war and to other things. In 1367, we find him receiving a pension under the particular title of *valettus*: a Court office which, quaintly enough, is sometimes translated as Valet and sometimes as Yeoman. It would be hard to find two words which have strayed farther from each other in their subsequent significance. Anyhow, the next glimpse we have of the poet is that of a ceremonial functionary, carrying a torch or lifting a curtain, in the ordinary small rituals that surround royalty: But it is plain that this was only a sort of interlude, and his missions to France were soon followed by the first of his missions to Italy. It involved his going abroad, apparently alone, with a little money and some letters of exchange; and its full object perhaps will never be known. In 1372 he went to parley with two citizens of Genoa about a port in England suitable to the Genoese trade. It is much debated, among

Chaucerian critics, whether the great enthusiasm he certainly showed later for Italian literature came to him through this first visit; but the best authorities now seem to think that all the really valuable 'Italianate' work was done after the second visit in 1378. Anyhow, his first important work, which is not Italianate at all, was the lament over the Duchess who was the wife of John of Gaunt: and the question of his relation to the House of Lancaster would suffice to bring us back to more practical and personal elements in his own life.

Among the very scrappy scraps that historians have had to piece together, there is mention in the year 1366 of a certain Philippa Chaucer being one of the attendants of the Queen. She was granted a pension, and later on we find the pension being paid through her husband Geoffrey Chaucer. This has given rise to endless disputes and difficulties; ranging from the suggestion that Geoffrey had revived the family fancy for Chaucers marrying Chaucers, and married a cousin of the same surname, to a deep and delicate dispute about whether he could possibly have been married in 1366, when a poem written about that year expresses the sentiment of a disappointed lover. Leaving the latter point for a moment, we may note that the theory of any close cousinship involves a non-existent dispensation from Rome, and in any case does not seem necessary. The alternative theory favoured is that he married Philippa de Roet; and if he did, a really interesting situation arises.

If he did, it would seem that two strides, both almost accidental, really took him into a world far above his own. For it so happened, merely by chance, that Philippa de Roet's sister was engaged in John of Gaunt's family as a governess; it seems too probable that she became John of Gaunt's mistress; and it is quite certain that she eventually became his wife. She was his third wife; and men at that

Public and Private Life

stage have often something a little senile about their sentiment. But something seems to tell us that she must have been rather a remarkable woman, whether in a pleasant or an unpleasant fashion; and it seems not altogether unlikely that some remarkable qualities ran in the family. Perhaps there was also something remarkable about her sister Philippa, that attracted the attention of the most subtle judge of character in that age. But beyond that, there seems very little material for judgment. What is much more to the point is, however, that if this identification be true, Chaucer had one wild leap of luck apart from all his services. By a sort of *mésalliance* nobody could have foreseen, the vintner's son became something very like a brother-in-law of the Blood Royal.

The present writer is prayerfully conscious that he was never meant to be a biographer; not having that eye for detail which can trace a tenable theory among many doubts. On the other hand, if unlearned in the more recondite documents, he has in his time studied about one thousand detective-stories, and is often struck by the resemblance between the ingenuity of their authors and the ingenuity of the learned biographers. The true biographer hunts down a hero as the romantic detective hunts down a villain; tracking him, so to speak, by lost buttons and cigarette ends; deducing his designs from his slightest scribbles or scraps of paper; drawing hints from eavesdropping on his most casual conversational remarks. Unfortunately, there is a fallacy in transferring these talents to the task of biography. A decent detective story is itself a selected bundle of clues, with a few blinds as carefully selected as the clues. If therefore the reader, or his romantic detective, finds that somebody has made a note of the latest train to Market Harborough, or observes somebody else wave his hat towards a particular window with a striped green blind, he knows that these

92

things have some connexion, however obscure or remote, with the great problem of who hanged Admiral Bundleton with his own bootlaces. But when we are dealing with the whole life of a real human being, and trying to trace its outstanding events, it is not in the least necessary, it is not in the least likely, that all the trivial incidents or allusions will refer to outstanding events. Many of them will refer to things that nobody can possibly discover, after five hundred years; many to things that were next to nothing even at the time; some actually to nothing at all. But some of the illustrious Chaucerian scholars, to whom the world owes such everlasting thanks for elucidating the text and many of the true facts, sometimes seem to be unable to realize this reality. They cannot believe that they are not sleuths, following a trail that was laid for them and cunningly darting upon clues that they were meant to see. Whatever Chaucer does or says, however idly or carelessly, can be taken down and used in evidence against him. Everything that could be an expression of his private feelings is supposed to refer to his private life. Anything, that could be twisted into the expression of an intention, must be an intention that he seriously entertained; anything like an intention that he seriously entertained must be an intention that he actually carried out. If he says anything, anywhere, in any connexion, referring to marriage, he must be referring to his own marriage. If he says, after writing a tragedy, that he would rather like to write a comedy, it must be some comedy that he actually wrote. If he should happen to say, or even happen to make one of his characters say, that he does not like the subject of some story, it must mean that he does not like a particular rival poet, who happens to have told the story. If he makes one of his characters claim to have gone somewhere where he himself actually went, then the fictitious character must be

93

meant for a portrait of himself. This sort of hunting for hints is wonderfully exciting and very profitable and edifying—in murder-stories. But it is not human; and it has no relation to real human life. And when they come to what is in fact the very foggiest and most fanciful phase of human nature, young love and sentiment about the other sex, they become all the more ruthlessly like policemen on the pounce.

Chaucer wrote a poem, apparently an early poem, called 'An Exclamation of the Death of Pity'. It is all about a young gentleman being in love with a young lady, and talking about her to various other people, allegorical and otherwise, in the medieval manner; and complaining especially that pity is dead and there is no hope of the fulfilment of his dream; which certainly seems a rather dreamy sort of dream. But the most elaborate scaffolding of scientific dates and details has been erected on this chance metrical exercise of Chaucer; calculations about when he was married; about whether it could have been written after he was married; about whether, in that case, it proves that he was unhappily married; calculations about the date of his falling in love, the date of his falling out of love, and (of course) the exact identity of the only possible lady whom he could ever have loved. I may be very irresponsible, but all this seems to me to be extraordinarily wide of the mark, touching a man's actual life in this vale of tears. I should imagine that there never was a man, not actually convinced of a vocation of virginity somewhere about the age of seven, who had not had enough in the way of day-dreams and dallyings to have written such sentimental verse by the age of seventeen. Sentimental verse of that sort has been written about a total stranger; about a face seen in a crowd; about a person who did not exist at all. Yet all this subjective side of youthful poetry seems to be entirely forgotten, because we are trying to make an objective biography of Chaucer out of any objects lying about; as the buttons and cigarettes lie about in the murder story.

Now the fact is that youthful brooding is so subjective that it hardly even needs a subject. Certainly its literary self-expression can often be quite easily transferred to another subject. The poet preserves what the lover has forgotten; and many a famous love-poem may have been begun about one lady and finished about another. The time at which it was published is no clue to the time at which it was written. The time at which it was written is no clue to the theme that it was written about. Save in a few very vivid and personal examples, the theme may have even begun and ended in thought. And it seems to me very unfair to Mrs. Geoffrey Chaucer to deduce, in a detective manner, that her husband was unhappy with her; or that her husband was unfaithful to her; or indeed that there was anything whatever the matter with either of them, from anything so flimsy as the fact that her husband is the author of some rather artificial love-verses, that he might have written to anybody at any time, or touched up at any time, or decided to publish at any time.

Some of the other evidences that have been found before now, by detectives hovering round the Chaucer household, are much more ridiculous than this. Somebody found a confession of domestic tragedy in the fact that Chaucer confessed that he was a little liable to be cross with the voice that woke him up too early in the morning. This may have been a tribute to his dreams, though more probably to his taste for dreamless sleep; but it can hardly be regarded as a very definite and detailed criticism of his daily or domestic life. As to the hundred and one jests and jeers that are thrown throughout his works at women or wives or marriage, they do not differ from the ordinary conventional joke of Mrs.

95

Public and Private Life

Caudle's Curtain Lectures, or the picture of any hen-pecked husband in *Punch*, except in being much more refined. For the author of the Miller's Tale was refined. That is, he could be refined; and a good many modern writers are most coarse and clumsy when they intend to be refined. These jokes certainly prove nothing either way about the happiness of his marriage. Such jokes have been made by hundreds and thousands of happy and un-happy husbands, and fill all the libraries of the world. The people who write them think they are funny; they write them because they think they are funny; not because they describe exactly the facts of their own private lives. There seems, in short, to be a curious oblivion of the purely literary reasons for literature. Poetry generally comes out of the poet's life, as distinct from his biography; not out of what he did, but of what he thought when he was doing nothing; not out of the self that he expressed in working or wiving or flirting, but of the self that he could only ex-press in writing. Certainly he does not sit down and keep a diary in verse, with all the details relevant and realistic. That is not the way poetry is written. But it seems to be the way biography is written.

I therefore delicately deprecate the idea of biographers thus appearing as detectives; especially as that not very superior sort of detective employed to collect evidence for a divorce between Mr. and Mrs. Chaucer, five hundred years after their death. I do not know whether Mr. and Mrs. Chaucer were happy or unhappy. Apparently it has not occurred to our bright psychologists that they were probably both. There seems to be a certain lack of vivid-ness in envisaging what marriage is like, as well as what poetry is like. But, as Professor Pollard has justly said, what evidence there is rather points to Chaucer having been both happier and more religious and respectable while his wife was alive than afterwards. It is more to the point that he was apparently poorer afterwards. Which may be rather a compliment to the wife.

I have said that I attach very little importance to the merely exclamatory or flippant phrases, on which the theory of the poet's conjugal tragedy has been based. It is a good rough rule with Chaucer to translate him into modern English, or a parallel modern passage. The passage about his wife waking him up might be rendered more or less correctly thus: 'A voice woke me up, rather as somebody I needn't mention very often *does* wake me up; but then, you see, the voice was very mild or gentle, so I knew it wasn't my wife.' That remark might pass in the patter of any comedian, or the half-impersonal confessions of any comic writer, without being supposed to throw any very blazing or blasting light on the actual misery of his actual marriage. And this is perhaps the most positive and pointed of the purely literary allusions that have been used for this purpose. But it is only right to add that there is one piece of actual record, that is not merely a piece of literature or a lark, which can be interpreted in the sense that the poet had been practically misbehaving himself. It is a rather mysterious legal document in which a young woman named Cecilia de Chaumpaigne releases a Geoffrey Chaucer from his legal liability in some charge of abducting or eloping. It is quite possible, of course, that the matter was concerned with some real wrong, though this does not fully explain it. The woman presumably had some reason for having once involved Chaucer (if it was Chaucer) in the affair. It is equally true, on that argument, that she presumably had some reason for releasing him from it. The best Chaucerian authorities seem to think that it was not exactly a personal matter, but part of one of those curious family conspiracies for getting hold of people and marrying them to other selected people, which were rather a recurrent scan-

97

dal in those times; in one case of which Chaucer's own father had been the victim. Quite apart from morality, in which any man may fail, it was not at all typical of Chaucer's temperament to engage in any personal or isolated violence or lawlessness; and it is certainly the only mark of the sort against his name. It is possible that he might play something like the part of Pandarus to some Troilus in his own marrying and remarrying family; it seems more probable that he would play the part of mentor or moderator; hence, possibly, the special pardon to himself. There may have been almost any sort of complicated comedy of relations; there may have been simply a bad break and nothing else. The incident forms the most thrilling and entertaining chapter in that Possible Life of Geoffrey Chaucer, which I am not writing and do not intend to write.

We have seen that Chaucer's first Italian mission was to Genoa; it has been conjectuʲed that he went from there to Padua, where it would have been possible for him to meet, as he certainly would have wished to meet, the most famous and in one sense the first poet of the age. Petrarch was in Padua at the end of 1372; and there is certainly something at least like a coincidence in the fact that he was then turning into Latin the same story of Griselda which Chaucer later turned into English. This (if one may say so) seems to me a good example of the difference between reasonable and unreasonable deduction from our fragmentary documents. There is a real objective concrete coincidence or convergence of facts, or at any rate approximation of facts, in Chaucer, Genoa, Padua, Petrarch and Griselda, *plus* the fact that the Clerk of Oxford, in telling the tale of Griselda, actually mentions Petrarch and Padua. Any one of these things might happen without any connexion; but it is odd that they were all connected. But when people pass from this to saying that Chaucer must have meant the Clerk of Oxford for himself, or

Public and Private Life

rather a double of himself (seeing that he already happened to be present in his own person), and when they mix up Chaucer's gossiping greediness for all sorts of books with the concentration on Aristotle which is a part of the character of the Oxford Schoolman and philosopher, they go a great deal too fast and indulge in fancy. No two Canterbury Pilgrims can ever be confused for a moment; and the Clerk of Oxford is the Clerk of Oxford, and Chaucer is very emphatically Chaucer. Nevertheless, Chaucer *was* interested in philosophy; besides being, in a really natural sense, a natural philosopher.

It is very possible therefore that Chaucer did here enter for the first time into that golden air of the Roman culture that was soon to be the golden air of the Renaissance; at the gates of which, crowned with laurel, stood great Petrarch clad in gold. That was how he seemed, at least, to his contemporaries to stand; and Chaucer certainly did not fail to admire him, however soon or late he began to imitate him; but he seems to have admired Dante more, though he could hardly be expected to imitate him better. Whether there be any connexion or no between the two turns of his fate, it is certain that the mission to Italy was like a golden gate for the practical prosperity of Chaucer. His real period of wealth, public importance and (it is fair to add) public industry, stretches from that St. George's Day in 1374, when the great English poet received from the English King the highly symbolic pitcher of wine (which he afterwards turned into a pension), right away past the death of King Edward in 1377 to the time of the revolt of Gloucester in the councils of his grandson. In the summer of the same year he became Comptroller of the Customs and Subsidy of Wools, Skins and Tanned Hides in the Port of London, and his salary seems to have been augmented by a variety of other payments, in a rather patchwork fashion; by a pension from John of Gaunt; two

99

wardships which carried remuneration, and a special grant from the King on some wool forfeited for non-payment or duty. He then went on another foreign mission to Flanders, of a smaller and secret sort, and we find that in such cases he was allowed to appoint deputies for his official work. But, in the ordinary way, he was a good hard-working official. It is apparent in everything, from such details as we know about the work itself to the particular tone of the relief he expresses at having balanced his ledgers and gone back to his books. In that way he was a good business man; though perhaps rather of the type that is a better business man for his employers than for himself. It is a type not uncommon among good-tempered, abstracted, secretly imaginative men; the type that goes on for years as an excellent Government Office clerk, but when once it is superannuated and at leisure, is not always wise in dealing with its own hobbies or investments. There has been much talk about whether the breakdown in Chaucer's fortunes, and the relative poverty that fell upon him, was entirely due to the later political accident which turned him for a time out of office. It has been suggested, for instance, that a hobby of Astrology, accompanied by a more expensive hobby of Alchemy, ran away with a great deal of his money. In this connexion only two facts can be noted in a mere skeleton of facts like the present. First, Chaucer seems to have had a son named Lewis; presumably by Philippa Chaucer, who is thought to have died about 1387. Chaucer wrote for his son a little treatise on the Astrolabe, treating that scientific instrument very much as a toy, and definitely stating that, whatever there may be in astronomy, there is precious little in astrology. This has been held to refer to a grievance against such medieval experiments. But it seems to me quite sufficiently explained by the fact that Chaucer was a Christian and a Catholic, with plenty of common sense and an acquiescence in the Church's protest against the superstitions of fatalism and doom. Even if he had not been sensible enough to be orthodox on that subject, a man of his nature would certainly be specially orthodox when writing something for his own child. That might not have prevented him playing the fool with sham sciences himself; but the thing is quite unproved. The other proof offered is the very violent explosion against the fraud and rascality of Alchemy in the Canon's Yeoman's Tale, which sounds to some good critics like the real recital of a real wrong. We cannot tell whether Chaucer had this experience; we can be quite certain that he had this conviction.

His second Italian mission first arrests the attention by bringing in certain figures who counted for a good deal, either in life or literature. We find here certainly, for the first time, that he was a close friend of his famous contemporary, the poet Gower; for he left Gower as a deputy to look after his affairs. Here we have another of these typical fancies, that have hardened into theories; the theory of the broken friendship and subsequent quarrel of the two medieval poets. Their relation is of some historical interest, but this sort of guesswork is very unhistorical. We can only speculate on the friendship. Chaucer was a man for whom the world teemed with quiet fun, as it says in the comic opera; and I have often wondered whether he felt the full irony of the patronage to which men such as he are subject. I do not mean the royal or feudal patronage, which was simply a part of the social order of the time, which a sensible man of his type would probably accept as we accept policemen or postmen. It was considered part of the province of a prince to support artists and such odd people; and, though the thing had obvious abuses, there was something to be said for it, if we compare it in all aspects with the problem of the best-seller or the man

Public and Private Life

who starves in Fleet Street. But I mean that more subtle
patronage that is extended to poets by poets, and not by
patrons. There is always something a little quaint in that
relation of the rich artist and the poor artist; or the old
artist and the young artist; or the successful artist and the
other who is not as yet successful. It is recorded with
rather savage irony in Mr. Belloc's sketch of 'The Good
Poet and the Bad Poet'. Remember that Hayley as a poet,
and not merely Hayley as a squire, was in a position to
patronize Blake. There is a grim humour in the fact that
a man like Swift felt bound to mention a man like Temple
as a literary leader, and not merely as a social protector.
The practical patrons of Chaucer did not, so far as I know,
appear also as the rivals of Chaucer. At least I never heard
of John of Gaunt dropping into poetry; or Henry of
Bolingbroke capping *The Canterbury Tales* with a little
thing of his own. But the thing has more subtle forms
when it comes from the seniors of the school of letters;
from those who are, for any reason, considered more established, or more learned, or more in the official limelight,
than a mere stray genius. I have always felt that there was
a touch of this in the attitude of Ben Jonson to Shakespeare. I am pretty sure there was a touch of it in the
attitude of Gower to Chaucer.

John Gower seems to have had a vaguely national or
official function, which was never entirely accorded to
Chaucer, for all his laureateship and his butt of sack.
Shakespeare, following some tradition of tragedy, and
more especially of morality, uses the name for the funereal
figure appearing before the curtain as a Prologue or prophet of woe and wisdom, to draw all the proper morals
from the historical plays; as if it were the name of the
licensed and labelled moralist of English literature. Chaucer addresses him as, 'O moral Gower', distinguishing
him, in a departmental manner, from 'the philosophical

102

Public and Private Life

Strode', whose province was presumably philosophy. But the delicate difference of tone appears when we pass from what Chaucer said to Gower to what Gower said to Chaucer. Gower was thoroughly friendly; entirely affable. He says that Chaucer is his poet; but he also says that Chaucer is his disciple and even 'his own clerk', who has taken down many of his thoughts, perhaps in somewhat lighter language. And in his doubtless sincere compliment to Chaucer's verse, we have exactly the same suggestion as that made by many graver poets about Shakespeare and his warbling of wood-notes:

> *Of dytees and of songes glade*
> *The whiche he for my sake made.*

One would not say that the graver poets disapprove of cheerfulness in the minor poets; but they mention it. Chaucer, like Matthew Arnold in Max's caricature, was not at all times wholly serious. Without claiming to have read every line and word of the moral Gower, which would be a boast of no little hardihood, I suspect that he was, for the most part, wholly serious. When I hint that it is barely possible that Chaucer saw some humour in all this, I do not mean to discredit the view that the two poets were friends. They were both, in their way, men of good will, and one of them was conspicuously a man of good humour. That sort of friendship need not go wrong, unless both the friends treat it wrongly. Blake abused Hayley like a pickpocket; but then Blake was as hard to please as Hayley was tactless in pleasing. Chaucer was not at all hard to please. It is written all over his work that he was very easy to please. George Macdonald finely said that God is easy to please and hard to satisfy; and there is something of that in many great men. I can believe that Chaucer was pleased with Gower's patronage, though I rather doubt if he was satisfied with Gower's poetry.

103

Public and Private Life

These being the human and rather humorous proba-
bilities of the case, the ingenious melodrama of the mortal
quarrel of the poets has apparently been made up merely
out of one chance remark in *The Canterbury Tales*. It is the
characteristic remark of Chaucer that he dislikes stories of
which the subject is some horrible perversion or monstros-
ity; he mentions one such legend, which does happen to
have been dealt with by Gower. We can only say that this
might conceivably have led to a quarrel; but I can find no
direct evidence that it ever did. To say it could only have
been written *because* of a quarrel seems to me simple nonsense. For the rest, Gower's place in the biography is that
of the friend whom Chaucer left to represent him when
he went to Italy for the second time: that second visit
which introduced him to other historical persons of importance; notably to Bernabo Viscounti of Milan, whose
tragedy attracted the sympathy of Chaucer, as remains
recorded in the Monk's Tale. He was not long in Italy
this time, but most critics hold that he saw more books and
manuscripts and received then his real introduction to
Italian letters. There seems to follow an expanding leisure
and importance at home; he was given a new Comptrollership; he was able to appoint a permanent deputy
for his old Comptrollership, and in the same year, 1385,
he was made a Justice of the Peace for Kent, and in the
following year a Member of Parliament, as Knight of the
Shire for Kent. Thus he seems to settle down and spread
himself in that very English landscape through which he
and his great company will ride for ever; when there came
the sharp turn in his destiny and something even like
disaster.

Richard the Second, the grandson of the old King, had
come to the throne as a mere boy; though a rather remarkable boy, to judge by the presence of mind and instinct, at
once princely and popular, with which in his boyhood he

Public and Private Life

faced and pacified the Peasant Rising. But he naturally suffered from uncles; generally either from John of Gaunt, the Duke of Lancaster, or from his other uncle, the Duke of Gloucester. Lancaster went abroad, leaving his protégés unprotected; Gloucester seized the power and almost the person of the young King, and in the overturn Mr. Geoffrey Chaucer lost all his comfortable jobs, which were given to the Gloucester party. There follow clear indications that he had fallen on evil days. He obtains protection for a year against being sued for debts; he sells some of his pensions for cash down. Relatively to his previous prosperity, his comparative poverty seems to have continued till his death. But relatively to these first pressing years of poverty, immediately after Gloucester's palace revolution, he makes a very considerable recovery; and seems to have received royal help once more, whenever he really required it. For Richard the Second, a year after he had become a man, determined to become a King. He suddenly rent the rod of office from Gloucester; summoned back John of Gaunt, and resumed that sort of rule which Victorian historians always called despotic, especially when it was slightly democratic. The effects of this, and of his ultimate fall, on English history were very great and have been considered elsewhere. But the effects on Geoffrey Chaucer were very practical and consoling; for he was appointed Clerk of the Works in the repairing of the greatest public buildings: the Tower of London and the Palace of Westminster, and St. George's Chapel at Windsor. He was later made a commissioner for the repair of high-roads, and though these jobs did not last indefinitely, he was never entirely neglected after the return of John of Gaunt. Richard the Second gave him a new pension in 1394, and later a tun of wine. Fortunately, also, even the fall of King Richard, which changed so many things, did not change this partial recovery of Chaucer's more moderate prosperity. Whatever else Henry Bolingbroke was, he was John of Gaunt's son, and had no quarrel with his father's old poet. He sent him a fresh pension in response to the humorous melancholy of the poet's 'Complaint to his Purse'; and with this Chaucer passed his last days in peace. But his last days had come. He died just after he had moved into a house near St. Mary's Chapel, from which he is said to have looked out in his last hours on the gardens and the great roof of the Abbey.

More than one portrait of Chaucer remains to give a general idea of his appearance, though that was the time of the first beginnings of portraiture in paint, at least in this country, as Chaucer himself may be called the beginning of portrait-painting in literature. The pictures we have represent him as he was in later life, when the Host of the Tabard chaffed him on his stoutness. It would be interesting to have an earlier impression, touching the days when he was light on his feet, and knew fighting and foreign travel, yet had already what was called his elvish face and the pleasant shyness that covered so much sharpness. The best existing portrait is that published by the poet Occleve, to illustrate one of his own poems. It shows the head in a black hood against a green ground; two tufts of grey beard and a wisp of whitish hair rather recall, at least to modern associations, the elvish comparison; but the face is sober and benevolent, not without something of that sleepiness touched with slyness, that is the mood of much of his later work. Red cords on his dress support writing materials and he appears to be carrying a rosary; at least, as it is certainly a string of beads, it seems most likely that it is a rosary. For I cannot suppose that Chaucer's quarrel with the Friar, even if it went to the point of assault and battery, would have prevented him from carrying what has been called the Layman's Breviary, devoted to the Virgin to whom he

Public and Private Life

had so much devotion, merely because the instrument happens to have been invented by St. Dominic. However that may be, the portrait is unmistakably a portrait; the person unmistakably a person. And it is easy to imagine the old man, in much that habit and condition, pottering about the Gothic lanes of Westminster, until he died, almost to a day (it is conjectured), coincidently with the death of the flamboyant, toppling and tottering fourteenth century.

He was buried, as we all know, in Westminster Abbey; the first of the poets to lie in Poets' Corner. There have been differences about the tomb, of late Gothic design, that still covers his bones; but it is certainly so far a genuinely Gothic thing, that it is the only thing in that Corner that suggests the idea of a corner. The more modern monuments do not suggest the sort of persons who would be content in any case to remain in corners. Even if it were erected much later, and not in the best medieval manner, it is so far medieval that it does suggest that the buried man is buried; not that he is impatiently and prematurely resurrected before the Resurrection. Even here we feel something of that *communis sententia*, or medieval common sense; which was so much less rhetorical, and therefore so much more really rational, than the rational eighteenth century. Few will deny that the figures which fill the Abbey to-day, mostly the relics of the eighteenth century, are in their nature rather rhetorical. I do not mind such rhetoric in its place; but I doubt if its place is a Gothic church, and I think it is made to look rather silly by the silent presence of the Gothic tomb. The latter seems to say, in the language of a simpler time, that Galfridus Chaucer had lived his life, and this monument commemorated his death; and that, *salva fide*, there was an end of it. He had swaggered a little in his day, and that cheerfully and pleasantly; but he does

Public and Private Life

not swagger solemnly in his death. He had served in arms, and been among swords and soldiers; but he does not stand wildly waving a sabre and bestriding a cannon, like General Sir Peveril Potts, whose services in the campaign before the Peace of Utrecht will leap to all our memories. He had done his best for his country in diplomatic negotiations with foreigners, and settled several questions of royal ransoms or marriages of considerable importance in their day; but he does not stand grasping a scroll or pointing to a map like the Right Hon. Benjamin Buffle, whose patriotic virtues have boiled over from his tomb in billows of bloated marble. He had written a little thing or two that some have admired; but he does not lean elegantly on an urn or look up at a laurel or invoke an invisible Muse, as does the immortal Timmins, whose works were so widely read by the fashionable world in the Age of Reason. He does not strike any attitudes as do the varied representatives of that remarkable company; including, I believe, five or six professional politicians and one butler; probably the most respectable person present. He does not offer any remarks, by means of post-mortem pantomime or sculptured signal or gesticulation. He lies prostrate as when death struck him down; in the last dark instant when he cried upon Christ.

Chapter IV

THE GARDEN OF ROMANCE

Chaucer advances into the light of literary history out of a forest of tangled traditions, translations, imitations, partial imitations and patchwork col-laborations, like a figure emerging from that chequered and glimmering forest of dreams in which such medieval figures so often walk; in which a half-human figure will carry two faces under a hood of allegory, and haunting half-recognizable voices speak from behind the golden masks of the gods. Most people realize more or less the curious sort of communism in culture that prevailed in those days. Some, however, hardly realize that there were two sides to it. Many medieval translators really were in-venting, even while they were translating—or stealing. While the modern egoist has the rather petty prudence of Polonius, and will neither a borrower nor a lender be, the medieval traditional translator would often lend as well as borrow. We first find a poem and read it as if it were an original; and then are surprised to find that it is a rather close translation. Then we read it as a translation, and are surprised again to find that it contains a great deal that is purely original. It is hard to say which of the two would seem the stranger, in the case of any strong and sincere talent to-day. Modern writers are intense individualists, and certainly none more so than the Socialists. If Mr. Bernard Shaw, say, or some more impatient intellect of recent times, had just begun his literary career, he certainly would not begin it by writing laborious English versions of the longest novels of Tolstoy. But still less, if possible, would he add to the length of the works of Tolstoy long passages entirely invented by Bernard Shaw. We should not find the whole dramatic story of Candida somehow embedded in the story of Anna Karenina. We should not find all the best speeches in *Arms and the Man* put into the mouths of moujiks, in the retreat from Moscow described in *War and Peace.* And that is exactly how the medieval translators used to go on. At the first glance, they almost seem to be publishing somebody else's book as their own. At the second glance, they seem to be gratuitously giving away their own work to improve somebody else's book. It cannot be understood without calling up a vanished world of the community of thoughts and themes, in which a tale or a topic was in some sense set up like a target; in which a romantic story was rather like a smoking-room story, which can be told over and over again, with variations by different story-tellers. One author did not so much rob the other as enrich the other. These ragged Northern poets may have taken refuge in the ruins of Greek temples or Italian villas, but not merely in the manner of bats and owls; they repaired the ruins not merely with new stones, but with precious stones. They often wore second-hand clothes; but they patched the old garment, not only with new cloth, but with cloth of gold.

It is necessary, to start with, to make this point clear about the spontaneity and sincerity of the translator. In this, even more than other things, the modern change has chilled the sense of scale or grandeur in Chaucer. There exists a fine French ballade, addressed to Chaucer by a contemporary in France; lauding his work up to the skies with a warmth it would be impossible to doubt; and it has for a refrain, like a burst of boisterous salutation: 'Grant

The Garden of Romance

translateur! noble Geffroy Chaucier.' Some English critics
have been a little sniffy (I can use no other word) in receiving this fervent foreign compliment; because it appears to describe Chaucer merely as a translator. On the
other hand, a brilliant French critic, who does full justice
to the poet otherwise, has in this matter also a faint suggestion of sniffiness (I apologize again to the academy of
pure English), in so far as he seems to insist that Chaucer
was merely a translator; touching certain words of which
much has been made. Chaucer was a translator; but his
French critic seems to me to miss his countryman's full
meaning in speaking of a *great* translator. It is not easy
nowadays to think of the thing on quite that scale; partly
because it is badly paid; partly because it is badly done.
Talking of 'a great translator' sounds like talking of 'a
great scrivener', or 'a great stenographer'. But this is to
leave out that vital medieval virtue; the enthusiasm of the
translator, his primary motive of admiration; sometimes
admiration for the author; sometimes simply admiration
for the subject. It will be necessary to note, in another
connexion, that it is indeed impossible to translate poetry,
in the sense of finding a precise equivalent to poetical
language. But it is none the less possible to be inspired
to write fine native verse by the inspiration of fine foreign
verse; or sometimes, even, of slight foreign verse. Indeed,
I am disposed to suspect that a translation is always either
much greater or much smaller than the original. Now
some of Chaucer's translations were much greater than
the original. All of them were, in a rather curious sense,
more original than the original. All of them seem to move
quite naturally in English poetry; though English poetry,
in a manner of speaking, had only just begun to move.
Indeed translations of this old natural sort do seem to find
it easy to get naturalized. 'Drink to me only with thine
eyes', is not a less lyric essentially English because it is

III

taken, almost line by line, from the Greek. 'When lovely woman stoops to folly', is none the less an English poem because it was taken, almost word for word, from the French. But in the case of Chaucer we are dealing with something much deeper than the eighteenth-century sentiment of Goldsmith or the robust pedantry of Ben Jonson. He was often dealing with those profound intellectual passions that concern themselves with the ultimates of the universe; with the philosophy that is even prior to poetry. He was moved to translate the original, he was moved to make the translation greater than the original, not by personal rivalry, or even by personal admiration, but by what he himself would call the *primum mobile*, or Great Mover of all hearts and heads; by a direct appeal, not to the original, but to the origin.

Those who do not happen to understand these emotions are at a disadvantage in the matter. This appears very clearly, for instance, in a composition which is generally placed by scholars among Chaucer's early works, and is certainly among his traditional works. I mean the alphabetical address to the Blessed Virgin, commonly called Chaucer's A B C. The French critic, to whom I have referred, pins the matter down to the single point that this poem is undoubtedly a copy of a similar French prayer, written by a French priest. He seems to make everything turn on the fact that the French priest wrote the poem in short lines, and the English poet was wise enough to widen them into long lines. In other words, while admitting the artistic effect, he tends to insinuate that it is an artificial effect. He congratulates Chaucer as an artist or artificer; but he congratulates him upon having selected a more ingenious form of verse, or made an experiment in metre. But this sort of technicality is not tenable in the presence of the poem itself. At least, it is not enough to satisfy any one with a strong sense of poetry.

The Garden of Romance

The original French poem is an honest but somewhat bald statement in very short lines; the first line being 'A toy du monde le refui'. Chaucer merely turns his mind to the same subject, and bursts out, 'Almighty and all-merciable Queen!' You do not produce that sort of line by counting the syllables.

Chaucer is not expanding his metre; he is expanding himself. He is expanding his lungs and his heart, like a man stretching out his arms in the pattern of the cross. He only breaks out of the framework of the French metre, because there was not room in it to stretch his arms. The mere words, as they stand, call up the image of a man so standing; and making some such wide gesture of worship. Of course, having once created his lyric metre, by merely breaking into his lyric cry, he has to sustain it throughout the poem, like any other poet; and sometimes sustains it with some difficulty, or (what is worse) with too great ingenuity; also like any other poet. But the poem is not a piece of ingenuity; certainly not a piece of metrical ingenuity. It is an original poem, in the sense that the emotions have their origin in the poet, and not merely in the other poet whose work he had read. I know that; as I know when a love-song is a love-song; or whether a drinking song could really be sung in chorus. Luckily or unluckily, as the case may be, this is a curious kind of lovesong. The writer quoted above, remarks, in a tone not uncommon also among some of the English writers on the subject: 'The learned critic Ten Brink, basing his opinion on this prayer as well as some other effusions addressed to the Virgin Mary, which are to be found in Chaucer's work, concluded that he must have passed through a period of intense devotion, more especially towards the Virgin Mary. That is possible.'

It is. It does occur from time to time. I do not quite understand why Chaucer must have 'passed through' this fit of devotion; as if he had Mariolatry like the measles. Even an amateur who has encountered the malady may be allowed to testify that it does not usually visit its victim for a brief 'period'; it is generally chronic and (in some sad cases I have known) quite incurable. And as Chaucer's work, practically beginning with translations like the A B C, practically ends with the almost excessive devotionalism of the Parson's Tale, and has any number of devotional declarations scattered between the two, I cannot understand why his very normal European religion should only be allowed to him during one peculiar period of delirium. But in any case, the point that concerns us here is that Chaucer wrote a poem as well as a translation. It is a poetical poem, not because of its relation to its original, but because of its relation to its subject. It is full of lines that have a certain large and liberal majesty, because they are filled with the greatness of the occasion: 'Glorious maid and mother, which that never were bitter, neither in the earth nor sea'—'O very light of eyen that ben blind, O very lust of labour and distress'—'And bringest him out of the crooked street; whoso thee loveth, he shall not love in vain.' If this were a translation of a heathen hymn to the sun, it would still be the sort which a man only writes by staring at the sun. If this were a Scandinavian song of the sea, it would be one which a man writes by knowing the sea, and not merely by knowing the Scandinavian songbook. And the purely literary moral, apart from any moral moral, of all this passage in the poet's life, is that he was already emphatically a poet, even if he was still a translator. He is a poet because he sings; because he opens his lungs and liberates his soul by a resounding and rhythmic utterance, the expression of love or admiration or passionate amazement. It is a primary and not secondary expression; as would be proved in answering the question: 'But what is he admiring?' Is he singing out in admiration

The Garden of Romance

of Guillaume de Deguileville, of Chalis, the original singer
of the French A B C? No; not at the moment. He is singing to the singer of the Magnificat.

I have begun with this example, not because it is chro-
nologically the first, or perhaps even one of the first,
examples of that dependence on tradition in which Chaucer's work begins; but because it is a clear and compact
case of the way in which a man may easily be expressing
the most positive and even passionate feelings of his own,
and yet be technically a traditional type of translator.
This double truth runs through the whole of the work
of Chaucer, the whole of the work rightly or wrongly
attributed to Chaucer, and indeed through the whole of
the works of his contemporaries, which are not by Chaucer at all. The disputes about the actual chronology of
Chaucer's first writings are such that the most learned
are those, confessedly, who know that they know nothing.
The controversy is extraordinarily complex, because of
this communal character in medieval literature which I
have already mentioned. When he was ostensibly writing an original poem, he thought nothing of quoting at
enormous length from anybody who happened to interest
him, for any reason. When he was avowedly writing a
translation, of a recognized Latin or French original, he
thought nothing of putting in chunks of Chaucer which
are not in the original at all. But this part of the problem
presents itself first, on fairly clear grounds, in the case of
the two longer and more important works, with which
Chaucer certainly dealt among his earliest experiments;
and in which he appears as a true translator, without any
particular doubt or disguise about the matter. The first
example is his translation of *The Romance of the Rose*; if
I may frankly translate the title as the poet did the poem.
The other was his translation of Boethius on *The Consolations of Philosophy*.

The Garden of Romance

The Romance of the Rose is rather like the Briar Rose of Pre-Raphaelite legend. It is very beautiful and rather difficult to get through. It is a long allegorical French poem, which was written in two parts by two distinct and indeed very different poets. If we compare it to the Briar Rose, we may say that the first half contains most of the roses and the second half most of the thorns. That is, the first four thousand lines were written by one Guillaume de Lorris, and are a grave and graceful allegory of the kind that can be traced like a tapestry in the background of the medieval mind; the description of a dream, a magical garden inhabited by Virtues and other valuable abstractions; much healthier company than many real persons in fact or fiction, but not very stimulating to a modern taste. The rest of the poem was added nearly half a century afterwards by the satirist Jean de Meung. He seems to have declined to accept the medieval convention that everything in the garden was lovely; with the result that everything in the garden became considerably more lively. Like Chaucer and Langland and the best men of the time, Jean de Meung was perfectly orthodox so far as theology was concerned; but, like them, and perhaps much more than they, he was critical of the growing corruptions and abuses of the Church. His satire was enormously fashionable, especially as some ecclesiastics had condemned it; just as if it were a modern improper novel. In any case, he was a man of ideas, over and above the one idea of the conventional though beautiful allegory; and he probably had a great deal of intellectual influence on Chaucer. But exactly how he and Chaucer stand to each other in connexion with the documents, it is very difficult to decide. It is enough to say here that a very long and continuous English version of the French poem does exist, and is apparently, or at least partially, by Chaucer; but that Chaucer himself (in the medieval manner of which I have

116

The Garden of Romance

spoken) is said to have confused the question further by putting in long passages that do not come either from his original or from himself, but are simply things that happened to please him in all sorts of other authors; chiefly ancient or classical authors. Possibly he may have thought that when something so luxuriant and unlimited as the Briar Rose had once begun to grow, there could not be too much of it. But this was in his early days, and I fancy that by the time he had developed the thrifty and cutting critical quality of *The Canterbury Tales*, he would have admitted that the beautiful entanglement of the Briar Rose was a bit too thick. Nevertheless, his work has never cut in two quite in the style of the work he translated; and in him the blossom and bramble remained a fairly recurrent design. There was always something courteous about him that would not obtrude a thorn without covering it with a rose; and something malicious about him which would not offer a rose without hiding a thorn.

Beyond this, the only general effect of *The Romance of the Rose* on his life is, as has been said, rather the effect of a decorative background. It was all this sort of thing that a poet meant by poetry, in the fourteenth century; as distinct from his own personal experiments or curiosities in poetry; which eventually became much more curious and experimental in Chaucer than they did in any of his contemporaries. But this is the starting-point of his poetical journey. This is the tradition which he took at first for granted as the tradition of his trade; this is the education as distinct from the evolution of a poet. All the medieval poets began with this story of a dream. We might say that they all began by walking in their sleep; a company of singing somnambulists. It is curious to think that *he* began so; who came to be, of all poets perhaps, the most conspicuously wide awake.

The business of the translation of Boethius touches a

general truth, even at the beginning, which will become more apparent and important towards the end. The relation of medieval men to philosophy, and enlightenment in general, was rather curious; and is not covered by the natural metaphors employed. We used to talk of the Dark Ages; most of us know by now that the true Dark Ages came before the true Middle Ages; and that in many ways the Middle Ages were far from dark. But, following the figure of an age of darkness, we are apt to think of an age of twilight; or perhaps, of grey morning light. But the metaphor itself is misleading. Twilight means an equally diffused light; and the difficulty of medievalism was the difficulty of diffusion. It would be truer to compare even the Dark Ages to a dark room, with certain chinks in the shutters through which particular rays of light could pierce. But the light was daylight, what there was of it; and not even a dull or troubled daylight. It was broad daylight that came through a narrow hole. Or it was like some long narrow ray of a searchlight sent out from a great city and falling like a spotlight on a remote village or a lonely man. And just as any man, however much in darkness, if he looks right down the searchlight, looks into a furnace of white-hot radiance, so any medieval man, who had the luck to hear the right lectures or look at the right manuscript, did not merely 'follow a gleam', a grey glimmer in a mystical forest; but looked straight down the ages into the radiant mind of Aristotle. There was indeed, as I have said, any amount of indirect transmission of light; any amount of reflection—in every sense. But I am not talking of the quantity, but of the quality of the light. Such light as they had came, not only from the broad daylight, but from the brilliant daylight; it was the buried sunlight of the Mediterranean. These men seem to be, and in some ways were, men simple or primitive. But their philosophy was not merely simple or primitive.

The Garden of Romance

In some cases it came from a ripe and rounded civilization; in some cases even from an over-ripe, from an autumnal civilization; from an over-civilized civilization. We might compare them to children in some cold and gloomy March, looking at the barns filled with the grain garnered by dead men in a forgotten autumn; but anyhow they fed their wild boyhood on things that were mature, and sometimes more than mature. Hence we have the paradox that a rude and primitive society, in some sense starting afresh, yet had so often for its guides, not merely the writers of the old world, but the writers of the world when it was growing old. All such paradoxes work back to the pardox: that the further we go back to the first ages of the modern world, the nearer we are to the last ages of the ancient world; as King Arthur stands in Britain at once as the first of the Britons and the last of the Romans. Thus a primitive poem, like Abbo's 'Siege of Paris', stops amid the storm of northern arrows rattling on rude roofs and walls, to make mythological conceits that had been copied from the copyists of Ovid or Virgil for five hundred years. But Ovid and Virgil are not the less civilized poets because barbarians continued to copy them. The men of a new civilization were not the less able to understand the civilized poets, because they had been continually copied. In a word, medieval men were not in the twilight; what they knew they knew. They had not read Homer at all; and (strange as it seems in a literate and enlightened age) did not despise him because they had not read him. They had read Virigil much more fully and thoroughly than we have. Anyone who doubts it may make the experiment of quoting beautiful Virgilian lines in a first-class railway carriage, full of politicians and captains of industry. In a word, though their knowledge of civilized antiquity was in a sense scrappy, though the scraps were not only old scraps but sometimes stale scraps, they had

The Garden of Romance

enough of them to understand what the great ancients had meant by wisdom; and, unlike some others, they had the great wisdom truly to try to be wise.

The case of Boethius illustrates specially the second truth; that the spring of medievalism had fed on the autumn of classicism. Boethius was a man who lived very late in the break-up of the Empire, under Theodoric. The period, with its power of amalgamating old and new, has been much underrated. Boethius hands on the Stoic memories; but it is not really necessary to deny that he was a Christian or assert that he was a nominal Christian. Many pagan philosophers were converted by Christian philosophy. His work was a sort of distillation of all that had been best in Paganism; small in quantity but good in quality. Thus he served very truly as a guide, philosopher and friend to many Christians; precisely because, while his own times were corrupt, his own culture was complete. Generally speaking, the cultured Mediterranean man had come to play this part towards northern men. His disciples had not read Homer, but he had; they did not remember one kingdom acknowledged from Scotland to Syria, but he did; they did not know in detail what fine shades of feeling or criticism had come with Catullus or Lucian, but he did. Thus (in the special case of Boethius) we find this mirror of maturity still reflecting a lost daylight in the darkest age; and playing a unique part, especially in the development of the English. Boethius, who had been martyred for justice by his barbarian master, wrote in prison a book called 'The Consolations of Philosophy'; in which he summed up all the truth and tradition of antiquity. Alfred of Wessex, the first great man of our own island story, wishing to educate his half-savage Saxons, assumes at once that it can be done best by translating Boethius. He also, like those who followed him, put a great deal into Boethius that is not in Boethius. He

The Garden of Romance

may be said to have completed the old Stoic's conversion to Christianity after his death. Chaucer, perhaps the last great Englishman of the same united Christendom, feeling the same need of portable philosophy, instantly turned to the same idea of a translation of Boethius. He also quotes from Boethius, consciously and unconsciously, in any number of his ordinary poems. Boethius was a point of view; it was a calm and cultured and well-balanced point of view; and the essential thing to realize is that a medieval man could have it as a common and normal point of view; and take it quite easily, like Chaucer.

All that we mean, in common talk, by 'taking things philosophically' was possible to a medieval man like Chaucer, even if we mean no more by philosophy than his whistling or shrugging his shoulders. The possibility is worth recalling, because it is generally rather left out of sight, both by those praising medievalism and those reviling it; by those who most admire its mysticism and those who rage most fanatically at its fanaticism. These elements, bad and good, did exist; but there were other elements; other fragments of the old Roman pavement of the world; other bits of the broken Christian empire of Constantine, that a man could pick up here and there. One of them was this Christian stoicism, or what would now be called manliness; and Chaucer was much attracted to it. We may mention here the handful of small poems in which the influence appears; though the dates of all of them seem to be rather doubtful. It stiffens the very virile and spirited little ballade with its familiar lines:

> Hold the hye wey, and lat thy gost thee lede:
> And trouthe shal delivere, hit is no drede.

Somewhat of the same sort is the moral appeal he addressed to Richard the Second on Steadfastness, decidedly a Stoic as well as a Christian idea. The remarkable poem, commonly called 'Gentilesse', in which he appeals to Christian equality against feudal inequality, might be said to savour of that remote concept of citizenship, which had once been left in the code of Justinian as the legacy of the Christian Caesars; anyhow, it suggests an aspect not always considered in the conventional conceptions of heraldry and chivalry. The poem called 'Fortune' opens with a self-sufficing defiance quite in the way of the ancients, and invokes the great name of Socrates: though Chaucer's sense of humour (a very Christian thing) leads him to let Fortune, as a lady, have the last word. The poem called 'The Former Age', a sort of Earthly Paradise, is almost altogether a paraphrase from Boethius.

Anyhow, as has been noted, he did deal thus with Boethius and *The Romance of the Rose*. These two translations were translations, whenever they were written or whatever was written along with them. When we come to the original poems of Chaucer, we come to much disputed matters, especially in the matter of chronology. We have very little to guide us except Chaucer's own references in his own writing, which are generally very amusing and rather disparaging references. We have also the dates of some historical events more or less clearly connected with the poems. Thus we know that by the time he wrote *The Legend of Good Women*, whenever that time was, he had already written the poem on the death of the Duchess, the wife of John of Gaunt; *The House of Fame*; *The Parlement of Foules*, and *Troilus and Criseyde*. For in the *Legend* he makes Love complain that Chaucer has mocked lovers in translating *The Romance of the Rose* and depressed their spirits with the tragedy of Troilus. But the leading lady, representing Woman, pleads for the poet, saying that although 'he can nat wel endyte' (that is, although this writer is unfortunately unable to write), yet he has done his best, by producing various very proper works in her praise; and the remainder of the list is given as above. As we shall note presently, it contains other matter; but it is not certainly a complete list. Many hold that these very early writings included the Legend of St. Cicely, as afterwards inserted in *The Canterbury Tales*; also perhaps the story, or a story, of Griselda, and some fragments of the Monk's Tale. There is also a group, of very doubtful date; *The Complaint of Mars*; *The Complaint of Venus*; *The Complaint to his Lady*; and similar things, all very complaining. On the whole, however, the list in the *Legend* is the important one. It is suggested by some that the passage in *Troilus*, in which the poet expresses the hope of writing a 'comedy', refers to *The House of Fame*, meaning that that vision is divided in three on the model of *The Divine Comedy*. It is possible, and we know that Chaucer venerated the epic. It seems much more probable to me that the promise of a comedy refers to the intention to write *The Canterbury Tales*, or perhaps the Knight's Tale as originally separate from *The Canterbury Tales*; or, most likely of all (for those who admit literary men to be human beings), some perfectly vague and general intention to go off and have a jolly time, after all that weeping; a hazy hope of writing something simply human and funny, such as was afterwards largely satisfied in *The Canterbury Tales*. Strictly speaking, indeed, the list is more enlightening about the life of Chaucer than about the argument of Love; for the poet slips into the list, not only the translation of Boethius, but a theological work by Origen on St. Mary Magdalene and a pronouncement of the great Pope Innocent III, about the miseries of the poor, which hardly seem at first sight to advance the cause of Lovely Woman in pleading before Cupid. For that very reason we may take it as certain that Chaucer had written these religious paraphrases, along with certain roundels and virelays, presumably lost.

On the whole, it seems most probable that he began his creative career by writing *The Death of Blanche the Duchess*, a sort of family service, almost a feudal service, to his patron John of Gaunt; that at some time later he wrote *The Parlement of Foules*, followed by the larger and more ambitious enterprise of *Troilus and Criseyde*, and then *The Legend of Good Women*. The Duchess Blanche actually died in 1369, which gives us one of the few definite points in the chronology. On our own calculations Chaucer would be about twenty-eight, and likely enough to be given a sort of minor laureateship to the Lancaster branch of royalty. There is a more shadowy possibility of dating *The Parlement of Foules*, because it involves a veiled and tactful allusion to proposals of marriage between Richard the Second and Anne of Bohemia: similar allusions to certain stages of this Royal courtship have been found in *The House of Fame* and in *Troilus*. But *The Parlement of Foules* is practically concerned only with these proposals, though in a highly allegorical fashion. Richard was actually married to Anne of Bohemia in 1382, but the preliminary proposals and suggestions began in 1380. Short of entering indefinitely, not only into details but into disputed details, this is about all that can be said with certainty of the time and order of these poems; save indeed for one separate problem, which arises out of several references to a poem called *Palamon and Arcyte* and an actually existing poem called *Anelida and Arcyte*. Some suppose the former to be simply the story afterwards incorporated in *The Canterbury Tales* as 'The Knight's Tale'; others an earlier experiment which is lost. The latter is a rather unconvincing fragment, full of the laments of some lady whom Arcyte has deserted, but linked with the other by the presence

The Garden of Romance

of that very English gentleman, Theseus, Duke of Athens, destined to play so breezy a part in English letters from the *Anelida* to *The Midsummer Night's Dream*.

Those who deal in labels for literature may be surprised to be told that the official ode, the feudal family duty, of a lament over the loss of John of Gaunt's wife, is in fact a very touching poem. First of all, it seems quite incredibly likely that John of Gaunt was really very fond of his wife, and that Chaucer was very sympathetic with so deplorably sentimental a state of mind. It contains a very noble description of love in marriage; of a deep comradeship that has never lost the last intimate veil of courtesy. The point is worthy of remark, because those hostile to such normal things have made a great hash of history, in their version of the medieval view of marriage. Because marriage was made merciless fun of, as it is still; and because love outside marriage, or even against marriage, was often pardoned as romantic or sympathetic, as it is still; above all, because certain fantastic fashions allowed of the public proclamation of the sort of beauty-worship and intellectual flirtation that exists still —because of all this, those who understand neither the fantastic nor the normal have pretended that all medieval men and women saw love and marriage merely as rivals to each other; accepted no marriage except as a dull duty; and enjoyed no love except as an illicit enjoyment. But this is all nonsense; not only to anybody who knows a little of human nature, but to anybody who knows even a little of medieval literature. The truisms remain true, however much fun people may get out of the paradoxes; the cynical paradoxes of satire, or the romantic paradoxes of adventure. A man imagines a happy marriage as a marriage of love; even if he makes fun of marriages that are without love, or feels sorry for lovers who are without

125

The Garden of Romance

marriage. That Chaucer was normal in this, as in nearly everything else, is abundantly proved by his own printed words. It is true that his printed words were poetical words, and will be less perfectly understood by those who can only read them as prosaic words. But even these can hardly misread them altogether. And anybody who can read poetry as poetry knows perfectly well when a poet is weighing his words, in a truly weighty fashion, and means exactly what he says. There is something in the sound and measure of the words, as of the tolling and swaying of a great bell; and it sounds unmistakably when the great Theseus lays before the lovers the Christian majesty of the mystery of marriage:

> *The first Mover of the Cause above,*
> *When He first made the faire chain of Love,*
> *Great was the effect and high was his intent*
> *Well wist He why, and what thereof He meant.*

Any man who really understands it does not see a Greek king sitting on an ivory throne, nor a feudal lord sitting on a faldstool; but God standing in a primordial garden, granting the most gigantic of the joys of the children of men. Poetry of this kind is not written by accident; it does not write itself. The poet who writes it takes a tone as unmistakable as a change in the human voice. Few will say that in this Chaucer was flattering the Duke of Lancaster. Fewer still, I imagine, will say he was flattering the Duke of Athens. He did not write that sort of thing in his sleep, or in a fit of absence of mind. 'Well wist he why, and what thereof he meant.'

The mixture of nonsense and normality in a healthy man, and the particular sort of nonsense which went to make up a medieval man, is very well illustrated, in the same connexion, in the case of *The Legend of Good Women*. At first sight they seem a very extraordinary exhibition of

The Garden of Romance

Good Women. They are selected according to a rather pedantic fantasy, which prevailed in the Middle Ages, concerning heroes and heroines who had died for love, as a sort of religion. Chaucer himself calls them the Saints of Cupid; the martyrs of romance who were to be a sort of decorative pendant or parallel to the martyrs of religion. Of the deeper meaning of this historic mood there may be something said elsewhere. But the modern reader may possibly be slightly amused, when Cleopatra makes her positively first appearance in the character of a Good Woman. He will be wise, however, in every sense, if he does not fix his eyes only on Cleopatra. He will be very unwise if he interprets the whole legend in the light, or shadow, of Cleopatra. I mean that he will be wildly wrong if he fancies it to be a Swinburnian hymn of harlotry; or supposes that the Legend of Good Women is really a Legend of Bad Women. Cleopatra finds herself among the saints, because she is credited with what would be called the final perseverance of the saints; with constancy, as distinct from inconstancy. But the poem itself proves that Chaucer did not think that constancy was necessarily the wild constancy of Cleopatra and Anthony, or even of Guinevere and Lancelot. For the great queen, the grand heroine, the perfect woman who rules the rest and leads them and speaks for them, the lady who is set up as the supreme lover, is neither Guinevere nor Francesca nor Iseult. She is Alcestis, the long-married woman who went down to Tartarus to deliver her husband. She is alone enough to show that Chaucer and his age did not merely separate love and marriage. She is obviously put first among the Saints of Cupid because she is one of the Saints of Hymen: and is called a Good Woman because she is a Good Wife.

The Parlement of Foules, presumed to come in between *The Death of the Duchess* and *The Legend of Good Women*,

127

The Garden of Romance

does not indeed give such scope to such sentiments. It is all about proposals for a marriage, but it hardly allows of any such serious emotion about the ideal of being married. It is a particularly graceful exercise in that sort of stately levity, which is suitable for compliments paid at court, by men who are rather more than courtiers. In form it is a fable about an assembly of birds, before whom three rival eagles advance their claim to the bird most desired as a bride; presumably a reference to the imperial princes who might have married Anne of Bohemia. It is not so easy to enter into the darker and more delicate psychology of a large bird of prey as of a bereaved husband, with whom you happen to be personally acquainted. Chaucer had not yet developed that divine impudence, which enabled him to make a cock in a farmyard talk like Aristotle and Aquinas about the mysteries of the supreme Will and Wisdom. In short, it is a charming parable; but we all feel that the Parliament of Fowls would have had a livelier session, if the Cock had been returned as a member. With *The Legend of Good Women* (leaving *Troilus* for fuller treatment) we pass to matters more purely Chaucerian, as being more personal and peculiar to Chaucer. In the prologue to this poem appears the picturesque and vivid, though quite light and unpretentious, personal sketch of the poet. In the livelier and more telling manner of his later tales, he tells us something of his own habits and humours; how he delights in books; how he is criticized for neglecting his neighbours for the companionship of books; how, when he has done his day's work with the accounts and ledgers of his various public offices, he does not want to go on a holiday but only to sit down with a book. Having worked the description up to this point, he gets the full effect out of the one exception, and makes quite a dramatic entrance for the Daisy. He owns that, when spring first comes on the fields, he suddenly

128

flings away his books and goes down into the daisy meadows to drink of a deeper delight.

The special feeling of Chaucer for the daisy, among the flowers of the field, has often been remarked, and both the personal taste and the popular tradition illustrate a sound instinct in medieval symbolism. A man might really learn more of the special spirit of Chaucer, by looking at daisies, than by reading a good many annotations by dons and doctors of literature. If he did toil laboriously in the long tangles of the Romance of the Rose, it is true to say that he opposed to it something fresh that might be called the Romance of the Daisy. We might even carry the figurative parallel further, and say that at one end or extreme of poetry is all that Walt Whitman meant by *Leaves of Grass*, the acceptance of the common even in the sense of the chaotic or incomplete, and at the other extreme the symbolic and almost heraldic Rose of the medieval allegorists; and that between that garden and that grass the exquisite and temperate medium or transition was really expressed in the daisy, or the first fresh realism of Chaucer. I am not denying the worth of any of the three types of poetry, from the wildest to the tamest; and I offer every apology to the grass. But when we talk of wild poetry, we sometimes forget the parallel of wild flowers. They exist to show that a thing may be more modest and delicate for being wild. And that atmosphere is exactly the atmosphere of Chaucer and of daisies. Certainly some of Gower's garden roses were tolerably tame flowers. But this is not meant in the modern 'ruthless' realistic spirit. When we say that Chaucer's flowers were wild flowers, we do not mean that they went on like wild beasts. We mean that there is a certain freshness and freedom about their very slightness or subordination, and it is this sort of unmistakable air that comes to us in Chaucer, like a cool wind across a meadow.

The Garden of Romance

I am aware, of course, that some industrious critics have suggested that all this was not only formal but even fictitious, and that Chaucer intended some elaborate compliment to some lady whose name was Marguerite. This is quite possible, as advanced by the best Chaucerian scholars, but there is a type of student who advances it to lay waste the whole daisy-meadow. He has a curious subconscious itch in the presence of poetry; an itch for explaining it, in the hope of explaining it away. But this sort of critic is in any case unreliable, because, in dealing with a poem, he cannot distinguish between its occasion and its origin. He is the sort of commentator who, listening to the enchanted voice of Oberon telling of mermaids and meteors and the purple flower, is chiefly anxious to assure us that the imperial votaress was certainly Queen Elizabeth, and that there actually was a pageant at Nobbin Castle, for a wedding in the Fitznobbin family, in which a cupid and a mermaid figured in such a manner as completely to explain William Shakespeare's remarks—and almost explain William Shakespeare. It is all quite probable; it is all quite true: by all means, let us be gravely grateful for the information. There were doubtless a good many pageants and a good many parades of Cupid and Dian; and I dare say a great many mermaids on a great many dolphins' backs. But, by an odd chance, only one of them ever, in the whole history of the world, uttered such dulcet and harmonious breath that the rude sea grew civil at her song, and certain stars shot madly from their spheres to hear the sea-maid's music. That is the kind of thing that has rather a way of only happening once. And if we really must find out where it came from, or why it came, we shall be wise to guess that it had a good deal less to do with the Mermaid at Nobbin Castle than with that other Mermaid at which Mr. William Shakespeare of Stratford sometimes took a little more wine than was

The Garden of Romance

good for him. In the same way, any appreciator of poetry as poetry knows that the medieval poet had a real kinship or sympathy with daisies and what they stand for, quite apart from whether or no he used them for personal purposes on particular occasions. It is quite possible that Chaucer took pleasure in the pun about the daisy when he was in love with some lady called Marguerite. It is much more probable that he had to pay some conventional compliment to a lady called Marguerite, and jumped at the chance of using a little thing he had already written about daisies. But anyhow it was he who wrote it, and it was about daisies that he wrote; and anybody who cannot see that cannot see that Walt Whitman liked grass because it is rank and ragged or that William Morris liked roses because they are symmetrical and symbolic. The whole picture he contrives to suggest, of his rising at the faint call of May, and leaving his books, and going forth like a shadow to find the green meadows under the grey dawn, is full of a certain kind of cool and colourless intoxication which would call up a crowd of daisies in any imaginative mind, even if he had never mentioned them. If he knew anybody called Marguerite (and shared with the professors that profound scholarship, of the school of Stratford-atte-Bow, which reveals that Marguerite is the French for daisy), he would very probably mention that. It has been similarly ascertained that a lady named Rose has sometimes been compared to a rose, and I presume, a lady called Rhoda to a rhododendron. But a poet, and his particular kind of poetry, are really to be judged by the fact that he prefers to talk most of roses, or rhododendrons, or sunflowers, or poisonous-looking orchids, or daisies in the fields of morning. His selection of such things strikes the note which he wishes to strike, and lets us realize the things of which he likes to dream. In this sense the selection and use of

131

The Garden of Romance

the daisy is Chaucerian; individually and unmistakably Chaucerian; it is one of the clues to Chaucer. It may be remarked that whenever he uses the word elsewhere, though in a casual connexion, it has the same sort of freshness and felicity. Among those splendid and spirited sketches in the Prologue of *The Canterbury Tales*, slashed in with a few strokes as verbally fastidious as Stevenson, we are told that the jolly red-faced Franklin, or country squire, in whose house 'it snowed meat and drink', had a beard 'as white as a daisy'. There could hardly be a better example of Chaucer's brilliant brevity of description. If he had said white as frost or snow, it would have been banal and suggested some senile decay. As it is, he conveys that even the blanching of the man's beard seemed to make him look more lusty and lively. Finally, as a last lesson from the daisy, it seems probable that the poet was quietly aware, so to speak, of the rather large and daring significance of the derivation of daisy from the eye of day; which gives to that small object something apocalyptic like the sunrise, and a sort of claim to be the eye of the whole earth. It is notable, because it connotes that something, which was kept rather quietly in the background, but which I have called elsewhere the greatness of Chaucer.

Anyhow, the personal preface of *The Legend of Good Women* naturally rather overshadows the legend itself, but even in the latter the interest is not altogether impersonal. Chaucer is chaffing himself, more or less, upon an imaginary charge of being a misogynist, and represents Love as charging him with having done great wrong to lovers, and notably to ladies. This, as has been said, seems to refer chiefly to *The Romance of the Rose*, which seems a little unfair; it is hard if a man, who has had the toil of copying out and translating such an interminable poem, should have also the burden of defending all its sentiments. But it is notable that the poet sets himself politely but decisively to the task of disproving his hatred of women. He does it all the more energetically because it was a very unnecessary task. Chaucer certainly did not hate women, let alone lovers; he did not hate anybody. At any rate, whether it be a strength or a weakness in him, he did not hate anybody much. All his talents were on the side of sympathy, even when they seem to take the form of satire. That is where he really does differ, for instance, from Dante; and there is something rather national about the difference. But indeed Chaucer had written or was about to write a more complete answer to the charge than is found in *The Legend of Good Women.* So far from thinking ill of women whom he was expected to admire, he managed to think well, or at least to think kindly, of a woman whom the whole world expected him to deride and despise. In the *Legend* he praised each woman in turn, for being a faithful lover. But he could not bring himself to curse a woman, even for being a false lover. The curious way in which this corner is turned, with a curve rather than an angle, is one of the most singular and individual qualities in the poem that probably he wrote most carefully and seriously, and intended to be the outstanding creation of his career.

There is nowhere a more whimsical, or even weird historical product than the story of Troilus and Criseyde. To begin with, it is a myth made out of a mistake; or what would now be a misprint. There never was any person called Criseyde, even in the sense in which there was a person called Helen. She is only the corruption of the name of somebody else, who was entirely different. And yet this walking misquotation walks the world as a more living creature than most legendary figures quoted on the highest authority; this talking typographical error not only talks to us, in an animated manner, in an unmistakably human voice; but also with a new voice that strikes a new note in human history. The tale of Troilus and Criseyde is an anachronism, an anomaly; in some sense a prodigy and a portent. It is a Homeric story of which Homer had never even dreamed. It is a posthumous Pagan myth belatedly born centuries after the death of Pagan mythology. It is a medieval romance, invented by medieval men, who seem to have managed to revere it as a part of pagan Antiquity, and to have practically forgotten that they had made it up out of their own heads. Finally, it is a Christian story entirely about Pagans; it is full of the particular sort of moral sensitiveness and sense of spiritual freedom which alone makes possible certain sorts of criticism; and especially of self-criticism. Criseyde is a Christian creation because she is a Minx; and a Minx is a product of the culture of Christendom.

Many even among educated readers may not be aware that the name of Criseyde is all that the Dark Ages had left of that very harmless person Briseis, the beautiful slave whom Achilles and Agamemnon each claimed as part of the spoil of war. It illustrates the difference between the two atmospheres, that the former lady is a passive instrument of fate, while the latter lady is a very active example of the abuse of free will. Briseis is blameless because she is blind. Cressida is even false, in order to show that she is free. Because Briseis was beautiful, the dogs tore on the Trojan plain the limbs of mighty chieftains: 'Such was the sovereign doom and such the will of Jove.' But because Cressida was something more than beautiful, was something of what men have come to call romantic; because she was wilful and mysterious and incalculable, Diomed is wounded and Troilus is slain; and bards lament, reproaching, not Jove, but Criseyde. Nobody had ever thought of reproaching Briseis. With this extraordinary medieval postscript to the Iliad, we come upon an entirely new world of curious and even complicated feeling; produced by the overflowing of medieval mysticism into the old jests and tragedies of love and lust. It is seen at its finest in Chaucer's version of the tale, because Chaucer was perhaps the man with the finest feelings in that age. It is a basic blunder to suppose that he was superficial, merely because he had a light touch. A light touch is a mark of strength and not weakness, in spiritual as in bodily things; and (in those days especially) to be in that sense superficial was a way of avoiding being intolerably sentimental.

It is a commonplace that this tale was treated both by Chaucer and Shakespeare; and it is rather a misfortune that we generally think first of the version that was written last. Anyhow, it illustrates a certain difference (of which there will be more to say later) to note that the Renaissance version, compared with the medieval version, is certainly livelier, and certainly not happier. It is the liveliness of the second fermentation; and what in Chaucer was still wine, in Shakespeare is very like vinegar. The chalice of Chaucer does indeed contain the dark wine of tragedy and the lamentation of lovers. But he laments chiefly for true lovers, and even when he implies the existence of false lovers, he never begins to imply that all love is false. Indeed his simplicity contains a subtlety that is not always justly valued, and can hardly be too carefully considered. When I say it is a new note, I do not mean of course that there was anything new either about jeering at lovers or raving at false lovers. I mean that there was something new in the particular way in which Chaucer balanced both so as to produce neither; the way in which Chaucer did not jeer and did not rave; but jested without jeering and reproached without raving. The charity of Chaucer towards Cressida is one of the most beautiful things in human literature; but its particular blend belongs entirely to Christian literature. Pagans had felt the agony and anomaly of true love given to the false lover; but the mixture was never a blend like this. Catullus, the most subtle and (as some would say) the most modern of the ancients, had reached the paralysing paradox of 'I hate and I love'. But the particular Chaucerian tone cannot be translated as 'I hate and I love'; it is something more like a combination of 'I adore and I pity', with 'I pity and I condemn'. Again we feel, if only for a moment, that it was not quite so absurd to talk of putting 'Daunt' into English; for many have felt the same fine shade in the feeling of Dante about Francesca.

But even apart from the more merciful view taken by Chaucer—even in the case of the rather merciless view taken by Shakespeare (which was indeed the view originally taken by Boccaccio)—there was a mystical medieval element in all this tragedy, or bitter comedy, about false love. It might almost be translated into theological language as a sense of the insecurity of the souls of others; though the theologians, to do them justice, generally urged us to begin with a sense of the insecurity of our own. I know of course that Chaucer does once, in a sort of noble weakness, snatch at a sort of fatalism as an excuse for his heroine; chiefly because he really cannot think of any other excuse. He is heart-broken about it: but this does not alter the new universal tone of *moralizing* about love. It is not fanciful to see something of a new spirit, even in the spiritual sense, in this closer vigilance touching the problems of the weak and wavering human will. It is really, for reasons on which we shall remark later, a sort of shadow thrown by a mystical and metaphysical cloud upon the classic and flowery fields of pure poesy. The medieval world did incessantly talk about true lovers and false lovers, where the classical world would often

The Garden of Romance

have been content to talk about lovers. And though there are many false lovers in classic fable, it is interesting to note that their falsehood does not really discredit them; and the false lover is the true hero. Theseus is not less the Athenian hero because he deserts Ariadne; nor Aeneas less the pious Aeneas because he deserts Dido. But a new note has crept into laments like that of Anelida and Arcyte; a suggestion that the false. lover is the false knight, and has broken some bond of chivalry. All this atmosphere, heavier with moral responsibility and self-determination, was not unconnected with the special social ideals of feudalism; and the notion of a wandering knight still owning dependence on a distant lord. But it was also deeply affected by that religious idea, which denied doom and substituted damnation or salvation determined by the will; the spirit that made Dante acclaim freedom as the first of divine gifts, or made Chaucer contradict Calvin, centuries before he was born, in the very first words of the Parson's Tale. In the very centre of that Christian cosmos, everything pivoted on the idea that the human heart could be given to God or withheld from him. The highest affections of the soul could turn this way or that, to the divine or the diabolic; and the supreme charity was valued because it was not enforced. It is rather a grim joke that the main tenet of the most orthodox creed might be summed up as Free Love.

Another new step, or rather a new stride, is taken in literary progress with the publication of Chaucer's version of Troilus. It concerns the character of Pandarus; and Pandarus really is a character. With him we have the first full appearance of Chaucer as a humorist; that is, of Chaucer at his broadest and best as a benefactor of humanity. The character of Pandarus does indeed sprawl through that very lengthy poem rather lazily, like the limbs of a giant where they have room to stretch themselves. The author has not yet achieved that brilliant brevity, that power of dashing in a whole personal description in a few strokes, which he developed later in *The Canterbury Tales*. The humour of Pandarus is not quite so humane as the humour in *The Canterbury Tales*; it is sometimes deliberately unpleasant; but it is the humour of a humorist. It is also important, in the matter of the general literary transition, to notice the points in which Chaucer changes the tale as he had read it in older versions. It is very significant of his independent craving for character that he turns Pandarus from a young cousin to an elderly uncle. Bernard Shaw said somewhere, very truly, that the vigour and virility of Rembrandt are best shown in his preference for painting old women rather than young ones. There is the same sort of clean and interested love of character in Chaucer's excellent descriptions of elderly men; such as the Franklin and the Knight. It must not be forgotten in relation to this change in the romance of Troilus. As has been noted already, the whole story has a very eccentric evolution from its Greek origin, and had already gone through curious changes. Criseyde was once Briseis; and Pandarus was not always a pandar. It seems to have begun with the usual graceful friendship of two youths, Troilus and Pandarus; pretty much like Damon and Pythias or Pylades and Orestes. But Pandarus had to take on, more or less, what was known in later theatrical circles as the part of Charles's Friend. And it was an almost inevitable implication, even in modern theatricals, that Charles's Friend was rather more cynical than Charles. Anyhow, Troilus's Friend became very cynical indeed; and the part he has to play, of bringing the lovers secretly together, lent itself easily to the less-pleasing jocularity of medieval and Renaissance literature. Thus, by the time of Chaucer, Pandarus has become a funny old man; and, by the time of Shakespeare, he has become a decidedly nasty old man. But, for the moment of medieval transition, the point is that Chaucer made the young man old, because he wished to make the character at once more ripe and more quaint, more experienced and more fixed. In that sense the character of Criseyde's uncle takes the new road as the first of the Canterbury Pilgrims; the first of that great and gay procession of the English comic characters, which has not ended with Falstaff or with Pickwick. We must not exaggerate the proportions of the change; the Chaucerian art is still mainly dominated by the serious romance of medievalism; with decoration for its form and sentiment for its substance. Only the less serious passages which are filled by Pandarus suggest the beginning of that new and powerful use of the comic, which seems sometimes almost more tremendous than the tragic.

I do not know whether it is one of Chaucer's jokes (and I am sure he made many jokes that nobody knows) when he appends to this apparently interminable poem, consisting of no less than eight thousand, two hundred and forty-six lines, the cheerful comment, 'Go, little book; go, my little tragedy'. But in any case it is profoundly significant that he adds to this the remark that he hopes some day to be able to write, 'Some comedy'. This has been variously interpreted; even in the sense that he meant *The House of Fame* to resemble *The Divine Comedy*. But it seems to me more likely that he had found the one comic character in his tragedy so amusing a study that he hoped to produce some more; or, in other words, that he found Sir Pandarus such good fun that he had already guessed, perhaps, that his greatest talent pointed towards such achievements as the Wife of Bath or the Nun's Priest's Tale.

On the whole, we may say that in *Troilus* we find that Chaucer, who was already a good poet, is beginning to be

139

The Garden of Romance

a great poet. There were depths and delicacies of regret, when the heroine entirely declined to be heroic, which were not possible in anything like *The Legend of Good Women*; where the heroines stood in a row, all being resolutely heroic. There could be a directness, even an excessive directness, about the jokes of Pandarus, which was not to be expected in the indirect diplomatic discussion of an international alliance, as explained by eagles. Chaucer has become Chaucerian, and emerges as a man of genius distinct from the many men of talent, who could then be counted on (if officially required) to go to sleep and dream of a house of gold or a garden of lilies. But when all this is allowed for, it will be well to realize also that all Chaucer's work, up to *Troilus* and including *Troilus*, come under a certain general description, that hardly applies to *The Canterbury Tales*, and are conducted within a framework of conventions, from which he afterwards broke away. In other words, the great poem of *Troilus and Criseyde* is possibly the last and certainly the best of the series of works written primarily under the power and magic of that special sort of Romance which turned love as it exists between lovers first into a sort of philosophy and then into a sort of religion; a thing that had both its grammar and its gospel; both its science and its asceticism. It is true that it would affect many robust rationalists as merely amounting to sentimentalism. But there was much more in it than that; as there was much more in Rossetti or Swinburne than appeared to the satirists of aestheticism in *Patience* or *Punch*.

Indeed that wood of wandering lovers, with their figured garments and burning pallor, and insistence on the kinship of desire and death, is a very easy thing to make fun of. A modern man may legitimately smile at the curious convention, by which it appears to be necessary for anybody in love with a young lady to collect a

The Garden of Romance

large number of other young ladies, and tell them all about it, and elaborately thánk them for their gracious sympathy and their highly exemplary patience; yet the man with the superior smile may not realize that he is being superior to Dante. He may think himself much more robust than the medieval lover who swoons when the conversation takes a discouraging turn; or the poet who weeps over the death of an abstract person called Pity, because his young woman (in more robust language) has turned him down. Yet it may be questioned whether the modern man really is more robust than Chaucer; or even half so robust. Nor would he find it easy to laugh at Chaucer very long, without beginning to have a dark suspicion that Chaucer was laughing at him. The truth is that Chaucer included this phase of romantic and vision-ary passion, and many other things as well. But he in-cluded it because God had given him a remarkable talent for seeing what good there was in things; and there was a great deal of good in this. A man vowed to this religion of romance may appear to us very effeminate in his emo-tions; but he might easily need to be very virile in his experiences. He could be called upon to fight; to die; and, what is worse, to wait. Professor Pollard, who cer-tainly has no medieval battle-axe to grind, remarks in his excellent study of Chaucer that the discipline of such lovers was rather severe and noble than merely weak and self-indulgent. The really important point, as a point of biography and history, is that, however stale we may find it now, it seemed at that time fresh, because it really was fresh. The *Vita Nuova* really was the New Life; there had been nothing exactly like it before, in all the history of love.

Romance was a strange by-product of Religion; all the more so because Religion, through some of its repre-sentatives, may have regretted having produced it. But it

The Garden of Romance

is quite obviously the transfer of the tragic responsibilities of the Faith to the field of almost pagan passion. It is sometimes said that Christianity has been weak and ineffectual. The truth is that it has been so powerful and effective that it coloured even the things it had not hoped to influence; and changed its enemies as well as its friends. Even worldliness, when it did not become otherworldliness, became another sort of worldliness. Even the Church, as imperfectly represented on its human side, continued to inspire even what it had denounced, and transformed even what it had abandoned. Anyone who judges by living facts, and not by dead details, can see the Christian ideal remodelling even the Pagan image in its own image. In a word, Chaucer was right (as he generally was) when he talked, with pleasant blasphemy, about the Saints of Cupid. They were in one sense saints; because they were in one sense martyrs. He could talk about martyrs of love more reasonably than modern rationalists talk about martyrs of science. But both are in this sense rational; that a martyr really means a witness. And these two types are indeed witnesses. They are witnesses to the necessity, which forces irreligion to borrow the terms of religion.

In short, whether or no this or that Christian may choose to oppose romance or chivalry, it is quite certain that without the Christians there would never have been any romance or chivalry to oppose. It is also perfectly true that there was a great deal of romance and chivalry which it would have been quite sensible to oppose. The period during which Chaucer lingered in this literary garden, extends from his first official poem on the Death of the Duchess to the completion of *Troilus and Criseyde*. But it includes one or two less pivotal poems, of more doubtful date, in which this sort of garden had perhaps rather run to seed. One is the work called *The Death of*

The Garden of Romance

Pity, to which I have already referred; another is *The Complaint of Mars*, and perhaps *The Complaint of Venus*; and *The Complaint to His Lady*, apparently a continuation of the former. These things are more shadowy and have a more shadowy relation to Chaucer; but they obviously have a relation to this contemporary Romance. Whether they are by the poet or no, they belong to this period of poetry; and it is well that this period should be understood. In the final phase of *Troilus and Criseyde* it can be fully understood; and Chaucer fully understood it, in its limits as well as its liberties.

This religion of romantic love had till lately all the advantages, and has now all the disadvantages, of having been revived by the Victorians. 'Love Is Enough', which was the title of one of William Morris's plays, might have been the motto of all William Morris's period. Rossetti and Browning, as well as Tennyson and Mrs. Browning, wrote always with this implication, right or wrong, of identifying the ideal morality with the higher sentiment of sex. We were all more or less brought up in that tradition, which contains a real truth; but we all know that there has been of late a reaction against it; rather an excessive reaction, beginning with Mr. Bernard Shaw and ending with Mr. Aldous Huxley. There are only two considerations in this connexion which affect a fair judgment of its earlier appearance in the age of Chaucer. The first is this; that, for all the advance of rationalism and science, the medieval romanticist was much more of a realist than the modern romanticist. The medieval poet did not deny that love stories could end badly; it was the Victorian novelist who invented the idea that they must always end well. The medieval man may sometimes have been a sentimentalist; but, to do him justice, he was not an optimist. He did not pretend that this particular kind of emotion, healthily popular as it is, and eternally attractive

The Garden of Romance

as it is, has only brought happiness and never unhappiness to human beings. The true lover was often tragic; the inspiriting thing about him was simply that he was true. Whatever therefore may be justly urged against the mere cushioned comfort or upholstered respectability of Victorianism, certainly cannot be urged against the thorny thickets and visionary vigils of medievalism. The second fact to remember is even simpler and more to the point. It is that Chaucer, having paid a magnificent tribute in *Troilus and Criseyde* to all that is really generous and humane in the worship of a highly medievalized and almost Christianized Cupid, does finally give his judgment; and his judgment is not in favour of the cult of Cupid but against it. In a series of verses of great beauty and power, as Professor Pollard has noted, he gives his ultimate decision that happiness is not to be found by dancing after any heathen god of love; but by looking up, as he bids all the 'young fresh folks' to look up, to where a more terrible but a more tender god of love hangs, not on Olympus but on Calvary. Thus, in relation to the whole of this business, of the medieval ideal of True Lovers, which Chaucer every bit as much as Browning can treat at its very truest, we may say that Chaucer was large enough to be delighted by the vision; but too large to be deceived by it. His claim to greatness gains on both sides; and he will not suffer by any cynical psychological discoveries, which the latest sceptics may imagine they have made about the falsity of Romance. If the nineteenth century deified Romance, if the twentieth century deserts Romance, the great medieval Maker is equally master of that vision; four hundred years ahead in seeing it; and five hundred years ahead in seeing through it.

Chapter V

THE CANTERBURY TALES

To watch the unfolding of the genius of Chaucer is to watch a pattern changing into a picture; or into a series of pictures. It is something like the illusion of a sick or sleepy child, staring at a wall-paper, for whom the flat plants seem to branch and blossom, or figures to begin to move among the formal trees. His work begins with the purely rhythmic decorative style that possessed medieval prose and verse, even more than medieval painting and carving. It ends with something more than the realism of Renaissance pictures; with something suggestive of the realism of modern novels. There is even a sort of paradox in it; that in his vigorous and adventurous youth he was formal; in his comparatively crippled and limited old age he was free. When he was a young soldier, fighting sword in hand against the spears of France, or a young traveller and political agent, dealing with delicate crises in the cities of Italy, his style of writing was still as rigid a pattern as the prison-bars that enclosed Palamon and Arcite. When he was something more like a shabby old pensioner, stout of body and lean of purse, limited, as it were, to the view from his own lattice looking towards the Abbey and his own future grave, he broke out into a dance of lively and dramatic detail that reminds us rather of Dickens or of Balzac. We see him gradually breaking those flowery chains of his youth, and then living to sow such very wonderful wild oats in his old age. It is in itself an inspiriting sight, and the outline of a gallant story. But, for all that, we must not exaggerate one side of the matter, or imagine that he merely escaped from a prison to a free hostelry and highway, when he fled from the House of Fame to the Tabard in Southwark.

For instance, it is well to remember that the purely medieval Chaucer has been an inspiration, even more, if possible, than the purely personal Chaucer. Art critics are now everywhere returning to that medieval sense of rhythm in art, and many literary men, long before, returned to it in literature. William Morris was a Socialist and in his time a typically modern man; what is very much more important, he was a typically manly man. He was eminently sane, hearty and healthy; and his broad face and leonine beard were in a sort of symbolic way felt as types of freedom and fraternity. But the Chaucer who inspired Morris was the Chaucer of the long elaborate pageants and allegories; even more than the Chaucer of the last brief excursion into the coarse comedies of daily life. A man wandering through the coloured corridors and labyrinths of the long decorative tales of The Earthly Paradise does sometimes feel a little like a fly crawling across a wallpaper. But that paper is a fly-paper that has attracted a good many flies. A Cambridge professor of chemistry whom I knew, a man whose whole main business was material modern science, had for his whole conception of a hobby or a holiday an endless journey in those realms of gold from the Glittering Plain to The Wood At The End Of The World. Mr. George Moore, who still manages to be a modern man of our time as well as his own, delights above all things in the decorative poetry of Morris; especially in the most meaningless parts of it, like the recurrent emblem of 'two red roses across the moon'. Now nearly all this inspiration was drawn, not only from Chaucer, but from the early romantic Chaucer as distinct from

146

the later realistic Chaucer. If the hero of *Troilus and Criseyde* seems to be an unconscionable long time dying, the hero of *The Life and Death of Jason* also seems a little leisurely in his life and slow in getting to his death.

The moral is obvious enough; that what we call the length and even the monotony of medieval literature is a human pleasure and a human need, in certain moods and moments of mankind. It lay like an infinite inviting sea in the background of the fourteenth century. It returned like a refreshing and copious flood to the dry and dusty respectability of the nineteenth century. And, in the case of Chaucer, our very admiration for his later discoveries may make us exaggerate the futility of the traditions he inherited. Sir Topas may create a false perspective, rather as Don Quixote creates a partly unjust retrospect. Readers infer from the novel of Cervantes that the old romances were all rubbish; though Cervantes goes out of his way to explain that they were not. Readers may remember the name of Sir Topas as a satire on chivalry, though in fact it follows on a very noble exaltation of chivalry in the person of the real Knight; the Knight who is without a name. Something of the same irony may even be found in the lives of the two men of genius. For Chaucer, who travesties Topas, had figured in armour and armorial bearings in the most florid period of the wars of chivalry; the terrible tourney of the Leopards against the Lilies. And Cervantes, credited with despising and destroying romance, had himself lived one of the most wildly romantic lives in history; escaping from slavery among the Paynims of Africa, and wielding a sword and losing a hand in the deathless death-grip of Lepanto.

There is, then, something to be said for the long poetical allegories eventually abandoned by Chaucer; as for the long prose romances ultimately satirized by Cervantes. Their very extension and expanse satisfied a psycho-

147

logical need now perhaps only felt by children and poor people, who like to have a very big book for their money. Yet there are few cultivated moderns who have not felt something of the pleasure of being able to lose themselves in the longest books of Dickens or Trollope. But there is more in it than that; for man lives by his devouring appetite for morality. The chivalric romance does really represent the Christian conception of life, which is at once a Quest, a Test and an Adventure. And the decorative allegories, that seem so dead to us, were once alive like a dance with the balanced morality of the Middle Ages.

Dante makes the very heavens dance, in the last pages of the Paradiso; sweeping the sky with swaying and spinning ballets of angels and spirits; and the symbol is very appropriate to the philosophy. It is appropriate; not because the dance stands for disorder, but because it stands for order. The dance is in its nature a rhythmic and recurrent thing, returning upon itself; and was therefore a perfectly correct and orthodox type of medieval moral theology. This, by the way, will be noted by the intelligent as correcting the exaggerated solemnity, with which some scholars have taken the tirades of fanatical friars, and other people, against the use or abuse of dancing. Doubtless there was much that was really pagan left in popular dancing, and doubtless there were plenty of donkeys in holy orders who found paganism in what was not really pagan. But in face of a fact like Dante's vision of the celestial dance, it is not tenable that the medieval mind thought of dancing merely as immorality or indecency. Nobody would describe people as doing in heaven what he had a deep and indignant horror of their doing on earth. Mahomet would not describe his Paradise as a place where the faithful were incessantly occupied in carving and worshipping idols. The Pacifist would not point happily to a future life in which everybody would be always waving sabres and firing off guns; the Prohibitionist would not picture heaven as a state of perfection in which the blessed could drink rum and gin for ever and ever. And Dante would not have filled the skies with dancing, if he had instinctively thought of the dance as degrading. The truth is, of course, that he instinctively thought of the dance as decorative and rhythmic, and therefore corresponding to a certain character in his whole conception of life. Indeed, it marks the whole difference between medieval life and modern life.

A certain break or sharp change in history can hardly be sketched more sharply, than by saying that up to a certain time life was conceived as a Dance, and after that time life was conceived as a Race. Medieval morality was full of the idea that one thing must balance another, that each stood on one side or the other of something that was in the middle, and something that remained in the middle. There might be any amount of movement, but it was movement round this central thing; perpetually altering the attitudes, but perpetually preserving the balance. The Virtues were like children going round the Mulberry Bush, only the Mulberry Bush was that Burning Bush which they made symbolical of the Incarnation; that flamboyant bush in which the Virgin and Child appear in the picture, with René of Provence and his beloved wife kneeling on either side. Now since that break in history, whatever we call it or whatever we think of it, the Dance has turned into a Race. That is, the dancers lose their balance and only recover it by running towards some object, or alleged object; not an object within their circle or their possession, but an object which they do not yet possess. It is a flying object; a disappearing object; and, as some hold, a disappointing object. But I am not concerned with condemning or commending either the religion of the Race or the religion of the Dance. I am only pointing out that this is the fundamental difference between them. One is rhythmic and recurrent movement, because there is a known centre; while the other is precipitate or progressive movement, because there is an unknown goal. The latter has produced all that we call Progress; the former produced what the medievals meant by Order; but it was the lively order of a dance.

When we understand this dance, we understand the order or pattern of the early poems of Chaucer; and above all why he does not seem to be in any hurry to finish them. Judged by our higher standards of hustle and pep, the Canterbury Pilgrims do not seem to be in a very great hurry to get to Canterbury. But they are like American tourists in the pace they observe, in getting to the pilgrims' goal, compared with the pace of Pandarus or Phoebus in getting to the point. But this leisurely quality is bound up in the very nature of the work, or play. A dance is a thing enjoyable in itself, and given such a dance of gods and heroes, it can go on for ever. A journey, if it is enjoyable on account of its object, is not equally enjoyable if it goes on for ever. I know that some moderns have tried to confuse at once the metaphor and the mind, by pretending that the joy of the journey is in something that can never be enjoyed. But this is a confusion. If they could express themselves clearly, they would either say that the journey is itself the goal, or else that the journey is hopeless and only an illusion makes it hopeful. Otherwise, they are out on a tramp that has no end, to find an inn that has no existence. The more reasonable progressives profess to envisage an end of some kind, and when praising the goal naturally tend to foreshorten the journey. These are the authors of Utopias and plans of perfect social reform. But the poet, who is describing a dance of virtues, or a pageant of beauty, has naturally no particular impatience that this should itself end. And something

The Canterbury Tales

of this lingering love of his own day-dream unduly prolongs his own description. It has the effect, especially for modern readers, of making much of such medieval writing dull. But even if we find it dull, let us not suppose it was the product of dullness, when it was the product of delight.

Of course, even these early works of Chaucer, on the old medieval model, are of very varying merit. *The Book of the Duchess* is a very affecting, because a relatively young and innocent, version of human grief; *The Parlement of Foules* has already more of the freedom of the fable about cocks and hens; *The Legend of Good Women* has moments in which it almost turns into a graver though certainly not greater *Canterbury Tales*; and the tale of Troilus and Criseyde, though to us inordinately long, has high and magnificent passages that are worth the toil of reading anything ten times longer. The point here, however, is that there is a sort of break in the story of Chaucer's style, and that the break came comparatively late in his story. He probably regarded the tale of Troilus as his supreme work, and the Canterbury Pilgrimage as a more casual postscript. His masterpiece is a kind of afterthought.

It might be maintained that, in the very act of leading his coloured crowd out of the Tabard and the town, and along the open road, Chaucer symbolized something of the change from the medieval balance to the modern march; from the philosophy of the Dance to the philosophy of the Race. Few modern racing men, fewer still among modern racing motorists, will regard the journey as much of a sporting event. Few journeys have a greater air of leisure; and nobody, certainly, will suggest that it was a race in which the best man was meant to win. The fact that the Reeve always rode at the tail of the procession will be sufficiently balanced by the fact that the Miller apparently rode at the head of it. Here at least the medieval poet can have meant no allegory of spiritual superiority. But there is also a serious element in the idea of the Canterbury Pilgrimage which makes the Pilgrims' Way something more than merely the open road. So far as having a definite purpose is concerned, the Pilgrim of Chaucer is as genuine as the Pilgrim of Bunyan. He is not in such a hurry because he is not in such a horrible fright; and there is no question of the Franklin or the Squire putting his fingers in his ears and fleeing from London as from a City of Destruction. But he is none the less really fleeing to Canterbury as a City of Salvation. Anyhow, he is not merely wishing to escape into the wilderness and leave all cities behind. I shall discuss in a moment the really new element which the poet half-consciously introduced into his long comedy of travel; the element of delay, or what a medieval man would have called dalliance. But though he admits a good many things besides pilgrimage and piety on this side of Canterbury, he does not admit anything beyond Canterbury. His scheme of travel is still dominated by the idea of a definite purpose, and the fresh forces which entered literature at this stage were more subtle, more subconscious, and more difficult to judge with delicacy, than a mere procession or progress into the void.

I know it was commonly said, both in medieval times and modern times, that the pilgrimage had become a mockery, by which it seems to be meant merely that it had become a holiday. But it was because it had been a popular shrine that it became a popular holiday. That this involved all the revelry, buffoonery, drunkenness and incidental swinishness of all sorts that belonged and still belong to a popular holiday, we could learn easily enough from Chaucer's own description, if we had not already learned it from our own common sense and experience. But Chaucer himself is very careful to put first the solid fact that a great many people, at least, did really wish to render thanks to St. Thomas of Canterbury for help in their past sickness; a good proportion of his own pilgrims are certainly religious people acting from religious motives. The truth is that, in this matter, I am again haunted, I might almost say tormented, by that little query which I put in the first pages of this book; the query that runs, 'But what of to-day—and what of to-morrow?' If it was a scandal to have religion mixed with riot or profanity, has it been such a complete cure to have riot and profanity unmixed with religion? If it was superstition to venerate the bones of a great man killed by a tyrant, is it any more intelligent that millions of clerks should go down and merely gape at the Sea, without having even the sense to worship Neptune? Is it more dignified that bankers should give us a St. Lubbock's Day on which nobody thinks of St. Lubbock; not even to the point of adoring colossal images of ants and bees? Simon of Sudbury, Bishop of London, had denounced the popular profanation of the pilgrimage. The Wycliffite tradition, and afterwards the Puritan tradition, has treated him as a hero. He may have been a hero, but he was not a prophet. He did not know what was going to happen to popular religion, when it had lost the Canterbury Pilgrimage. The truth is that anybody who tries to look at Simon of Sudbury's problem from both sides, from front and behind, will realize its real difficulty; but will incline to a simple if slightly impatient conclusion. He will be tempted to say that human beings are not to be trusted with a religion. But are they therefore to be trusted the more without a religion?

Chaucer died and left his last great work unfinished; his most perfect achievement still imperfect. Though he lived a long and busy life, he, more than any other great writer, died young. He had only come to the beginning when he came to the end. He was already old when his work became suddenly and entirely new. There have been cases of men trying a new trick or experiment and breaking down in the middle of it, as did Dickens in the detective story of Drood. But the experiment was a small one; which he might have made at any time, and one which many others had already made. There are cases of an author in his last days writing something rather separate and unique, like a last confession or farewell; as did Shakespeare with the unearthly loveliness of *The Tempest*; or, in another way, Ibsen in the rather incomprehensible outbreak of *When We Dead Awaken*. But these were things not to be developed or extended further, even by their authors, let alone by anybody else. For good or evil, they were not things that could be done twice. Nobody could write another play like *The Tempest*; nobody, I should imagine, wants to write a play like *When We Dead Awaken*. But *The Canterbury Tales*, the last unfinished work of Chaucer, is in quite another sense unfinished and finished. It is not only a new scheme, but a new style. It is not only a new style, but potentially a new school. It is as if he had been an architect, who through a long and successful life had planned out the round arches of the Romanesque and the squat pillars of the Norman churches, and then, almost on his death-bed, had dreamed of and designed the first Gothic cathedral. For indeed *The Canterbury Tales* do remain rather like a huge, hollow, unfinished Gothic cathedral with some of the niches empty and some filled with statues, and some part of the large plan traced only in lines upon the ground.

Just as in such a case, the arches would stand up more strongly than the statues, or the walls be made first and more firmly than the ornament, so in Chaucer's work the framework is finer than the stories which correspond to the statues. The prolonged comedy which we call the

Prologue, though it includes many interludes and something like an epilogue, is made of much stronger material than the tales which it carries; the narrative is quite superior to the narratives. The Wife of Bath's Tale is not so good as the Wife of Bath; the Reeve's Tale is not so vivid as the Reeve; we are not so much interested in the Summoner's story as in the Summoner, and care less about Griselda than about the Clerk of Oxford. The Miller does not prove even his own rather brutal energy, by telling a broad and rather brutal story, half so well as the poet conveys it in those curt and strong lines about his breaking a door by butting it with his red-bristled head. And the whole conception and cult of Chivalry is no better set forth, in all the seventy pages that unfold the Knight's Tale, than in the first few lines that describe the Knight. It is impossible to say for certain, of course, whether Chaucer realized how much more real and original were the passages which concern the Pilgrims than those which concern their imaginery heroes or martyrs. It is possible that, like many another great original genius, he did not know which parts of his own work were really original, still less which were really great. It is likely enough that Shakespeare attached more importance to some laboured conceit, in the manner of the Euphuists, than to such stabs of staccato speech as 'Kill Claudio!' or 'Undo this button'. It may be that Chaucer really did regard the Prologue as a mere frame in the sense of a picture frame. In that case, we can only say he invented a new kind of picture gallery, in which the picture frames are much better than the pictures. Still, a word must be said for the understanding of the pictures, even when he had boldly stolen them out of other people's picture frames. In other words, we must understand something about stories as stories, before we even open this medieval story book.

I have taken too much notice, perhaps, of those who

The Canterbury Tales

are still so childish as to talk about the childishness of Chaucer. I mean in the sense of bearing with him, as if he talked broken English. It would be truer to say he talked the unbroken English, which we have since broken up into bits and snippets of American slang or jaded journalese. There is rather more sense of a rounded whole, in expressing the religious sentiment in words like 'Almighty and almerciable Queen', than in saying, 'Up-to-date scientists admit worth-while qualities in religious urge'. I leave it to the most modern critic to decide which sounds like English and which like Pidgin English. I have pointed out that the poet was not in fact infantile or immature in any contemptible connotation of the words; but in many ways an experienced and even a polished person. He was an artist who picked perfect words to produce his exact effect; he was a diplomatist who was probably himself picked out for his power of picking his words tactfully and persuasively; he was a philosopher who drew theoretical distinctions, along the lines of contemporary thought, with almost the delicacy of a theologian; he was a well-read man, who could collect stories of all shapes and colours from the ends of the earth; whose fancy could follow the mazy mythology of Ovid, and whose intellectual imagination could measure the starry stature of Dante. But I confess that there is a real element which might rightly be called childishness, if the term be used in a healthier sense, for something that may or may not have grown up, but has not grown old. There is a quality in Chaucer, and in the whole civilization that produced Chaucer, which men of rather wearier civilizations must make a certain effort to understand. It is something that moderns have mainly praised in childhood; because moderns have not preserved it in manhood. It is gusto; it is zest; it is a certain appetite for things as they actually are, and because they actually are; for a stone because it is a stone, or a story because it is a story. If that is merely simplicity, he was simple. If that is merely stupidity, he was stupid. That is, if we would appreciate him or his age, we must go back to something that stirred in us when we first found that the door of a doll's-house would open; or when we first found that the end of a story could be the point of a story, as in the surprise that ends the admirable story of Puss in Boots. Chaucer and his friends were really capable of reacting to those surprises; of waiting patiently for the point of those stories; of treating the whole narrative process as a pleasure in itself. Most modern people cannot really do this; they have read too many novels. They have forgotten the very verbal meaning, by which novels once meant news. They have lost the positive pleasure in a double fashion; partly because they have been bewildered by too many plots; partly because they have been even more bewildered by the newer sort of novels, which have not got any plots.

Now when we talk of Chaucer, or for that matter of Shakespeare and many others, as borrowing plots, or copying plots, or repeating plots, we must always remember that the age was really simpler in the sense that there were fewer plots; and that a plot was a very precious thing. It was really prized, unlike many other precious things. It was prized because it had a point, and people were normal enough in their nervous system to start at the prick of the point; instead of having their dead minds punctured all over with old pricks, like the diseased arm of a drug fiend. A mere anecdote was thought worthy of careful presentation, as a relic was worthy of a casket of jewels. The medieval man spent, or wasted, music and ornament and developed detail upon a pointed story; just as the more subtle modern novelist wastes them upon a pointless story. The point to seize is that the people involved were really so far simple, or (as I should say) so far receptive, as to regard a mere story as something rich and rare; something that was a gift; something that was a good in itself. Most of the Canterbury Tales, and especially the first and most finished of them, are good in themselves. I mean they are good even apart from the way in which this particular man of genius presented them. We may say, if we like, that Chaucer's stories are excellent, only they are not Chaucer's. But we must realize that Chaucer thought they were excellent, and enjoyed them as much as if he had invented them. We must not leave out the love of mere naked narrative in the men of medieval times. Everyone knows, for instance, the outline of the Knight's Tale; how two friends quarrelled for the same lady-love and were condemned to settle it by combat; how one knight prayed to Mars to give him the victory, but the other knight prayed to Venus to give him the lady. It is a good story; it would make a good play; if a play were still a thing with a plot. Everybody knows, I suppose, the plot of the Pardoner's Tale, which is a plot in the precise sense; of how three thieves went to find Death to slay him, and found only a heap of gold; and how one was sent to fetch food and wine, which he poisoned, while the others plotted to stab him and did so; so that they all found Death on their heap of gold. That is a good story, and contains a grim crescendo of dramatic action. This element of mere pleasure in narrative must be allowed for, in all accounts of the atmosphere of the age. For instance, the story of Griselda, as a moral story, must be balanced with a great mass of medieval jokes and satires about the woman ruling the roost, and the grey mare being the better horse. But the story of Griselda, as a story, is simply one of the numberless legends and fables about a person passing successfully through a series of tests or trials; like the weird tasks of Michael Scott or the Twelve Labours of Hercules. Men listen to it, as

The Canterbury Tales

children would listen to it, merely to see how the person
passed through his or her misfortunes to the end. If this
sort of innocent intensity be called childishness, it is true
that the age of Chaucer was childish. But we must recover something of the spirit in order to understand the
age; we must sink back into that barbaric past, and far
beyond it into dark depths of primitive instinct, and even
endure to hear some cry out of prehistoric savagery com-
manding us to become like little children.

Nevertheless, there is another side; and an aspect in
which the pictures are extremely picturesque. It is a commonplace of the critics that the actual stock of stories,
which fill up the framework of *The Canterbury Tales*, is
a borrowed stock from all sorts of sources, like the plots
of the plays of Shakespeare. But the narrative poet had
at least one opportunity of showing dramatic talent which
was denied to the dramatist. Shakespeare did not have to
offer each of his comedies as the creation of one of his
characters. We only know that Hamlet liked a particular play about Hecuba and that Theseus could put up with
a particular play about Pyramus and Thisbe. We are un-
illuminated touching the theatrical tastes of King Lear
or Macbeth. But Chaucer had a collection of characters
almost as diverse in dignity or indignity, and had to select
a story for each. The stories are chosen with admirable
art; with much more aptitude than some speeches in some
dramas. Nothing could be more fitting than the sustained
nobility of the Knight's Tale; a tapestry of heroes clad in
gold, except perhaps the ragged and rending contrast that
tears it at the end, when the Monk is just about to begin
his dignified recital of the deaths of kings, and the drunken
Miller roars him down with his cataract of coarse, not to
say foul narrative; an admirably managed collision of
comedy; as if the ruffian had thrown a pail of slops over
the statelier story-teller. But other examples, which are

159

The Canterbury Tales

less well known, illustrate the same persistent neatness of impersonation. What could be more apt than making the dignified anti-clerical Doctor careful to narrate, not a Christian or even romantic story, but a story of the stoic virtue of heathen Rome; the story of Virginius, precisely the sort of hero whom such secularists have always preferred to the saint. How right it is that the chivalric romance of the young Squire should differ from that of the old Knight, in having a touch of the Arabian Nights about it; a more irresponsible and fabulous flight, upon a winged horse, into the golden horizons of Tartary. Equally delicate is the instinct which makes the Prioress, the refined and charming spinster, tell the beautiful legend of the child singing down the street on his way to the crown of martyrdom; or the Father Confessor of the nuns, a comfortable humorist of the type rather common as the male adviser of devout females, tell a sort of playful parable, full of nods and winks, in which the weaknesses of humanity are courteously covered by the feathered costume of cocks and hens. It is more generally recognized that the quarrel between the Summoner and the Friar is vigorously illustrated in their respective narratives, and the same sort of interplay of tales occurs in many places throughout the whole. Perhaps nothing is more characteristic of the Wife of Bath's Tale than the enormous and inordinate length of the Wife of Bath's Prologue. One is momentarily reminded of the proportions between one of Mr. Bernard Shaw's plays and one of Mr. Bernard Shaw's prefaces. Nobody will say that the Wife of Bath bears a marked resemblance to Mr. Shaw; for of all the Pilgrims she was possibly the least Puritan. But her glorious and garrulous egotism, her unfathomable and inexhaustible vitality, are quite admirably hit off in the mere fact that she talks about things in general at such interminable, if not intolerable length, long before she gets to the beginning of her story at all. Chaucer, with his typical shrewdness, has not supplied any such long personal preface to any of the other stories. There are, of course, any number of other minor examples of the same aptitude; indeed there are very few of the stories that are in themselves entirely impersonal, or could have been shifted to any other person. It is not for nothing that the comfortable and prosperous Merchant tells a tale that is rather naughty, in the manner of a French farce, but not gross in the manner of the Miller's Tale. I will not debate the case of the Cook's Tale, specially called 'Gamelyn', because I know its authenticity is very doubtful. Finally, there is the supreme example that I have already given, of the irony of the Rhyme of Sir Topas. I mean the fact that the poet's own story is the only unpoetical story. The tales are always appropriate; and the inappropriate is the most appropriate of all. Chaucer has distributed caps to fit the heads of the whole company; and when he reserves the dunce's cap for himself, it is all the more fitting because it does not fit.

If, then, we regard the stories in a dramatic light, as connected with the characters and quarrels of the story-tellers, we can stretch our minds to take in a general conception of the work which Chaucer was doing, whether he knew he was doing it or not. The whole work takes on the character of a Novel, the first true Novel in history. In it the fundamental logic of most previous story-telling is already reversed. The story-tellers do not merely exist to tell the stories; the stories exist to tell us something about the story-tellers. The novel of character has appeared, and the novel of character is something rather different even from the epic, let alone the allegory or anecdote or story with a point. For though the great epic poets, Homer above all, have sometimes a very strong sense of character, still their ultimate motive is a true

The Canterbury Tales

movement towards a crisis or an act; a turning-point of time illustrative of the fate of man or the will of God. Homer has made a real character of Hector, but the subject of the Iliad is not the character of Hector, or even the life of Hector; it is the death of Hector, and the death of Hector is the doom of Adam. It is quite different with that more modern form of art for art's sake, which may be called character for character's sake. We could not expect to have Hector talking for ever in his tent; as we should like to have Falstaff talking for ever in his tavern. One could not go wandering aimlessly with Orlando and Ruggiero as one could with Don Quixote and Sancho Panza, or with Mr. Pickwick and Sam Weller. There would have to be a Quest of some kind, that is, an ultimate epic action; the epic is always a *chanson de geste*. And in the same way, nobody perhaps would have been more surprised than Chaucer to be told that he had added or discovered something that is not to be found in Virgil. Yet it is true that we might be interested in a Knight who never got to Canterbury, as we could hardly be interested in a Trojan hero who never got to Rome. In the novel of character, characters are companions; and *The Canterbury Tales* is the grand original of all such works, because they appear in companionship.

Indeed I rather wonder nobody has tried to turn it into a novel. Many have made a paraphrase; including some cases in which it might rather be called parody. But, oddly enough, the experiment which would be the most frivolous seems to me the most fascinating; and I am rather surprised that it has never been tried. There have been renderings of the medieval poet into modern verse, and renderings into a sort of medieval prose. There have also been renderings into a more or less modern prose. But I have never seen what I may call a rendering into modern fiction. I wonder that somebody, especially among the novelists, has not tried his hand, merely as an experiment or a joke, at turning the Prologue and framework of *The Canterbury Tales* into the form of a modern novel. The thing might be done, of course, in very different degrees of seriousness or silliness or pure satire. It would be quite unhistorical to turn the medieval crowd into a modern crowd; for in a thousand things all the characters are really medieval. But, like many anachronisms, it would be a great joke. It would be amusing to see how far we could really get along with the Host as a modern hotel proprietor, the Knight as a retired Colonel knighted for his military services, the Clerk of Oxford as an Oxford don, the Franklin as an ordinary country gentleman with a good estate, the Doctor as a modern doctor, the Parson as a modern parson, and so on. It would be historically illuminating to see what could be done; still more historically illuminating to note what could not be done. For the moment, however, I do not mention this imaginary modern novel with any wild intention of attempting to write it. I mention it as the shortest and sharpest way of conveying, to the modern reader, what seems to me the amazing genius of Geoffrey Chaucer as a novelist.

It is not a question of the broad comedy or farce which is most commonly mentioned by the critics, as in the unedifying quarrels of the Summoner or the Miller. It is a thread of thoroughly sound and thoughtful psychology that runs through almost all the interchanges, rather especially in the passages that are comparatively quiet. I will take only one example to illustrate what I mean. It is an example that I have never seen noticed, though doubtless some of the very able Chaucerian students have noticed it. But I rather fancy most people have not noticed it, because it is not anything in the way of an insult, but is rather a compliment. Only it is exactly the compliment that would be paid by that particular sort of person, to the

The Canterbury Tales

other particular sort of person, at that particular time and place. I mean the passage in which the Franklin, the hoary but hearty old squire, with the big appetite and the beaming geniality, listens to the tale told by the other or medieval sort of Squire, the young gallant who is the son and attendant of the Knight. This young gentleman has pleasing manners, and I suspect a certain modest self-complacency, but he has been taught to treat his elders with respect, and to mingle such courtesy with his natural high spirits. He tells a tale which is of the nature of a fairy tale, as compared with many of the others; a fine fantastic fable about a king who had a magic ring and a magic horse; there is nothing else notable about it, except that he evidently tells it with fluency and gusto and makes himself, more or less consciously, rather a fine figure in the company. At the end of his story comes one of those minor humours which reveal the real novelist's grip on human nature. The old Franklin, who has been listening, I imagine, with a slightly gaping gravity, impressed by the continuity rather than the content or precise meaning of the monologue, seems to shake himself, assumes an air of massive and venerable solemnity, and ponderously compliments the young man on having said his little piece. He informs the youth (if we may so translate him) that he is a credit to his family and upbringing; that he has performed his duties in an eminently satisfactory manner, and generally that he is almost a model to his generation. Then the thought behind all this begins to shape itself, and the old gentleman introduces the lamentable subject of his own son, who is (it would seem) a most prodigal and unprofitable social character; quite unlikely to go out of his way to entertain the company by telling, or even leaving half-told, the story of Cambuscan bold. The rest of the old squire's speech consists entirely of regrets and gloomy prophecies about his own absent

164

and unpresentable offspring. Now that is a living incident that leaps at the eye; a story that comes straight out
of the things that really happen. It is as quiet and as real
as Jane Austen. It has only to be translated into the language of a modern novel, and it would be as vivid even
to the modern novel reader. He would instantly see the
poor old gentleman shaking his head and saying (entirely
irrelevantly, because some other young man had just
finished a recitation), 'Ah, I only wish *my* boy could be
made to understand, etc. etc.' It reminds one of that situation which Stevenson truly said would make an excellent comedy; in which two grumbling old fathers had
each a sort of half-jealous, half-argumentative, admiration
for the son of the other.

Now there are any number of little lively scenes like
that, in the intercourse of the characters in *The Canterbury
Tales*. They are filled with that truth that is especially the
truth of fiction. I mean that Chaucer knew exactly what
sort of person he meant by the Franklin and exactly what
sort of person he meant by the Squire; and therefore knew
exactly what they would say to each other, even in a con-
tingency that he had not yet especially considered. The
characters have been already built up by innumerable
small touches, and, improbable as it may sound in such
a connexion, nearly all the seemingly accidental touches
are actually used, or do actually tell, in the full development of the comedy. There would not be that particular
touch of comic pathos, about the poor old Franklin's disapproval of his son, if the Franklin himself had been primarily a moralist or a model of austerity and abnegation.
The fact that we know the old man to be himself rather
a jolly old heathen, enormously fond of food and drink,
gives him somehow all the human helplessness of a very
normal father. Similarly, it was not for nothing that we
were told of the young Squire, long before he began to tell

The Canterbury Tales

the Squire's Tale, that, with all his gaiety, he was meek and serviceable, and carved before his father at the table. It was exactly that touch of deference in the young dandy, that probably produced the vague but vastly favourable impression which moved the Franklin to speech. We can imagine the young man anywhere, even in a modern novel. He would be the sort of young man from Oxford, who is very careful to address an older man as 'Sir'.

And all this was done when the world had never so much as dreamed of a novel, in the modern sense of a mere study of the fine shades of fictitious character. This was done in an age of rigid religious allegories, of flat and decorative romances of chivalry, of stories having indeed a hundred merits of harmonious pattern or verbal melody, of spiritual idealism or intellectual symbolism; but hardly as yet even the beginnings of what we now call the psychological element in narrative. Chaucer did it alone; he did it almost by accident; he did it by sheer moral imagination, in a style of which there were as yet no models to emulate and no rules even to break. It was like the first portrait drawn in a world that had known nothing but patterns. Beautiful patterns indeed, and ingenious and intellectual patterns, and patterns showing a profound knowledge of mathematics and their relation to metaphysics; but with never a line or a curve in them calculated to teach anybody how to begin the particular picture of a face. It may be said that this is too sweeping a description of the world of literature to which Chaucer had access, and so in a sense it is; but it will be found, I think, that the exceptions really prove the rule. Dante, for instance, most certainly had a profound sense of a human character, in the deeper sense of a human soul. I think it probable that it was this sense of individuality in Dante that so profoundly attracted Chaucer; and made Chaucer, with an insight remarkable at the time, prefer the bitter exile of Ravenna to the resplendent Laureate of Rome. But even the case of Dante does not meet the particular point I mean. The reason is not merely that Dante could not, by the very nature of his work and plan, develop the delicate and light comedy in consideration here. Nobody would expect to find the joke about the Franklin and the Squire cheerfully introduced into the Circle of Ice or mentioned in passing by St. Bernard when discoursing on the Beatific Vision. But the reason is deeper than that. It is the reason given, with great insight and wisdom, by Mr. W. B. Yeats, when he said that tragedy swamps character while comedy consists in character. Dante deals with those huge and heroic passions which are simply human or superhuman; but in any case overwhelm the small differentiations that make all the fun of comic fiction. The Franklin is essentially one particular father grumbling over one particular son, in one particular set of highly amusing social circumstances. But the cry of the father in Dante, as it comes out of the Tower of Hunger, is simply the cry of fatherhood. I am not claiming for Chaucer the very highest power of tragic or typical expression, which is not so much the voice of men as of man. But I do claim for him that his comedy of character was of the finest; but above all, that it was the first.

Nevertheless, if we are to understand the medieval world, but still more if we are to understand the modern world, we must recur to the real limit or term set to the long-drawn-out comedy of the Canterbury Pilgrims; the limit which is Canterbury. It is true, as I have said, that this original and astonishing adventure in literature does bring in all that we value most of the fiction of the present; but it also brings us to a certain blank or doubt about the fiction of the future. The Novel was a speciality of the nineteenth century; precisely because it did seem, in the lull of the liberal enlightenment, possible to study mere individuality or idiosyncrasy; and to study it in a world of eternal leisure. It was not for nothing that the three-volume novel was found in the seaside library. There was a sort of suggestion of an endless holiday, in that study of character for character's sake. I do not mean that it was not, or is not, or will not always be, a normal and even noble intellectual interest. I mean that the age of the great novelists took the holiday for granted: assumed that the basis of the human brotherhood could never be broken up. The real trouble is this; that after a certain point of intellectual differentiation, the brotherhood is broken up. In a revolution, men will not stand still to be studied. In a fundamental philosophical disagreement, men will not even agree about what is worth studying. This modern division is masked by the mildness of modern manners. The Conservative clerk and the Socialist clerk do not bawl and bellow at each other as did the Miller and the Reeve; but they disagree with each other much more than did the Miller and the Reeve. And when the Socialist actually acts as the Communist, even the mildness has been known to be modified. It is also masked by a modern mysticism, which leads many to feel quite honestly that they can do without the definite goal of the journey. But while this may mean for some a growth of sympathy, it means for most a break-up of sympathies. There is nothing to keep the Pilgrims on the same Pilgrimage.

The truth is that the broad religion creates the narrow clique. It is what is called the religion of dogmas, that is of facts (or alleged facts), that creates a broader brotherhood and brings men of all kinds together. This is called a paradox; but it will be obvious to anyone who considers the nature of a fact. All men share in a fact, if they believe it to be a fact. Only a few men commonly share a feeling, when it is only a feeling. If there is a deep and delicate and intangible feeling, detached from all statements, but reaching to a wordless worship of beauty, wafted in a sweet savour from the woods of Kent or the spires of Canterbury, then we may be tolerably certain that the Miller will not have it. The Miller can only become the Pilgrim, if he recognizes that God is in the heavens as he recognizes that the sun is in the sky. If he does recognize it, he can share the dogma just as he can share the daylight. But he cannot be expected to share all the shades of fine intellectual mysticism that might exist in the mind of the Prioress or the Parson. I can understand that argument being turned in an anti-democratic as well as an anti-dogmatic direction; but anyhow the individualistic mystics must either do without the mysticism or do without the Miller. To some refined persons the loss of the latter would be no very insupportable laceration of the feelings. But I am not a refined person and I am not merely thinking about feelings. I am even so antiquated as to be thinking about rights; about the rights of men, which are extended even to millers. Among those rights is a certain rough working respect and consideration, which is at the basis of comradeship. And I say that if the comradeship is to include the Miller at all, it must be based on the recognition of something as really true, and not merely as ideally beautiful. It is easy to imagine the Knight and the Prioress riding to Canterbury and talking in the most elegant and cultivated strain, exchanging graceful fictions about knights and ladies for equally graceful legends about virgins and saints. But that sort of sympathy, especially when it reaches the point of subtlety, is not a way of uniting, or even collecting, all the Canterbury Pilgrims. The Knight and the Prioress would be the founders of a clique; as they probably were already the representatives of a class. I am not concerned here with whether the modern mind prefers its pretensions to popular breadth or its claims to creedless spirituality. I am only pointing out that it cannot have both at once; that if religion is an intuition, it must be an individual intuition and not a social institution; and that it is much easier to build a social institution on something that is regarded as a solid fact. Now, however strange it may seem, the men of the Middle Ages did regard the miracles of St. Thomas of Canterbury, and the help given them from heaven by his intercession 'when that they were sick', as examples of a solid fact. There was any amount of human historical evidence for such miracles; and they were too ignorant and primitive to have learnt to prefer determinist theory to historical evidence. And as all men desire health, and as even the worst men may ask heaven for help in ill-health, and as few except the very worst would refuse altogether to be thankful for being healthy, the whole purpose and attitude of the Pilgrimage rested on a reality recognized by all sorts of people, good, bad and indifferent. A religion of miracles turned all this crowd of incongruous people into one company. A religion of moods would never have brought them together at the tavern, far less sent them trotting laboriously to the tomb.

That is perhaps the deepest difference between medieval and modern life, and the difference is so great that many never imagine it, because it is impossible to describe it. We may even say that the modern world is more religious, in that the religious are more religious. Anyhow, there is nothing to prevent a modern mystic being as mystical as St. John of the Cross; and doubtless many students of St. John of the Cross are even now approaching his sanctity. But we may be practically certain that if there is a modern man like the Miller or the Reeve, he has not got any religion at all. He certainly would not go on a religious pilgrimage, or perform any religious duty at all. One of the quarrels in *The Canterbury Tales* sounds exactly like a quarrel in a public-house to-day, between a boisterous bookie and a surly north-country groom. It is still possible to find two such persons in a public-house; it might be possible to find them in a public conveyance going down to the Derby. But how are we to stretch our minds so as to imagine the bookie and the groom deliberately going together to Glastonbury, solely to inquire into the recent psychic phenomena supposed (by some) to be connected with the Holy Grail? That is the measure of the difference between Chaucer's age and our own. That is the measure of the difference between an objective religion, worshipped as an object by the whole people, and a subjective religion, studied as a subject only by the religious. There is something much more dramatic and challenging than the disagreement of the Summoner and the Friar: and that is the agreement of the Summoner and the Friar. They would never even have come together to quarrel, except in a social system that fundamentally assumed them to agree.

Thus, the Canterbury Pilgrimage takes on a very symbolic social character, and is indeed the progress which emerged out of the medieval into the modern world. All modern critics can take pleasure in the almost modern realism of the portraiture; in the variety of the types and the vigour of the quarrels. But the modern problem is more and more the problem of keeping the company together at all; and the company was kept together because it was going to Canterbury. It will be another business, if the variety of companions discovers a variety of aims. It will raise a new problem if the Miller, with his appetite for more vulgar noises, refuses after all to go to Canterbury and insists on going off to Ramsgate; possibly the scene of sports in which he bore away the Ram. It will be a different thing, if the Merchant firmly refuses to ride beyond

The Canterbury Tales

Chatham, because all his interests are limited to the progressive industry of that wealthy and dirty town. Darker days will come, when the Prioress, not content with pitying mice, will withdraw to a Vegetarian Hostel on the hills of Westerham, inhabited by cranks; while the now aged Knight, swearing that the Service is going to the dogs, and that these damned pacifists haven't a damned patriotic instinct left, shall devote himself furiously to the fortifications of Dover. As their counterparts stand to-day, it is easier to imagine the Wife of Bath wanting to go sunbathing at Margate, or the Clerk instantly returning, with refined disgust, to Oxford, than to imagine either of them wanting to toil on together to a particular tomb in Canterbury. For the moment, this division of heart is masked by a certain heartiness, in the modern pursuit of mere games and pleasures; but you cannot make a complete social system out of games and pleasures. You cannot, in some dark hour of peril, ask thousands to die for the Derby, or even to be taxed to death for the International Golf Championship. A nation that has nothing but its amusements will not be amused for very long. Moreover, the amusements are at least as narrow as the devotions and dedications. You will not persuade the Clerk of Oxford to go to Ramsgate, merely to see the Miller win the Ram. You will not persuade the Miller to go to Oxford, which might well have been named, at that time, after the Dumb Ox of Philosophy: St. Thomas of Aquin. But they were both ready to go together to the shrine of St. Thomas of Canterbury. The real modern problem is—what pilgrimage have we on which these two different men will ride together? I mean, of course, one on which they will ride together and remain different. There are many forces making for a superficial sameness in modern life; far too many. There is standardization and the stunts of journalism and the various forms of conscription and coercion rather peculiar to our time; such as Prohibition. But you do not re-consecrate the Cathedral by shutting up the Tabard; or make men want to go on a pilgrimage by forbidding them to go to a public-house. There are many modern forces, commercial or scientific, tending to make men look or talk the same. But the Clerk and the Miller did not look and talk the same. They had nothing in common but their purpose; but they had a purpose. It is very puzzling to look at the real society around us at this moment, and consider whether it has a purpose. For the present, at least, there is no Canterbury in sight for the Canterbury Pilgrims. The coloured cavalcade is halted somewhere in the suburbs, and suffering the bewilderment dating from that day, when sectarians and journalists and jerry-builders between them decided that every man should live in the same villa and every man in a different universe.

Some of these conclusions are inevitably coloured with my own convictions; but I do not think that those most opposed to them will differ greatly about the contemporary facts. Few will deny that a certain kind of straightforward story, with a plot and a point, but adorned with vivid portraits of different persons, began to enter the world in Chaucer's time. Not many will deny that the development of that straightforward story is doubtful and perplexed in our own time. It is possible, of course, that somebody will make something out of it; something that is another story; something that is not a story. Something may be done with the subconsciousness of the Miller or the dual personality of the Wife of Bath. But I doubt whether it will be what we have known as a readable romance, if it cannot hold together the Wife of Bath as one person or the Canterbury Pilgrimage as one party. I am not alone in thinking that we are likely to see the break-up of the particular culture made by the Renaissance, at least

173

The Canterbury Tales

as much as Chaucer was in a position to see the break-up of the particular culture of the Middle Ages. Nor am I alone, I fancy, in suspecting that this special creation called the modern Novel, which began with him, may end with us.

At least, in this lighter and (dare I say) lesser matter of letters, may we who are burdened with conclusions, or even convictions, be suffered to entertain a suspicion? A suspicion that in the secret matter of happiness (not prosperity, or efficiency, or even equality, but happiness) men do not merely progress indefinitely, but rather pass a flashing moment of maturity; pass it, for instance, when they drink just too much good wine at the Tabard and fall under the table, or progress beyond Canterbury and fall into the sea. That there is an instant of radiant ripeness which the drunkard does not recover, and to which neither does the dead return; and that this crisis of perfection, in literature and the love of literature, comes when what is old and simple can still mingle with what is new and strange. When men can still listen to a story like children, but can already savour the humours of men like men; when men can still be surprised at the logical turn of fate that swings round and strikes down the victorious Arcite, but can already be ironically entertained by the torrent of self-expression from the Wife of Bath, who exults in sheer egotism for pages before she gets to any story at all; when they were still so unsophisticated as to be moved by the mountainous yet ever mounting crescendo of magnanimity in the generous rivalries of the Franklin's Tale; and yet have gained enough of culture to appreciate some verbal felicities in the telling, as in the Dantesque touch of the woman's wild prayer that all the high black rocks be sunken into hell; when a man could yet weep like the Host (that sentimentalist!) over the mere death of a simple maid, and yet roar down a bore or a bully with the joyful contempt of Rabelais; when they could find a melodious pleasure in the mere flow of a narrative and yet remain sufficiently wide-awake to react when it ended with the point of an anecdote; when the world was young enough to be capable of hero-worship and old enough to be capable of humour; and that this flame of the highest happiness flashed for a moment in the mirror of the genius of Chaucer; like the noonday sun upon a naked sword.

Chapter VI

CHAUCER AS AN ENGLISHMAN

We have heard much of late of something called Emergent Evolution; a phrase which, like many scientific phrases, we may find rather useful so long as we do not use it scientifically. Evolution as explanation, as an ultimate philosophy of the cause of living things, is still faced with the problem of producing rabbits out of an empty hat; a process commonly involving some hint of Design. But evolution, and especially emergence, as a convenient and compact description of a sort of relative growth we can all see for ourselves, is very useful in many connexions, and especially in connexion with the problem of England in the later Middle Ages. The Englishman, as a national figure now fully nationalized, stands in the modern world for certain associations or impressions, true or false, but anyhow fairly familiar. We could hardly say simply that, in Chaucer's time, the Englishman was non-existent. We cannot exactly say that the Englishman was existent. We can say that the Englishman was emergent. But it is necessary to state more exactly the stage of his emergence, and the true proportions in which he was like and unlike ourselves.

The nineteenth-century version of the Englishman would be entirely false in the fourteenth century. It may be urged in answer (by curious and restless minds) that the nineteenth-century version was entirely false in the nineteenth century. It is easy enough to point out con-

Chaucer as an Englishman

trasts and inconsistencies that might seem to make the whole ordinary English legend a lie. The normal Englishman was supposed to be a sturdy and stoical figure, who hated to show his feelings for fear of seeming flashy; or making anything so theatrical as 'a scene'. And his most popular novelist was Dickens and his most fashionable statesman was Disraeli. But though it is obvious that he was much more romantic than he thought he was, it is true that his romance about himself was the romance of being unromantic. That is, it was the romance of being practical; even the romance of being prosaic. There was a multitudinous English type made on that model, and they really were more national as well as more normal than the quacks or geniuses whom they admired. It is obvious that the 'unpatriotic' Cobden was a hundred times more of an Englishman than the patriotic Lord Beaconsfield; and perhaps the humdrum Trollope more representative than the dazzling Dickens. When all allowances are made, it is true that a type had appeared, by about the end of the eighteenth century, which was commonly regarded as the English type and is even now only partially transformed; a type compared with which most foreigners appeared volatile or violent or exuberantly vivacious. Its story had been one of two or three centuries. Its foundation, like every foundation, was religious: its first basis had been Puritanism; on this was erected all the ugly opulence of Industrialism; and then there had matured another influence, most modern but perhaps most fascinating and fashionable of all; what may be called the genteel stoicism of the Public Schools. The gentlemen who governed England, the gentlemen who *were* England, received their two great commandments. They must play the game and they must not play at it. Above all, they must not play at it playfully. A singular seriousness must be directed towards the sports that most

Chaucer as an Englishman

other people think merely sportive; and they must be made the rites of a religion of patriotism. With this went all the kindred things: the pride in evading emotion; the contented confession of a certain ignorance of music or foreign refinements; the hazy identification of the vices of industrialism with the virtue of industry. This Englishman did exist; at any rate he did try to exist. And there is a sense in which the ideal is more important than the real. The real is only useful to realistic novelists. It is the ideal, or in a better language the god, who really leads the masses of men and turns the corners of history.

When we have firmly and clearly modelled the image of what the whole modern world has meant by an Englishman, we must instantly and utterly destroy it. When we have once vividly understood what was really meant by the national ideal in the nineteenth century, we must utterly sweep it away from the whole field of the fourteenth century. Nothing whatever resembling that conscious ideal of common sense, or cold virility, existed for Chaucer and his contemporary countrymen. Indeed, so far as there was a general atmosphere and attitude, it was all the other way. If the Victorians could have actually had a vision of Chaucerian England, they would have thought the Englishman was a Frenchman. All the jokes against the Frenchman would be jokes against the fourteenth-century Englishman. All the emotions and expressions of emotions were there, especially those considered most un-English. If Jules and Jacques kissed each other, it would seem altogether absurd to Thackeray. If Palamon and Arcite kissed each other, it would not seem in the least absurd to Chaucer. That men should on occasion weep, and even weep in public, seemed no more unnatural to the writers of the older England than it did to the writers of the Old Testament or the Iliad. But the contrast is even plainer in the gesture of joy than the

178

gesture of grief. The tag about Merry England is not unhistorical; for many historic witnesses did regard it as rather merrier than the neighbouring nations. The Victorian Englishman was rather prone to regard a damned fiddler as a damned foreigner. The medieval visitor to England described it as full of fiddling; as especially addicted to music and minstrelsy and dance and song. From the Victorian point of view, in so far as England did differ from France, it was in being rather more French than France. And indeed the Victorian, or the man who finds virtue only in the modern Public School ideal, must frankly face the fact that in the fourteenth century what he has called England did not exist. Not only was there another nation, but it was in a sense a Franco-English nation. It was partly because France and England were so nearly one nation, that the kings struggled so long to make them one kingdom. Anybody can see in history how near were the national types to each other then, and how far apart they are now. The Black Prince and Bertrand du Guesclin understood each other much better, as enemies, than French and Foch could understand each other as allies. Behind all was the great unity of Christendom, more than twelve hundred years old, which the later insular Englishman had never even heard of. Such was the condition when the first cracks appeared in that Continent. France and England did not unite; and the great English nation was founded, very largely by Joan of Arc.

Now it is when we have frankly and fully realized this that the fun begins. It is when we have cleared our minds of the last lingering notion that the proverbial practical Englishman existed then, as he exists now, that we can begin to consider what is meant by saying that he was not existent; but he was emergent. Geoffrey Chaucer no more regarded himself as John Bull than a prehistoric Red

Chaucer as an Englishman

Indian regarded himself as a Regular Guy. He no more prided himself on being a plain blunt Englishman, with a Bible under one arm and a business ledger under the other, than a Cossack of the twelfth century prided himself on being a Communist of the twentieth. It was an utterly different world, the old world of Christendom which had once been the Christian Roman Empire; a world in which the local loyalties were still feudal; the larger loyalties still often imperial; and the ultimate loyalty entirely religious and long centred in Rome. Nine-tenths of the mind of a man like Chaucer were busy with things that have entirely vanished from the world, as seen by an English patriot to-day. The vast, if shadowy, suzerainty of the Emperor that had reared itself against the supremacy of the Pope; the assumption at the back of every Christian mind that the Crusades ought really to be continued, though they had already been practically abandoned; the serious juridical argument about the Plantagenet claim to the French throne; the vast and crowded ways of medieval travel, which followed so largely the great roads to the great shrines of the Continent. It can all be summed up by saying that Chaucer would have thought it quite as natural to go on a pilgrimage to Compostella as on a pilgrimage to Canterbury. It is also worth remarking that, if he had gone on a pilgrimage to Compostella, or to any Christian shrine in Hungary or Poland or the other end of Europe, he would very probably have seen a statue of St. Thomas of Canterbury looking down on him in a strange land.

But the point is this; that while nine-tenths of his mind made him a citizen of the old empire of Christendom, there was another tenth of his mind; and it was beginning to tell. Canterbury would not suggest to him anything resembling what we mean now by a cathedral city or an Archbishop of Canterbury. It would be more likely

Chaucer as an Englishman

to suggest the Pope who had avenged St. Thomas on the tyrant who had him slain. But he was beginning to feel, with a part of his mind, that Canterbury was Canterbury and not Compostella: that it had a Kentish and not a Spanish smell about it; that, while it was an international shrine, it was a point of pride to have an international shrine inside one's own nation; and that, while it was only one of the holy places, it was convenient and comfortable to have a holy place so near home. We may say, if we like, that his subconsciousness was more national than his consciousness; I suspect that it was as yet only a corner of his subconsciousness; but it was growing; it was evolving; it was emergent. And it is really a subtle and fascinating study, far more fascinating than anything offered by a cheap simplification, modernization or nationalization of the Chaucerian phase, to trace out the first faint beginnings of the separate national character that exists to-day; the real roots of the difference that afterwards, in its later exaggeration, divided England from Europe.

There are several very curious, and even mysterious, things about Chaucer, which do already mark him out as a man somewhat different from the same sort of man in the France or Italy of his day. There are moments when we can truly say that the medieval Englishman is already beginning to be the modern Englishman. Something, often something oddly negative (as is often the case with the quaint qualities of the English), has begun to appear, in such a way that we can say now, though it is doubtful if we could have said then, 'This man is beginning to look devilish like an English Gentleman', or, 'If he does not look out, this will end in being a Good Sport'. Not that I would imply any lack of sympathy with these modern ideals, in moderation; I merely mean that, in this time of transition in which Chaucer lived, we sometimes sud-

181

Chaucer as an Englishman

denly see them looming far ahead; things not perhaps inevitable, but certainly unmistakable. These possibilities already existed; they need not eventually have been so much exaggerated; above all, they need not have been so much isolated. Anyhow, Chaucer could already boast of being distinguished from his fellow-Christians; though he could not yet boast of being divided from them.

I will take first one very strange example; the position of the poet in relation to fame and fashion. He was not an unsuccessful man. For the greater part of his life he was a successful man and a poet; and yet we cannot say exactly that he was a successful poet. That is, he was not successful as a poet in the way in which some of his contemporaries were successful as poets: praised and applauded as poets; crowned and enthroned as poets. In this respect there is a curious parallel between the mystery of Chaucer and the mystery of Shakespeare. They were neither of them failures or outcasts; they both seem to have had a good deal of solid success, though Shakespeare was wealthiest in later life and Chaucer in middle life. But they were more successful than famous; and more famous than glorious. The odd obscurity of Shakespeare, in some aspects, which has been the negative opportunity of so many cranks and quacks, is a real fact so far as it goes; and it can best be measured if we compare it, for instance, with the flamboyant fame of Ronsard a few years before in France. Some say that Shakespeare's death was disreputable; it is a far more creepy and uncanny fact that his life was respectable. He lived and died, not like a first-rate failure, but like a fourth-rate success. He lived and died a proper provincial burgess, a few years after Ronsard had gathered round his gorgeous death-bed that great assembly of nobles and princes in the robes of religion, and proclaimed to all Europe as with a trumpet that no man born had known so much glory as he, and that he was weary of it and thirsty for the glory of God. The obscure death of Shakespeare is almost as startling a contrast, whether it was disreputable or respectable.

Now Chaucer moves in almost exactly the same manner, on what may be called a lower level of moderate success. As we can compare the respectability of Shakespeare with the public glory of Ronsard, so we can compare the respectability of Chaucer with the towering splendour of Petrarch. Petrarch was not, I fancy, a much greater poet than Chaucer; certainly not so original a poet as Chaucer. Petrarch had a public triumph like the triumph of Julius Caesar; like the triumph of an Emperor who had conquered the world. He passed through the streets of Rome with an army of banners and trumpets, to where he was crowned with laurel, the eternal crown, upon the high rock of the Capitol, and went to Mass like a king in state, to leave his wreath on the altar of St. Peter's. And all this time we find the English poet, greater or at least as great, moving about busily, but entirely lost in the crowd; noticed by nobody in particular except the few people who sent him on his rather mysterious errands; apparently having a good deal to do, but always of the sort that rather involved his avoiding observation than obtaining fame. He seems to be all over the place; but he is always under the surface. Nobody says, 'I met old Chaucer in Westminster'; nobody writes, 'I had the honour to meet no less a person than Mr. Chaucer when I was in Italy'. He was in Italy when the radiant and resplendent Petrarch was there; certainly in the same country, probably in the same town. It is highly probable, though by no means certain, that they met. The question has been debated down to the last detail by men much more learned than I. But a much more important point, as I should consider it, is this: that in any

Chaucer as an Englishman

case people would have said that Chaucer had managed to
meet Petrarch; not that Petrarch had managed to meet
Chaucer.

Now we may easily note this, to begin with, with the
somewhat melancholy moral, 'That is about as much as
England will do for literature and literary men'. Probably it was true then, as it is certainly true now, that
France and Italy would lend themselves more naturally to
a great popular enthusiasm for a poet as such; to a great
national and even political pageant in honour of pure
Beauty. It is also true that they have preserved, perhaps by their more direct hold on pagan antiquity, more
of the ancient idea of an *officium* or official status of the
Bard or the Orator; a sort of sacred position like that of
the Priest or the Sibyl. Compared with that, we may say
that in England all authors are amateurs. Many of them
were primarily what used to be called humorists; that is,
many of them were characters and some of them pretty
queer characters. Even as early as Chaucer's time, it
would seem, there was something of this aversion to the
public carnival for the crowning of a poor literary gent.
But, unless I am mistaken, there was something else in it,
much more deep and subtle. Mr. Geoffrey Chaucer, with
his unobtrusive way of going off on Government business, his taste for being trustworthy and not conspicuous,
his carrying of important dispatches and trying to look
like anybody else, has something extraordinarily English
about him. We almost feel that he has given 'his man' a
holiday and quietly packed his suit-case at the club. Already, in the fourteenth century, there is faintly fore-
shadowed that indescribable tone of the English gentleman on such a job. He is the unofficial official. He has
the official obscurity of numberless gentlemen in Government offices. He has even a touch of the strong silent hero,
who goes on Secret Service in the novels of Sapper and

184

Chaucer as an Englishman

Le Queux. All this, of course, is a wild exaggeration like the novels in question; for, as I have said, the thing had only just faintly begun to be a tendency and had not yet ended in a type. Still, we cannot dismiss a dim impression of that sort of gentlemanly understanding, of that sort of impersonal personal mission, when we compare the sort of success that was allowed to Chaucer with the sort of success that was allowed to Petrarch. We have, perhaps, a hint of the sort of man who really, in his heart, thinks it more important to share a secret with his country's rulers than to be acclaimed like a god by all the crowds of his countrymen. Anyhow, it seems to me that there is already a subtly national note in this odd use of a man of genius; and this concentration on public affairs as private affairs. Chaucer was not in the least like a modern Englishman; but he was the beginning of something of which the modern Englishman was the end. The point here is that it had already begun.

Second, there is something symbolic in his social rank. There is even something symbolic in the doubts about his social rank. Something was already growing, and was especially developed in England, which was not quite explained by the logical system of ranks and guilds in the Middle Ages. For logic (or what reasonable people call reason) was almost the very soul of the Middle Ages. Yet something more indeterminate is already detaching itself; and in England it has become most detached. It is symbolized, as I say, in the very fact that one aspect or tradition of Chaucer shows him as the child of a common vintner selling barrels of wine to ruffians like the Shipman; while another shows him not so much a courtier as almost a cousin of some great prince like John of Gaunt. Something individualistic in English development made this really true of individuals, though not of classes. It must not be confused with that lifting of men from the

185

lowest to the highest estate, which was a common action
of medieval monarchy, as of all genuine monarchy. King
Henry could raise the butcher's son as King Cophetua
could raise the beggar-maid; that true personal authority
often had a touch that seemed like magic. The thing I
mean concerned the way in which the upper middle class
abutted upon the upper class; and how particular people
could cross the line in a particular way, especially in this
particular country. Nor must it be confused with that
opportunity often offered to the poorest to rise by the
ladder of learning, and the assistance of the Church,
which was the peculiar glory of the Middle Ages. This
matter I mention now is more of a social accident; it
would always be rather a chance for the richest than for
the poorest; but they probably had more of a chance here
than elsewhere. One way of putting it would be to say
that the system of nobility was no longer mere nepotism;
but it was still mere favouritism. Another way of putting it would be to say that the vintner's son, in the words
of the comic opera, was appointed by a job; and a good
job too.

Our England has been an aristocracy˗which denied
that it was aristocratic. In this queer inverted pride there
has often been hypocrisy, but often only inconsistency;
the desire to combine limited privileges with liberal sentiments. Anyhow, its story for the last century or two has
been that of a governing class which pretended not to
govern. Now nothing of that last phase was possible to
the philosophy of the Middle Ages. Princes they knew
and citizens they knew, and the authority of superiors and
the equality of brethren; but accepting social superiority
as an atmosphere, while not asserting it as an institution,
would have seemed to them mere nonsense. A medieval
man would have thought it simply a mad paradox for
anybody to give a man a coronet and a coat of arms to

Chaucer as an Englishman

make him admirable, and then call people snobs for admiring him. When they crowned a man king, they made him king; and would have thought it silly to crown him, if he were only what we now call a constitutional king. Sometimes they preferred a republic; occasionally it degenerated into an aristocratic republic. But they did not explain that aristocracy is more democratic than democracy. All this singular way of talking is entirely modern, and we must not look for anything like that in the social position of Chaucer. Nevertheless, there is already something distinctively English in the social position. There is something private and occasional in his way of slipping into the social class above his own. We can almost hear the County, or the Club, saying that after all he is a damned good fellow; not without the implication of a damned useful fellow. But the point of the admission was, as it continued to be at least until very lately, that the exception was exceptional. It was exceptional even if it became pretty frequent or general. It was exceptional because it was personal. The word went forth that the vintner should be accepted; not that the vintners should be. So, until lately, the whole object of English aristocratic diplomacy was to admit the greengrocer without admitting the greengrocers; to admit the pork-butcher without admitting the pork-butchers; and especially of late, to admit the pawnbroker and the moneylender on the same principles and in even larger numbers. With the last phase of all (which has begun to happen in our time), in which the gentleman no longer patronizes the pawnbroker, because the pawnbroker patronizes the gentleman, we are not here concerned.

Thus, though the social status of the poet was only a sort of far-off signal, that might hint to historians that a long historical process had begun, there is something satisfactory and almost soothing in its embodiment in so

187

Chaucer as an Englishman

great and so magnanimous a man. For it is not fair to forget the good side of this curious opportunist aristocracy adopted by the English. It has certainly proved the only human and workable way of preserving aristocracy, which has really not been preserved at all, as a method of govenment, by anybody except the English. Everywhere where aristocracy was logical, that is, where nobility and heredity and heraldry went together in a consistent scheme, that nobility has ceased to govern the nation. It has always been elbowed aside either by democracy or by despotism. The working of the English method does really require a certain kind of geniality and good humour; a certain spirit which, if we wish to see it at its very best, we could hardly find more vividly embodied than in the personal character of Chaucer.

I do not think it fanciful to find in Chaucer's work, not only the first faint outline of the English Gentleman, but also the first faint outline of the English Lady. There is no doubt that the Prioress in *The Canterbury Tales* is a Lady; but she seems to me to be an exceedingly English Lady. The considerable social importance of her little dogs would alone strike the special note. She was a spinster with exactly the right amount of sentiment; as exhibited in the motto on her brooch or clasp. She was particular about manners at table. She did not like to see a mouse caught in a trap. And indeed we may once more indulge our fancy, in finding one of these ancestral adumbrations; the suggestion of the whole temperamental tendency expressed in the special kind of kindness to animals so much valued by the English gentry to-day. It is a special kind; and some critics might even find it a paradoxical kind. The Prioress was more logical than many a modern lady, whose favourite cat (if he is anything of a logician) must be profoundly puzzled at being allowed to kill mice but not to kill birds. The same

188

Chaucer as an Englishman

critic (if he were in a mood to be merely critical) might possibly describe the gentry of England as a nation of fox-hunters perpetually boasting that they are not bull-fighters. But the critic would be too critical, if he implied that the inconsistency was an insincerity. There really is a particular kind of affection for animals, which is very marked among the modern English; and in some indefinable but very vivid fashion, it does rise up before us in the presence of this medieval English lady. Somehow, she does waft across the ages a delicately mingled atmosphere of refinement and fuss. It is indeed an error to suppose that our ancestors were merely barbarous and benighted to a man, about difficult questions like our relation to the lower animals; or that the notion of avoiding cruelty is merely new or modern. It is not even true, as some more sympathetic people imagine, that tenderness to wild animals was the isolated individual discovery of the great St. Francis of Assisi; original as he was in many ways. There are any number of old medieval stories about hermits and holy men who protected animals from the hunters, for instance; and might not have been so popular after all with the North Blankshire Hunt. It was a characteristic of St. Anselm a century before St. Francis. The truer way of stating the case is that men have always been pretty patchy and inconsistent in their attitude to animals, and that we ourselves are pretty patchy and inconsistent still. In every age there are a few who are very careful and many who are very careless, and a modern lady with a devotion to mice might find herself almost as much in a minority at a modern tea-table as did the Prioress at the Tabard.

I only mention the matter here, however, as another example of that almost creepy unconscious fashion, in which we can feel the mind of Chaucer beginning to work towards the things that afterwards went to make up

Chaucer as an Englishman

the peculiar modern mood of the English nation. As I have suggested that there was something, so to speak, of pre-natal nationality about Chaucer's way of going about his business, I may add that there is an even more unmistakable social savour about Chaucer on a holiday. In all his remarks about his companions, as well as in his few remarks about himself, there is all that particular sort of self-effacing sociability which has really, when all cant is disposed of, made the English gentleman the best companion in the world. It has been complicated by all sorts of inconsistencies, and by many that have arisen since Chaucer's time. It has been often narrowed by aristocracy and sometimes soured by Puritanism, but it is there still; and in the Catholic Canterbury pilgrimage it is there already. It is marked off from the same kind of courtesy among Frenchmen or Italians by two unmistakable marks, which still exist; a certain casualness and flippancy, especially to fill up silences, and a certain half-conscious policy of avoiding deep disagreement on matters that really matter. Chaucer is all for letting sleeping dogs lie, including the greyhounds of the Prioress. He is not fond of fuss. He rather evades the questions asked of him, and does not mind looking more of a fool than he is. It is when I consider the man at this particular moment, in this particular aspect, in the hour of holiday when he was most himself, that a vague notion occurs to me that may be the explanation of the difficult problem of his politics.

Chaucer lived in a time that was the turning-point of English history; more truly the turning-point, I think, than even the time of Shakespeare. Being, like Chaucer, made free of a free religion, I do not admit that men or societies are bound to any inevitable doom. So I will not say that after what happened in the England of Chaucer, nobody could have avoided what happened in the Eng-

Chaucer as an Englishman

land of Shakespeare. But I will say that in the time of Chaucer a turn was taken and a road was partly travelled, which it would have been necessary to retrace in order to avoid the destruction or transformation that lay ahead. What happened in Chaucer's time was that the Nobles broke the King, and could actually set up a new man to call himself King, though he was no more than a Noble. These things always happen by stages; and this could not have happened so early, except that the Noble was the nearest to the royal blood. But he was almost admittedly a usurper, and his success stood for the breakdown of many medieval principles that nobody before had ventured to break. What Chaucer himself thought of the political position we have no certain means of knowing. The catastrophe occurred late in his life, when he was probably willing enough to receive occasional help from the Court he had known in his youth, without interfering further in its quarrels. It has sometimes struck me as rather curious and interesting that when he addressed to the new King his humorous ballade about the emptiness of his purse, he accompanied that very broad hint with an Envoi which might have more meanings than one. It begins, 'O conqueror of Brutus' Albion' and, though he hastened to add more formal salutations, this might possibly be read as a reference to the violent and untraditional origin of the reign. Something of the same oddity has always struck me in Andrew Marvell's admirable Horatian Ode on Cromwell, which is supposed to be a compliment to Cromwell, but sounds to me like a prolonged sneer at him. The long parenthesis on the dignified and courageous death of Charles the First can hardly have been very cosy reading for Cromwell. And the last lines, about 'the same arts that did gain a power must it maintain', sound to me uncommonly like saying, 'You've got everything by brute force, and you'll jolly

191

well have to hang on to it'. However this may be, I do not pretend that there is even this amount of criticism necessarily implied in Chaucer's action, when he addresses Henry of Bolingbroke as a Conqueror rather than a King. Still, it is one of those half-shades that seem faintly suggestive where all is shadowy; and I think it likely enough that Chaucer's mind was somewhat divided on the matter. On the one hand, he had been of the party and group of poets whose patron was John of Gaunt, the father of the usurper; on the other hand there is nothing to prove that John of Gaunt himself, let alone all his poets and protégés, would have approved entirely of the usurpation. Then, again, the tone of Chaucer's previous poem, addressed to the dethroned King before his dethronement, lends some support to the idea that he thought that prince was reckless or almost riding for a fall. He continually repeats, in no very courtly tone, that what the realm needs everywhere is Steadfastness; with the possible inference that its ruler was not sufficiently steadfast. This was certainly a charge made against Richard the Second, both in his own time and in ours, but here again the inference is very insufficient. To take another parallel from the age of Marvell; there were many Cavaliers who continually reproached Charles the First with his errors in the earlier stages, but who supported him at the last and to the last, from Wentworth who died for him on the scaffold to Falkland who died for him on the battlefield. I think, therefore, that there is very little that can be inferred from the fragmentary evidences of Chaucer's political attitude. He had been a diplomatist, but not a politician, and the common desire of almost every intelligent diplomatist is to keep as far as possible out of politics. He had been ready to represent the country and the court among foreigners, but it does not follow that he had any particular partisan interest in

192

Chaucer as an Englishman

the quarrels of native factions among themselves. With
the question of whether there was any political significance in his disappearance from office, and interlude of
obscurity, I deal elsewhere.

In any case, all such speculations are conditioned by
the great historical limitation called human life; the fact,
too often forgotten, that such a man never saw the sequel
that we see. Shakespeare, who on the whole upholds the
legend of a lack of steadfastness in Richard the Second,
could see far too much of what followed to think that
steadfastness was secured by the accession of Henry the
Fourth. Though Shakespeare seems on the whole Lancastrian in his sympathies, he was much more conscious
of the inevitable perils of pitting Lancaster against York.
He looked back at his princely but pathetic Richard, the
last pure Plantagenet, across a valley of dry bones, of
death and futile destruction; of which Chaucer could
never have had a hint. There was no way in which the
old court poet, brought up in the splendid court of the
victorious Edward, could guess the ghastly evisceration
of England by feudal rebels up to the exhausted peace of
Bosworth. Chaucer was brought up in a time when the
Lilies could be triumphantly quartered with the Leopards,
as if France and England had become one country. He
never knew that the time was coming when England
would become two countries, or perhaps three or four
countries, and her shield be quartered in a very different
sense. Yet that disruption of England in the Wars of
the Roses was of some curious concern to Chaucer, as a
poet as well as a patriot. For I cannot but suppose that
the desolation of that dynastic war was the explanation of
something that needs not a little explaining; the comparative barrenness of the Chaucerian tradition in literature after his death. He had, if ever man did in the world,
started a new impulse; yet it seemed to have stopped

193

Chaucer as an Englishman

almost as soon as it started. It would be an exaggeration to say that we had no medieval poets before Chaucer and precious few after him. But there was nothing like the poetic progeny or dynasty we had every right to expect, until long afterwards when the Renaissance came to England. And I suspect it was due to the conqueror of Brutus' Albion, who did more by his example to encourage potential conquerors than to encourage potential poets. If Chaucer did expect steadfastness from the Lancastrian usurpation, he suffered a post-mortem punishment for his mistake.

Thus the readiness of Chaucer to support the party of the son of John of Gaunt, though regarded by good historians as probable, is certainly not proved. But I confess that I come to regard it as more probable, when I contemplate, as I am doing here, his curiously casual English attitude as expressed in the comedy of *The Canterbury Tales*. With so much about him of what has made the English glorious or generous or genial, there was something also of what has made them gullible and indifferent and too much controlled by events. Chaucer was not a snob, but he was something of what they call in America a regular guy or in England a clubable fellow or a man's man. I could easily believe that he was never so much in revolt against the success of Bolingbroke as Shakespeare was against the success of Burleigh; for Shakespeare was a tragic poet with a touch in him of the revolt of Timon. It is a possible fancy, where all is fanciful, that the greatest Englishman of that age did not rebel against the tragic turn of the age, because he was too English to be a rebel. He may even have been duped by that dull cynicism that talks about the need of practical politics, and then gives itself up to be plundered by practical politicians. He may have been so far infected by such opportunism as to accept Henry of Bolingbroke as a practical politician. He

Chaucer as an Englishman

would not be the less English for having joined in the biggest blunder of English history. But I repeat that there is no proof of the fact; it is little more than a possibility, and it is a possibility that only interests me here because it goes along with all the other hints that there was already something in the medieval Englishman pointing towards the particular idiosyncrasies of the modern Englishman. It had nothing to do with the higher part of his mind and work, which was concerned with that everlasting light in which all things stand bright and solid; but on the lower level it is likely enough that he may have let things slide like sand. He may have let sleeping dogs lie; little knowing, like many another opportunist, that what he really did was to let slip the dogs of war.

There is one comment which may well be added at this point. It is agreed that in the modern sense of novelty, the production of new nostrums and notions, to be worked into systems like Socialism or Christian Science, Chaucer was not a man who troubled about ideas being new. It was quite enough for him, strange to say, that they were true. He was in many ways really conservative and even his talents did not lie in the direction of new definitions or demands. A critic might put it in the form of saying that Chaucer was a true son of the feudal system, in that he was even proud of being a dependent. He was, as we have seen, proud of being a dependent of the poet Ovid, a dependent of the philosopher Aristotle, a dependent of the theologian Aquinas. All this is true, and it is a truth that disposes at a blow of all the dreary attempts that have lately been made to represent medieval society as utterly servile or brutal or bigoted. Every man who has ever opened a book of Chaucer, every man who has ever opened the doors of Chaucer's mind and world, knows all that to be nonsense, even when it is nonsense supported by detailed or laborious learning. Chaucer was a great poet; he was a great man; but he was not a great revolutionist, not even in that sense a great reformer; certainly not a great iconoclast or heretic. He was not a man to hurl Bolshevist opinions like bombs into the crowd of conventional people with whom he lived so courteously and contentedly; he did not have them to throw, and he would not have thought them worth throwing; certainly not worth the explosion. If anybody thinks this sort of 'taking the world as he found it' a proof of littleness, such a person cannot be expected to accept my view of Chaucer's largeness. But the critic, in withdrawing the compliment from Chaucer, must withdraw the slander from the Middle Ages. It is quite certain that the reader of Chaucer instantly breathes an atmosphere of breezy and cordial brotherhood, of charity towards all sorts of men, of a sense of the worthlessness of rank and wealth in comparison with worth, of a sense of fundamental freedom and fraternity in the commonwealth of Christian men. These notions must have been normal medieval notions, or a man like Chaucer would never have had them, or bothered about them. He was not the sort to go digging for abnormal notions. There is that amount of truth in calling him a conservative or even a courtier. They must have been ideas that a man could casually express; or Chaucer would not have remained a court favourite all his life, when he was always expressing them so casually. If that is what is meant by denying originality to Chaucer, the charge is true. There was nothing of the New Morality about him; there was nothing of the man who wears no clothes in Hampstead or cannot keep cats because they are carnivorous. It was not so that he held the view that men of rank should be rebuked or that gentility was not mere ancestry. If these liberal sentiments had been fads in that sense, to the medieval mind, nobody with a notion of personal character can think that Geoffrey

Chaucer as an Englishman

Chaucer would have joined the faddists. Some may hold, but I do not hold, that a man cannot be really original who has this huge appetite for what is normal. Anyhow, Chaucer had it, and he was so native to his age and country that his attitude must have seemed tolerably normal to them.

So far we have seen in faint outline a figure very familiar to us in modern literature and to some extent in modern life. He minds his own business; he does not talk shop; he is even content to remain under the mystical cloud of being Something in the City; he does not make scenes, and has a particular kind of limited politeness to servants; he is rather silent and yet somehow sociable, in the sense of being able to get on with other fellows at the club or (it is right to add) in the camp; he is manly; he is modest, at least in external manners; he is well-bred; he is well-groomed; he is solid and reasonable and reliable; but he has his good points, for all that. And the greatest of these is something that neither Puritanism nor the Public School has contrived to kill; he is generally fond of a joke. His great national contribution to the culture of Christendom has been that quality. It is the English sense of humour, like the Spanish sense of honour or the French sense of right reason. It is true that a certain sort of pompous ass like Sir Willoughby Patterne or Mr. Dombey has been exhibited as an Englishman; but he has generally been exhibited by Englishmen. Podsnap would not have been so absurdly English, if Dickens had not been an Englishman. True, there is only one Dickens, but there are a million Dickensians; a great many more Dickensians than there are Podsnaps. On the whole, the prevailing spirit of the English is an appreciation of this sort of fun, especially when it broadens into farce. Indeed, when it is properly understood, there is something in it that breaks out beyond the limits of mere farce, and becomes a sort of poetry of pantomime; a climax of anti-climax. Dickens is full of wild images that would be nothing if they were not funny. They would be not merely nonsensical but non-existent, if they were not (I say it with some firmness) so damned funny. Mrs. Todgers's wooden leg; Mr. Swiveller's gazelle who married a market-gardener; the toothpick of the gentleman next door, which if sent to the Commander-in-Chief would produce such marked results; the effect of Henry the Eighth's little peepy eyes on Mrs. Skewton's view of history; these are things that would simply cease to exist in a really rational universe. They are not symbolic; they are not really satiric. They are upheld by an invisible power and lifted without support upon the wings of laughter; by a power more unanswerable and more irresponsible than pure beauty.

Now compared with the fun of Dickens, there is certainly something altogether shrewd, sensible and solid about the humour of Chaucer. He was, as has been said already, only the seed of that separate growth; but it was growing separate and it was soon to be growing wild. We shall note elsewhere the way in which the medieval common sense of Chaucer differs from the almost maniac laughter we sometimes hear from the Elizabethans, even from Shakespeare. But for all that a frontier had been crossed, and there is already in Chaucer an element of irrational humour, which is not the same as the old rational humour. The old humour had been a form of satire. Chaucer often sounds satirical; yet Chaucer was not strictly a satirist. Perhaps the shortest way of putting it is to say that he already inhabits a world of comicality that is not a world of controversy. He makes fun of people, in the exact sense of getting fun out of them for himself. He does not make game of them, in the actual sense of hunting them down and killing them like wild vermin or

Chaucer as an Englishman

public pests. He does not want the Friar and the Wife of Bath to perish; one would sometimes suspect that he does not really want them to change. Anyhow, a softening element of this sort has got into his satire, even if he really meant it for satire. But, with this step, he is already on the road to the Dickensian lunatic-asylum of laughter; because he is valuing his fools and knaves and almost wishing (as it were) to preserve them in spirits—in high spirits. In a hundred other ways his humour is English, and not least in this, that he often uses flippancy to avoid an argument and not to provoke it.

For I have so far confined myself strictly to considering what (unfortunately) a great mass of modern Englishmen mean by an Englishman. I have taken the matter from this end, so to speak, and started with the strictly national type produced by Protestantism and the modern division of nations. And I have pointed out that, even in terms of this familiar type, Chaucer is readily recognizable as English: that he contains the seeds of some of the things that have since become even extravagantly English. But I apologize to England for talking as if these things alone were English; and to Chaucer for supposing that he did not know and love an England that was relatively free from all these things. There is matter much larger than these little social tricks in the real heritage of the English; and Chaucer was the true trustee of that heritage; above all of the great national heritage of humour. It is the custom to boast that it is more than wit, but the really interesting truth is that it is more even than humour. It is not merely a critical quality; in a sense it is even a creative quality; a sort of crooked creation that is called the fantastic or the topsy-turvy. Here again it is possible to quote things from Chaucer that seem to have come into the world centuries too early, and to be of the type of the nursery nonsense of to-day. That this wild spirit runs through all English literature can be proved by a single quotation from Lear. I do not mean the comic Lear but the tragic Lear; who was almost equally nonsensical. There was never a crazy touch in that crack-brained style done better than that of Shakespeare's fool, when he says:

> *'This prophecy Merlin shall make; for I live before his time.'*

This poetry also Mr. Lewis Carroll shall make; but Chaucer lives before his time. Even in the Father of English Poetry that far-off cry of pure folly can he heard, perhaps for the first time in human history.

There is in English humour something that can not only be compared to art for art's sake, but might more truly be described as adventure for adventure's sake. It is not unconnected with the sense in which the more honourable part of English conquest and colonization was adventure for adventure's sake. I mean that it was not really directed towards a consistent policy of rule. Grave historians have expressed a mild astonishment that the British were so long unconscious of the British Empire. It is a possible explanation, to suppose that they were unconscious of it because it did not exist. It was not an empire in the logical sense of an *imperium*; a scheme for extending a type of civilization over countries that had not got it; as other empires wished to extend the Roman Law or the Spanish religion. It had first the practical purpose of trade; but after that its purpose might more truly be described as fun; the satisfaction of seeing strange places—and leaving them strange. If we like to put it so, the adventurer had something nobler than greed; which was curiosity. Now that curiosity always delighted in curiosities. They were like the curios that sailors brought home from strange seas; parrots and monkeys and tropical shells. But there was even more interest in the curiosities

200

Chaucer as an Englishman

the sailor could not exactly bring home to his landlady; such as Cannibal Kings or Chinese temples or Arctic whales. There runs through the English adventure the vague desire that these funny things should *remain* funny. He does not specially wish to convert the yellow men in the temple; though he might attempt a constitutional compromise about cannibalism. And there runs through the English humour the same notion of amusing monsters, to be stared at. And Chaucer is at the spring of this spirit; because to him the Wife of Bath is an amusing monster. We do not approve of her; but we do not feel responsible for her, any more than for a whale or a white elephant. There is a wise fool whose eyes are in the ends of the earth; and the English invented that phrase of yet more imaginative folly: 'The other end of nowhere.'

It is a very extraordinary fact, when considered historically, that Chaucer should have been so unmistakably English almost before the existence of England. It is the details of language, like the details of landscape, that give this entirely unique and unmistakable touch. It is an elvish touch, to use a term that was actually used about the poet. It almost suggests that the other name of England is Elfland. Yet it has nothing whatever of the thin ethereal spirit of faerie; as we see it, for instance, in the Celtic myths and the poems of Mr. W. B. Yeats. It is a solid and almost smug sort of goblin market; a real town where the goblins are really marketing. The nearest we can come to a more serious definition is that it is a certain spirit of nonsense even in landscape. We find it in the names of some real English villages, which might have come out of the wild geography books of Mr. Edward Lear. We feel it in some of the impossible places invented by Mr. Edward Lear, which might be the names of real English villages, valleys or downs; such as that typical title, 'The Hills of the Chankly Bore'.

Chaucer as an Englishman

Now this touch is instantly felt in Chaucer. The Pilgrims' Way does not run merely, in the medieval manner, through meadows patterned with flowers or forests dark with enchantment. But neither does it run merely through reasonable and recognizable places like Southwark and Sittingbourne. There is something selective in the eye of Chaucer, which is already open for other and special things. Nobody at home with the nonsense element I mean can read that phrase, in the account of the pilgrimage, about passing a town 'which that i-clepd is Bob-Up-and-Down', without his heart leaping with joy, and bobbing up and down with that buoyant and unconquerable city. I do not know exactly what it means; and there have been all sorts of speculations about it. I do not know whether Chaucer made it up out of his own head, which is quite possible; or whether it was a real English village, which is also quite possible; or whether it was a nickname connected with some local jest, which is perhaps most probable. Some have suggested that it was so called because something in the winding, rising and falling road made it appear to be on different levels at different stages; and that sort of rambling road probably was then, and certainly is now, rather specially characteristic of the English countryside. But the feeling of the curious primeval kinship between England and Chaucer is justified in either case. I do not care whether it was something that England invented and Chaucer glorified; or whether it was something that Chaucer invented and England glorified. The spirit of a man who loves that landscape, can sometimes run so close to the land, that it invents something that exists already. I remember composing, when I was quite young, the first rough form of a song about the round hills and rolling, almost revolving roads, of which a man dreams after a day in Sussex. In that song I invented an entirely imaginary town of Roundabout as the mystic

Chaucer as an Englishman

centre of this rotatory landscape. And it was some time afterwards that I discovered that there really is a town in Sussex called Roundabout, because the men of Sussex had seen the same scenes and dreamed the same dream.

Therefore there is, it seems, something primitive about this poet, because he is as large as the land and as old as the nation. There was little enough in him of the mystic, in the narrow or special sense; yet it is impossible not to feel something mystical about his magnitude as an emblem of England. He had somehow got into his head and into his note-book a certain national quality, centuries before the nation attempted to understand or describe its own quality. He had, for instance, the humour that is at once broadened and blunted by good humour. He had the particular *sort* of soft-heartedness that can be seen in the English; sometimes an incomplete and illogical sort; but not far removed from that of Chaucer's Prioress, who might have been frightened of a mouse, but wept over its being in a trap. He had the English type of tolerance and in some things the English type of irresponsible individualism; there is that amount of truth in Matthew Arnold's view that he was lacking in 'seriousness'. He was not the stuff of which Reformers are made. He took things as they came, and the world as he found it, and men as God had made them, or even as they had made themselves. He had a curious sort of abstract liberality underlying concrete conservatism, which was very national, and can be seen in many Tories who are devoted to a Monarchy and explain that it is just as republican as a Republic. In all this he is the First of The English; and his figure has therefore this quality of a type and even an archetype. That figure is seen in the sunlight of history walking among the gay pavilions and palaces of French kings and French-speaking knights and nobles; negotiating war and peace in what was practically a French quarrel about a French pedigree; he is seen learning a thousand things from the sonneteers of Italy and the troubadours of Provence; but within him something is born, and it is the name by which we live. He may or may not have made the somewhat dreary attempt to translate *Le Roman de la Rose* into English. But nobody could possibly translate *The Canterbury Tales* into French.

There is something personal about England. Rome or France or Bolshevist Russia or Republican America, each in its own way, is a principle; but England is a person. And it is very like the very indescribable sort of person this book has to describe. I will not be so daring as to define what William Blake meant by The Giant Albion; but we may agree that if the country called by poets Albion could be conceived as a single figure, it would be a giant. And when I think of Chaucer in this primary and general fashion, I do not think of a Court poet receiving a laurel from the King or a flagon from the King's butler, nor even of a stout and genial gentleman with a forked beard setting forth from the Tabard upon the Canterbury road; but of some such elemental and emblematic giant, alive at our beginnings and made out of the very elements of the land. Perhaps if we were caught up by that eagle that whirled away the poet to the gates of The House of Fame, we might begin to see spread out beneath us the titanic outlines of such a prehistoric or primordial Anak or Adam, with our native hills for his bones and our native forests for his beard; and see for an instant a single figure outlined against the sea and a great face staring at the sky.

Chapter VII

CHAUCER AND THE RENAISSANCE

It will be noted that many quotations from Chaucer in these pages are recast in a manner that may well distress Chaucerians; though it is done with the hope of increasing the number of Chaucerians in the world. I can only say that I am acutely sensitive to all that can be said against what I am doing. To say that I have modernized Chaucer has a very ugly sound, and might stand for a very ugly thing. The first difficulty about disturbing any ancient language, that is good of its kind, is that the man who turns it into new language may turn it into pretty thoroughly bad language; in the sense of something worse than slang. There is also this paradoxical but practical fact: that the very examples in which the meaning of a word has changed are the examples in which we know what it means. If we substitute a very modern word, we may find that everybody uses it and nobody knows what it means. It marked the use of an old phrase, of which the meaning has changed, when the Prayer Book said, 'Prevent us, O Lord, in all our doings'. But nobody does imagine that the vicar, who reads it out in the parish church, means that he wants to be tripped up with booby-traps and butter-slides in everything he attempts. The dead word, like the dead language, does in a sense remain sacred. 'Prevent' is a Latin word and still makes sense in Latin. But there is always the peril that turning it into modern English might mean turning it into more modern

American; and ghastly possibilities open before us, of some future reformer altering 'prevent us' to 'put us wise'. Or, to take another example, it is now extremely archaic English to talk about the Holy Ghost. But it is perfectly intelligible English, although it is archaic English. Indeed it is intelligible English because it is archaic English. It stands for a certain idea which was strong when the language was made, and it stands exactly where it did. Whereas, even so reasonable a change as that of 'ghost' to 'spirit', may bring in a nuance of change, owing to modern uses of the word 'spiritual' and the looming spectre of Spiritualism. Similarly, it is archaic to talk about ghostly counsel or ghostly consolation. But nobody does in fact imagine that ghostly consolation means consoling people by telling them ghost-stories. Whereas, if we begin to think of what does give spiritual consolation, or appear to give it, to a great many modern people, the most horrid possibilities begin to close in upon us. We may end by altering old English to something that is not English at all; and talking about an Uplift or (heaven defend us) about an Urge.

Therefore, while I believe in occasionally changing the Chaucerian speech or spelling, I believe in changing it as little as possible, and indeed only where the original is utterly unintelligible to an ordinary modern reader; or where (what is far worse) the accidental look of ugly unintelligible words makes a passage appear undignified which in fact is full of dignity. Several excellent attempts have been made to modernize Chaucer; nor is the idea itself confined to the times we call modern. It strongly possessed the great critical imagination of Dryden; a poet whose greatness, humanity and English breadth were in many ways very Chaucerian, but who was persistently underrated in the nineteenth century, merely because he had voted Blue instead of Buff in the party quarrels of

Chaucer and the Renaissance

the seventeenth century. It would be truer, of course, to admit that the prejudice had real roots; and that Dryden's crime was his lack of enthusiasm for the establishment of plutocracy and his Catholic dislike of the Puritans. Anyhow, he had every right to recur to the great English tradition of the medieval poet; and he did admirable work in paraphrasing and popularizing whole sections of the Canterbury Tales. His version shows very clearly the particular limitations of his age, and we may be absolutely certain that all our versions will show posterity the very obvious limitations of ours. But it is on the whole much better than many experiments of the sort in our own time. A modernized version of four of the Canterbury Tales has recently come from America. It is ingenious and intelligent; but it shows very clearly the danger of needless modernization of what is merely medieval, without being, for any reader, in the least meaningless. What is wanted is not the reconstruction of every line of Chaucer so as to make it fit metrically and grammatically into a modern line. What is wanted is a careful preservation of the old construction of every line, except where it is quite impossible to keep the construction and yet put the right construction on it.

For there is another objection, far deeper than the first I mentioned. It is really true to say that the best guide for doing this job is to remember that it is impossible to do it. After all, by trying to do it at all, we are treating medieval English as a foreign language. And there never was, is not, and never will be, a translation of a poem from a foreign language. There have been some beautiful poems written in one language, more or less parallel to beautiful poems in the other. There have been reasonable translations into the one language, which were good enough to goad people into really learning the other language. There have even been great poems, which professed to be only translations of small poems. But no man has ever reproduced the atmosphere and magic of one single word by the use of another word. Nobody could put the exact equivalent of 'revisit thus the glimpses of the moon' into any other English words; and he certainly could not put it into German or Russian or Chinese words. It is this separation that makes necessary such intermediate explanations as these; it may be that the Tower of Babel was indeed the chief tragedy of mankind. But anyhow, it is strictly true that we can translate anything in reason. We cannot translate anything that is beyond reason; like the way in which mere sound and spelling can be a spell. The American edition, of which I have spoken, does really translate everything in reason. It explains the ordinary sense of Chaucer's narrative with sustained and competent clearness, but it works on the assumption that everything must be translated from the foreign language called Chaucerian into the other language called English—or perhaps American. The consequence is that while the style and the story go forward energetically, something has gone out of the story and the style; and what has vanished is the song. Thus, to take the test case of a passage so often quoted, the dying speech of Arcite, I should think it quite satisfactory to leave the lines substantially as they stand:

What is this world? What asken man to have?
Now with his love, now in his coldë grave,
Alone withouten any company.

But the conscientious transatlantic translator thinks it his duty to make it scan in modern grammar by saying:

What is this world? What asketh man to have?
Now with his love, now cold within his grave,
Alone, alone, with none for company.

Chaucer and the Renaissance

Now somehow or other, with the best intentions, he has broken the backbone of the tragic line with a load of repetition, like the repetitions that fill up bad blank verse; while the original simple line 'alone withouten any company' is like a desolate yet living cry, echoing in a vault of stone. That is the intangible trick that we call poetry. And that is the paradox of dealing with the present problem of Chaucer. The same thing that convinces us that he must be translated convinces us that he cannot be translated.

In my own citations, therefore, I have adopted the principle of altering the lilt or accent or form of the line as little as possible, and only altering the words where they are in actual fact foreign words. But I am quite conscious that even by doing this I lose a great deal, and can only say that there are readers who could hardly get anything, if this were not lost. If I criticize other experiments, I would accompany the criticism with a profound groan of gratitude, to St. Thomas of Canterbury or my patron saint, that I have not got the job of carrying out my own principles of interpretation through a complete translation of Chaucer's works. The thing is so stupendously difficult that even to do it decently is to do it admirably. I for one (if I may excuse myself in the polite manner of the poet among the story-tellers) do not propose to do it at all. But it seems only right, since I have quoted the poetry in a particular form, according to my own taste and fancy, that I should insert here this brief note upon the practical rules I have observed. For the rest, I am quite sure that the translator need not avoid slight variations of speech, such as are no longer used but are still understood. On the contrary, I think he should preserve them rather carefully, for they very often have a unique quality lost in the later development of the language. The old word can actually strike a new note. We have all

observed the fine touch of distinction given in Shakespeare or Milton by the mere shifting of the accent on
a familiar word, or the variation of a customary termina-
tion; the pleasure there is in realizing that Hamlet says
'I'll wipe away all trivial fond recòrds', merely because we
always say 'récords'; or in repeating Milton's ending,
'And summons given, the dread consult began'. I hope
no American will translate Milton into English and turn
it into a consultation—the common consultation one has
with a doctor or a dentist or a trustee. There is not a little
of this pleasure, among the many pleasures of reading
Chaucer. Aristotle, the teacher of medieval men, said very
truly that the language of poetry has a perpetual slight
novelty. It is none the less so, when the slight novelty is
a slight antiquity.

In my own unscrupulous experiment, I should aim
at two things; first, as far as possible preserving the original word; and second, preserving the originality of the
original word. Now in some cases we cannot keep the
force of the word, if we keep the form of the word. Men
cannot think a strange word striking if they do not know
what it means; but short of that, it may be all the more
striking because it is more strange. There has been very
little recognition of the possibility of such an intermediate
course. Chaucer is either copied in a style that is not popular, or translated into a style that is not Chaucer.

There was never a better criticism of Chaucer than that
written within a hundred years of his death by old Caxton
the printer; nor has this particular aptitude with words
been expressed in words so apt. The medieval master
printer's estimate is worth libraries of the patronizing
pedantry, that has been written in the four hundred years
that followed. 'For he writeth no void words; but all his
matter is full of high and quick sentence'; that is, sense;
sententia. The melodious but monotonous etiquette of

Chaucer and the Renaissance

much medieval poetry was a perpetual temptation to write void words; like the void words of modern journalese; except that the medieval words at least were graceful and the modern words base.

Very tentatively, therefore, and with all the mingled tact and terror proper to an amateur in a field where so many scholars must have speculated, I am in favour of doing for Chaucer something like what has already been done for Shakespeare. I mean publishing a popularized version, in so far as this can be done by the mere simplification of spelling or clarification of common words, where the difference is a difficulty; and nowhere else. I do not mean modernizing Chaucer, in the sense of making him appear modern; I mean only elucidating him just enough to permit him to appear medieval. I imagine that a multitude of medieval things have already, in fact, been treated in this way; Malory and the Paston Letters and any number of Border Ballads, especially those in the original Scots. It is unfortunate that Chaucer happens historically to stand, as if he were a Borderer himself, on the exact frontier between writing in a foreign language that is translated and writing only in an old-fashioned language that needs only to be brought up to date. This makes the thing much more difficult to do; but not the less worth doing.

Broadly, my principle would be this; that no reader minds meeting an old word, but is only bothered when he meets a new word. I mean, of course, a word that is new to him; a word that is old enough to be new. He does not dislike, but likes, any ancient medieval monument as such, so long as it does not block the road, and hold up the ride to Canterbury. For instance, in the famous line I have quoted from the Knight's Tale, what in the world is the use of altering the word 'withouten'? If there be any human being who can read the line, 'Alone withouten any

Chaucer and the Renaissance

company', who does not know at once that 'withouten' means 'without', I should imagine he must be a very rare and isolated sort of reader; withouten any company and certainly withouten any common sense. But when, in another passage I have also quoted, the poet lamenting over Troilus speaks of 'this false world's brotelness', then I should boldly alter it in the modern version to 'brittleness', precisely because it would be quite natural to suppose that it meant 'brutalness'. Where there is an ambiguity of that sort, for a modern reader, I would not give the word a modern meaning, but merely give it back its own medieval meaning. I admit that the task would be terribly delicate, and I have not the faintest intention of trying to do it myself. It would be a matter of tireless and sustained tact, every touch of which would look like caprice. It would have to turn perpetually to different solutions for different problems; sometimes alteration, sometimes accentuation, sometimes annotation. Anyone rushing lightly upon it may well be checked at the very start; for I think the very first line of *The Canterbury Tales* presents the greatest difficulty of all. Many a modern reader may have been induced to try Chaucer, as merely a rather old-fashioned English writer, and found, 'Whan that Aprille with his schowres swoote,' a slight obstacle at the start. Merely to show what I mean by using different methods, I should be frankly inconsistent in dealing with the difficulties of that line. I should leave 'Whan' (who would be such a fool as not to know that it meant 'when'?) but I might in compassion alter 'schowres' to 'showers', lest the consonants be really misleading, and because the syllabification is just the same. I should put an accent on the second syllable of 'Aprille', and the mark showing that the 'e' is not mute. Finally, if I could not change 'swoote' to 'sweet' (because, curse it, it has to rhyme to root), I would put a footnote to say that it is

212

Chaucer and the Renaissance

meant for sweet and pronounced more like 'sooty'. I see a vast and varied task open before me; from which I cheerfully turn away.

Now my only excuse for dwelling on this literary possibility is that I do think it a matter of vital importance to open up the English past at least as far as Chaucer, in the sense that it has been opened up as far as Shakespeare. As I shall try to point out here, the great river of the national culture and character did in some sense grow narrower as well as swifter and stronger, at the moment when it came over the rocks in the cataract of the Elizabethan Renaissance. But, anyhow, it falsifies everything to suppose that, because all modern intellectual life still moves with the impetus of that mighty fall, therefore the fall is the same as the fountain. A man does not understand England who has read Shakespeare and not Chaucer, any more than a man understands Italy who has read Tasso and not Dante, or a man understands France who has read Ronsard and not Villon. Anybody can see that these ancient inspirations are constantly coming to the surface again, sometimes much later than the later fashions; that much cynical French writing derives rather from Villon than from Ronsard, or that the new vision of Italy may find more in the imperialism of Dante than in the ornamental chivalry of Tasso. So there are all sorts of things in Chaucer, or for that matter, in Langland, which should come out in a complete consciousness of the English destiny; and which happened, by historical accident, to be more or less out of sight for the very greatest of the Elizabethans. In a word, the ordinary modern Englishman will considerably enlarge his mind by reading Chaucer; and it is my humble desire that he should to some extent be able to read Chaucer, even if he is unable to read Middle English or Anglo-Saxon or Norman-French; or if he is, by mere sloth and moral weakness, unable to read the learned books in which the structure of these various languages is set forth. I do believe, as Dryden did, that it would be a good thing to make Chaucer an ordinary possession of ordinary Englishmen; and I should not think the thing thrown away, even if, like Dryden's experiment, it had to be done over again about three hundred years hence. In the future, for all I know, men will say that our culture began with Dryden. In that case our culture will stop short with Dryden. Even at present, as I do know, many men talk as if our culture began with Shakespeare. In that case their culture stops short with Shakespeare. And, as I propose to suggest in this chapter, there really are matters in which even Shakespeare stops short of Chaucer.

But in these opening words I only claim to maintain that Chaucer is readable, or can readily be made readable by ignorant people like myself; I am not in the least concerned to conceal my ignorance. It will be noted that nowhere in this book have I made any pretence of pronouncing upon the purely philological or grammatical or metrical problems, with which the study of Chaucer, for the students of Chaucer, teems on every side. There is a whole labyrinth for grammarians and the scientific students of language in the development of the medieval English dialects, and the degree of their absorption in the French-English of Chaucer. There is a world of inquiry, and very interesting and important inquiry, in the matter of his adoption of Continental metres or schemes of scansion, and the order in which he adopted them. But it is the whole point of this book that Chaucer is literature and not linguistic study for the learned; that it needs very little to make him popular in the sense that literature can be popular; and that learning is a totally different thing. I have learned some rudiments of Chaucerian problems at school, or rather neglected to learn them at school, and I have read and forgotten a good many facts on the same subject since. But I should no more think of setting up to be an authority on Chaucer than an authority on Punch and Judy; or Pickwick; or the Christmas pantomime. These things are not studied, but appreciated. What little I remember of earlier instruction leads me to think that it has changed a great deal, and that some parts of it were always rather crabbed and perverse. I remember that the jokes of Chaucer were the subject of specially serious discussion. Doubtless there does exist this second class of Chaucerian difficulties, but I doubt whether I am particularly suited to overcome them.

There is something faintly irritating in the fact that so many popularizers of Chaucer have described his humour as 'sly'. And yet there is something in it; or something to be got out of the right understanding of it. Doubtless it is partly due to a more or less external and technical trick of expression; he is very fond of laughing in a parenthetical manner, like the aside of a comic actor; so that even when the joke itself is jolly and obvious enough, it has the grammatical shape of a broad grin in brackets. This is common enough; perhaps the best example is that charming passage in the charming fable of the Cock and Hen, in which the former bitterly exclaims in Latin, *mulier est hominis confusio*, and Chaucer gravely adds the explanation:

> *Madame, the sentence of this Latin is*
> *Woman is mannës joy and mannës bliss.*

When the critic calls this sly, we can see what he means; but in fact the effect is produced not so much by being secretive as by being simply impudent. Anyhow, the general effect is produced by being large and simple and all of a piece. Chaucer's humour is spread over so wide a surface of himself that it is always partially present, when he seems most serious and especially when he seems most simple. But there is a third accidental aspect in which Chaucer may truly in some sense be congratulated on his slyness. I suspect that he has made a good many jokes that his critics and commentators cannot see; and one or two which the commentators have sat down grimly and resolutely to prove not to be jokes at all. True, their serious explanations change. I remember how a schoolmaster explained to me with desperate seriousness, in the days of my youth, that Chaucer's remark about the French language, as spoken by the Prioress, was pure and unstained by any adulteration of amusement. Chaucer says that the Prioress spoke French very well according to the school of Stratford-at-Bow: 'For French of Paris was to her unknown.' The authority then proceeded to prove, with academic passion, that French, so long the language of the English court and aristocracy, really was talked correctly at Stratford; and therefore Chaucer can be acquitted of the grave charge of flippancy, when he said she was unacquainted with the French of France. I fancy that the smile of Chaucer, as he left the court without a stain on his character, might truly be described as a little sly. For it might occur to simpler souls than the academic, and intelligences more in touch with Chaucerian simplicity, that even if correct French is talked by foreigners, there is still something a little funny about pitting it against that national tongue as talked by the natives. If I were to say, 'Professor Hiram Q. Hike spoke the most correct and cultivated English that Boston can produce, though he ignored some nuances adopted in London, England', I think it barely possible that I might be suspected of irony. And the charge would not be answered by saying that the people of Boston do talk English, or something they have a right to call English; that they talk much better English than the people of Bison City, Texas; and that Boston is justly proud of a great tradi-

tion of English scholars and critics. There would still remain the faint possibility that critics even more English
might be found in England. If somebody said, 'Our
Guatemalan guide talked a vivid and picturesque Spanish,
which would have considerably puzzled the inhabitants
of Spain', it would not entirely extract the sting to say
that Spanish is the official language of Guatemala. And
so, when even a poor medieval poet goes out of his way
to compare the French talked by an English lady with
the French talked by Frenchmen, I am, and was even as
a boy, disposed darkly to suspect that he saw the fun of
it. Of course this individual authority may have been only
an individual and not an authority. I only know that the
criticism was confidently imposed on me in my school-
days. But what amuses me most is to discover that a
totally opposite criticism has been confidently imposed
since. Later on, I discovered that the serious commentators were saying (at another stage) that the passage
about the Prioress means, not that she spoke French well,
but that she did not speak French at all. And they quote
certain phrases two hundred years later, which suggest
that knowledge acquired in Stratford-at-Bow had become
a proverb for total ignorance. This seems much the more
plausible dogma of the two; but even of this I am daring
enough to have my doubts. Saluting in all seriousness
men better informed than myself, and being myself in
every way a citizen of Stratford-at-Bow in the matter of
ignorance, I still think that the emphasis of such expressions varies much from age to age; that a suggestion might
be positive under Elizabeth which was relative under
Edward III; and that the nuance of Shakespeare's language might be different from the nuance of Chaucer.
I still think that the best way of finding the nuance of
Chaucer is to look for it in Chaucer. Given the character
and the context, I think it most likely that Chaucer

meant the Prioress to speak French as an English school-mistress speaks it, stiffly and imperfectly but not alto-gether without pretension. The joke against this sort of *parly-vooing* might easily have been broadened and blunted until it came to mean common insular ignorance. But I may be quite wrong; and I do not attach much import-ance to the question of being right. I only note that if the learned are now right, some of the earlier learned were very wrong.

A somewhat more serious reason, however, led me a few paragraphs back to bring into consideration the attempt of Dryden to popularize or modernize Chaucer in his own day. For the whole of this business of the modern trans-lation of Chaucer, or the medieval difficulties of Chaucer, is bound up with the general destiny of literature and lan-guage after his death. He was indeed saluted after his death in tones of very noble loyalty and gratitude by the few fine English poets that were at all worthy to praise him; by Occleve and by Lydgate. But we hardly have that impression of a literary dynasty that we might have expected as following such a king and conqueror in the world of culture. Curiously enough, as many acute critics have pointed out, the richer and more romantic quality of Chaucer's tradition was carried on rather more con-tinuously in Scotland than in England. The Wars of the Roses, I suppose, had something to do with it. Anyhow, when a full poetic inspiration came to England, it came as the influence of de Meung or Petrarch had come to Chaucer; direct from foreign lands, but from lands now in the full noonday of the Renaissance. Everybody can see the sense in which that noonday sun was brighter even than the brightest star in the medieval night of the north. But there is something more to be said about the com-parison, which has never, as it seems to me, been said sufficiently clearly. And as the matter arises directly out of an attempt like that of Dryden, and the suggestion that it should be repeated, I will deal with it here.

To many in the nineteenth century the notion of Dryden paraphrasing Chaucer was very like their notion about Pope translating Homer. It was the notion of a primitive giant being introduced by a dwarf who was also a dandy. They thought that Pope had done nothing but provide the golden-haired Apollo with a gilded peruke, or the swift-footed Achilles with a pair of high-heeled shoes; giving a new irony to the weakness of the heel of Achilles. They exalted Chapman's Homer against Pope's (as did Keats, the greatest of the Romantics) merely because Chapman was full of the particular Elizabethan type of fire and fancy. Only, as Arnold and others eventually hinted, there was something to be said on the other side. Pope is not very like Homer; but he is so far like Homer that he talks like a sane man; and the great Elizabethans did not always do so; neither indeed did the great Romantics.

In the same way, the critics of the more romantic nineteenth century felt sure that Dryden could do nothing in the red-rose thicket or daisied lawn of the medieval poet, except clip the hedges with the extravagant trimness of topiary; or turn a Dantesque forest into a Dutch garden. It was owing to the particular angle at which they stood at that moment to historical research and political theory. They exaggerated very much the antiquity and simplicity of Chaucer; they also exaggerated very much the artificiality and decadence of Dryden. They did not understand the many respects in which Dryden stood much nearer to Chaucer than they did themselves. And we may repeat, with all respect to them, that one of these was the same as in the other case; that Chaucer and Dryden both talked sense. There was indeed, as I have suggested before and shall more fully explain later, a sense of which

Chaucer and the Renaissance

Chaucer talked nonsense; and a somewhat different sense in which Shakespeare talked nonsense. But they did not talk nonsense with that high seriousness, that earnest belief in effort, that faith in the utmost for the highest, which was sometimes the special glory of the Victorian era. There was even a quality of objective rationality, which separated them in some degree from the imaginative ambitions of the Elizabethan era. Chaucer may be a very ancient well of English undefiled; and Dryden may be only a seventeenth-century specimen of an artificial lake, not to say an ornamental pond. But both the well and the pond have this in common; that they are still waters that may possibly run deep, and do at any rate reflect calmly the real objects of earth and sky. Whereas the torrent of the Renaissance in the sixteenth century, and the torrent of the Romantics in the nineteenth century, are much too splendid and inspiring as torrents to be useful for any sort of reflection. In other words, we need to look a little more carefully into the real merits of these various phases of literary history, and to note especially what there was about Chaucer that does in some ways separate him from Shakespeare; and may even in some ways unite him to Dryden. I think the quickest way of approaching it is through something in the particular nature of his humour, even though it is so elusive as to have caused disturbance among the learned, some of whom call it sly, some of whom refuse with dignity to see any humour at all.

However, this particular sort of slyness, and its distinction from a darker kind, does give us a key to certain very vital changes following on the Chaucerian simplicity. I know that commentators, or those critics who chiefly shine as commentators, are often gravely anxious to clear great men of the charge of talking nonsense. They apply it to Shakespeare; who has whole passages in which he talks

Chaucer and the Renaissance

nothing but nonsense. When Hamlet says, 'I am but mad north-north-west: when the wind is southerly, I know a hawk from a hand-saw,' the remark strikes his critics as one eminently suitable for scientific and rationalizing treatment; some hastily amending it to 'I know a hawk from a heronshaw', and the other, I think, inventing some new tool or utensil called a hawk. I know nothing of these things; they may be right. But seeing that the man was a fantastic humorist in any case, and pretending to be a lunatic at that, and seeing he starts the very same sentence by saying he is mad, it seems to me, as a humble fellow-habitant of Hanwell, that he probably meant to say, 'a hawk from a hand-saw', as he might have said, 'a bishop from a blunderbuss', or, 'a postman from a pickle-jar'. Now this sort of wild fantasticality is Shakespearian but not Chaucerian. Chaucer has in the background too much of that logic which was the backbone of the Middle Ages. The Renaissance was, as much as anything, a revolt from the logic of the Middle Ages. We speak of the Renaissance as the birth of rationalism; it was in many ways the birth of irrationalism. It is true that the medieval School-men, who had produced the finest logic that the world has ever seen, had in later years produced more logic than the world can ever be expected to stand. They had loaded and lumbered up the world with libraries of mere logic; and some effort was bound to be made to free it from such endless chains of deduction. Therefore, there was in the Renaissance a wild touch of revolt, not against religion but against reason. Thus one of the very greatest of the sixteenth-century giants was almost as much of a nonsense writer as Edward Lear: Rabelais. So another of the very greatest wrote an Orlando Furioso which might some-times be called Ariosto Furioso. So, in the same way, the narration of Raphael Hythloday is a wild jest. But there are some who still believe, quite literally, that Thomas

Chaucer and the Renaissance

More's Utopia describes the Utopia of Thomas More. For all I know, there may be some who believe that his friend Erasmus wrote *The Praise of Folly* because he thought that all fools were truly deserving of praise. As the Latin exercise-book said, there are some who laugh; and there are some who apparently don't, under the most extreme provocation. There may be some, for all I know, who would quote the anti-feminist observation of Chaucer's cock, with its cowardly parenthesis, as solid and scientific proof that a dead language was used to keep the people in ignorance; and that woman was oppressed by refusing her the benefits of education.

In any case, the truth in this suggestion of slyness is that it is a suggestion of sense. Chaucer was a man much more prudent, and in some ways much more balanced, than the great men of the Renaissance who came after him. Just as it was not in his temper, so it was not in his tradition, to let a joke run away with him, or to indulge a fantasy at the expense of everything else. It was the essence of the medieval philosophy that there is danger in all directions, just as there is good in all directions. That is the meaning of that balanced scheme of Mortal Sins, of Pride and Sloth and Avarice and the rest, with which Chaucer actually concludes and crowns the whole huge design of *The Canterbury Tales*; and of which Mrs. Haldane, the wife of the professor, recently remarked mysteriously that they are all 'quite out of date'. Whether she really meant that nobody nowadays runs after money, or neglects any of his duties, or thinks too much of himself, I do not know. But what the medievals meant, by thus dividing and labelling the vices, was that a man might fall into one of these vices even when fleeing too far from another. A man who neglects his business may fall into sloth; a man who pursues his business may fall into avarice. And what the wreckers of the medieval system really

did, practically and in the long run, was to let loose some
of the vices on the excuse of exterminating the others.
After the Renaissance, the Pagans went in for unlimited
lust and the Puritans for unlimited avarice; on the excuse
that at least neither of them was being guilty of sloth.

The poets, who take the tone of the time, had often a
touch of this lawlessness, and of something that can be
worse than lawlessness; concentration. That is, the time
tended sometimes to be not only maniac but monomaniac.
Chaucer inherited the tradition of a Church which had
condemned heresies on the right hand and the left; and
always claimed to stand for the truth as a whole and not for
concentration on a part. He came indeed in days when that
tradition was not at its best, and was beginning to de-
generate into bitterness and abnormality; but he is himself a living embodiment of what that tradition had really
been. *Communis sententia*; the phrase is Latin and very
medieval. It marks the real effects of 'the vulgar tongue'
that everybody knew what it meant while it was in Latin,
and nobody notices what it means now it is in English. A
modern man using the term does not even notice the word
'common' and means the very contrary of 'common'. He
means private judgment; his own personal incommunic-
able sense. But Chaucer was very medieval and he was
pickled in common sense.

The point is worthy of note, because it is one of the
points in which his greatness has been rather unfairly over-
shadowed by the greatness of Shakespeare. When all is
said, there was in the very greatest of the sixteenth-century men of genius a slight slip or failure upon the point
of common sense. That is what Voltaire meant when he
called Shakespeare an inspired barbarian; and there is
something to be said for Voltaire as well as for Shakespeare. Let it be agreed, on the one hand, that the Renaissance poets had in one sense obtained a wider as well

as a wilder range. But though they juggled with worlds, they had less real sense of how to balance a world. I am sorry that Chaucer 'left half-told the story of Cambuscan bold', and I can imagine that that flying horse might have carried the hero into very golden skies of Greek or Asiatic romance; but I am prepared to agree that he would never have beaten Ariosto in anything like a voyage to the moon. On the other hand, even in Ariosto there is something symbolic, if only accidentally symbolic, in the fact that his poem is less tragic but more frantic than 'The Song of Roland'; and deals not with Roland Dead but with Roland Mad. Anyhow, what is here only accidental becomes in the Elizabethans rather anarchical. When all is said, there is something a little sinister in the number of mad people there are in Shakespeare. We say that he uses his fools to brighten the dark background of tragedy; I think he sometimes uses them to darken it. Somewhere on that highest of all human towers there is a tile loose. There is something that rattles rather crazily in the high wind of the highest of mortal tragedies. What is felt faintly even in Shakespeare is felt far more intensely in the other Elizabethan and Jacobean dramatists; they seem to go in for dancing ballets of lunatics and choruses of idiots, until sanity is the exception rather than the rule. In some ways Chaucer's age was even harsher than Shakespeare's; but even its ferocity was rational. Chaucer describes a whole crowd of many-coloured personalities of all possible types and tendencies. But I do not remember that, in the whole five volumes of Chaucer, there is such a thing as a madman.

In other words, the medieval mind did not really believe that the truth was to be found by going to extremes. And the Elizabethan mind had already had a sort of hint that it might be found there; at the extreme edges of existence and precipices of the human imagination. That is

Chaucer and the Renaissance

why there followed in theology and thought, after the Renaissance, such extremes of speculation as the Calvinist or the Antinomian. I am concerned here to point out a difference rather than a preference; my own preferences are pretty obvious, but they are not the obvious truth involved here. The point is that even those who see the change as bringing more liberty may admit that it brought less sanity. Chaucer was not on the edge of a precipice, but in the middle of a solid meadow of daisies. And he not only was sure of his own common sense; he was also sure that the sense was really common.

Somebody said, and eventually everybody said, something about 'the spacious days of Queen Elizabeth'. I fancy it has falsified history more than any other popular quotation. If they had said, 'the spacious days of King Richard the Second', it would, in some ways, have been much more true; that is, in the sense of a consciousness of the whole problem of the whole people, of community with other countries and the Continent as a whole, or the vision of life in the light of a general philosophy. The Elizabethan epoch was of intense interest; of intensive intelligence; of piercing sharpness and delicacy in certain new forms of diplomacy and domestic policy, and the arts of the ambassador and the courtier; and, especially in one or two great men, of vivid and concentrated genius in the study of certain particular problems of character. But it was not spacious. If there was one thing it did not possess, it was that particular sort of fresh air that blows over the daisied meadows of Chaucer. Its special and specialist studies involved men in almost everything except fresh air. I have used the word 'involved' by accident; but it is applicable as well as accidental. Everything, even the great poetry of Elizabethan times, was a little too much involved. In literature it was the age of conceits. In politics it was the age of conspiracies. In those conspiracies

Chausage and the Renaissance

Chaucer and the Renaissance

there is a curious absence of the fresh popular spirit that often blew like a wind even through the heresies and horrors of the Middle Ages. None of it was in the same world with the Peasants' Rising. The age of Richard the Second was an age of revolutions. The age of Elizabeth was an age of plots. And we all know that this was mirrored more or less even in the mightiest minds of that epoch. It is almost in a double sense that we talk about Shakespeare's 'plots'. In almost every case, it is a plot about a plot. He has even a sort of restlessness vaguely connected with the sixteenth-century sense of the importance and the insecurity of princes. 'Uneasy lies the head that wears a crown'; and also the head that has crowns on the brain.

That Shakespeare is the English giant, all but alone in his stature among the sons of men, is a truth that does not really diminish with distance. But it is a truth with two aspects; a shield with two sides; a sword with two edges. It is exactly because Shakespeare is an English giant that he blocks up the perspective of English history. He is as disproportionate to his own age as to every age; but he throws a misleading limelight on his own age and throws a gigantic shadow back on the other ages. For this reason many will not even know what I mean, when I talk about the greater spaciousness around the medieval poet. If the matter were pushed to a challenge, however, I could perhaps illustrate my meaning even better with another medieval poet. It is vaguely implied that Shakespeare was always jolly and Dante always gloomy. But, in a philosophical sense, it is almost the other way. It is notably so if, so to speak, we actually bring Shakespeare to the test of Dante. Do we not know in our hearts that Shakespeare could have dealt with Dante's Hell but hardly with Dante's Heaven? In so far as it is possible to be greater than anything that is really great, the man who wrote of

226

Chaucer and the Renaissance

Romeo and Juliet might have made something even more poignant out of Paolo and Francesca. The man who uttered that pulverizing 'He has no children', over the butchery in the house of Macduff, might have picked out yet more awful and telling words for the father's cry out of the Tower of Hunger. But the Tower of Hunger is not spacious. And when Dante is really dealing with the dance of the liberated virtues in the vasty heights of heaven, he is spacious. He is spacious when he talks of Liberty; he is spacious when he talks of Love. It is so in the famous words at the end about Love driving the sun and stars; it is the same in the far less famous and far finer passage, in which he hails the huge magnanimity of God in giving to the human spirit the one gift worth having; which is Liberty. Nobody but a fool will say that Shakespeare was a pessimist; but we may, in this limited sense, say that he was a pagan; in so far that he is at his greatest in describing great spirits in chains. In that sense, his most serious plays are an inferno. Anyhow, they are certainly not a Paradiso.

I only use Shakespeare here as a parallel, and I will not continue it indefinitely as a parenthesis. Otherwise I should, of course, qualify the word paganism by well-known facts about his life, as well as by the whole tone of his literature. That Shakespeare was a Catholic is a thing that every Catholic feels by every sort of convergent common sense to be true. It is supported by the few external and political facts we know; it is utterly unmistakable in the general spirit and atmosphere; and in nothing more than in the scepticism, which appears in some aspects to be paganism. But I am not talking about the various kinds of Catholic; I am talking about the atmosphere of the sixteenth century as compared with the fourteenth century. And I say that while the former was more refined, it was in certain special ways more restricted, or properly speaking, more concentrated. Shakespeare is more concentrated on Hamlet than Dante is upon Hell; for the very reason that Dante's mind is full of the larger plan of which this is merely a part. But, it may reasonably be said, I have no right to take the case of Dante in order to make out a case for Chaucer. I am not likely to pretend that Chaucer absorbed every detail of the Thomist theology and purely theoretical ethics of the Divine Comedy. What, it may be asked, has Chaucer to do with Dante; what did he actually inherit from Dante? I answer, the spaciousness. The general sense of not being himself in prison; for Chaucer does not himself go to prison with Palamon and Arcite, as Shakespeare does in some sense go to prison with Richard the Second. Nay, to some extent, and in some subtle fashion, Shakespeare seems to identify himself with Hamlet who finds Denmark a prison, or the whole world a prison. We do not have this sense of things closing in upon the soul in Chaucer, with his simple tragedies; one might almost say, his sunny tragedies. In his world misfortunes are misfortunes, like clouds in the sky; but there is a sky. And there is a quite indescribable serenity that comes from security, in the thought that the sky is settled in an accepted order; or, as the medieval men used to put it, that the heavens are incorruptible. This sense, which Chaucer has vaguely and Dante vividly, is in all its variations quite different from the later mood that culminated in Ford and Webster; where the storm has become more than the sky. It appeared in Chaucer in a leisurely and allusive fashion, but it is there all right; and it is the consciousness of a cosmic philosophy at the back of the mind. It is enough to a man of his temperament to joke about it; to say that it can all be found in 'olde bookes'; to feel a sort of satisfaction that somebody somewhere has a hundred books, clothed in black and red, of Aristotle and his philosophy. But it is the feeling that was

Chaucer and the Renaissance

lost at the Renaissance, when so much else was gained;
the feeling of a sort of reasonable repose in the common
sense of Christian philosophy; especially the colossal common sense of St. Thomas Aquinas.

Thus we have the paradox that the spirit of the Renaissance, at the very moment when it seemed to most men to
be emerging into the daylight, was, in another sense, at
that very moment plunging into the dark. It was plunging into those dark problems of scepticism with which
the world is wrestling still. But it is not a mere question of
some calling scepticism an enlightenment and others calling it a benighted gloom. There really was something of
mystification and secrecy in the very air which Shakespeare breathed; which remains in the sort of biographi-
cal problems which he left behind him. I have said elsewhere that there is a certain parallel between the obscurity
of Chaucer and the obscurity of Shakespeare, in a practical or political sense. But the cases are very different in
this spiritual or atmospheric sense. The mystery of Chaucer is mainly negative; it simply arises from the fact that
we happen to have few official records and no private
memoirs. It is a *hiatus valde deflendus*; but it is not, thank
God, a Cipher. Nobody can imagine *The Canterbury Tales*
being a Cryptogram. It was only possible to suggest it of
Shakespeare because Shakespeare had the bad luck to live
in an age of cryptograms. That is, he lived in an age of
conspiracies. But, in fact, there are real riddles for Shake-
spearians; quite apart from the mad riddles of Baconians.
There is no Mr. W. H. to distract our minds from the
poetry of Chaucer. Chaucer's purely personal poems are
mostly of the sort that anybody could understand; such
as frank and hearty demands for more money. There are
problems about his private life, as is noted elsewhere; but
they are not presented in a manner at once deliberate, de-
fiant and tantalizing, as are some of the relations adum-

Chaucer and the Renaissance

brated in the Sonnets. His Dark Lady was never so dark as all that. She is rather, so to speak, a wash-out; a figure so faint and pale that we cannot be certain whether she existed, or whether the poet is really writing about her at all. Here again, the obscurity is merely negative; but in the Sonnets there is a positive obscurity, a darkness visible. It was said that Shakespeare unlocked his heart with this key; but it sometimes seems truer to say that he hampered the lock.

It is well to remember that this particular *kind* of perplexity has really come into the world since the breakdown of the medieval order; even though the breakdown was accompanied by brilliant diversions in all other directions. It is true, for instance, that the Renaissance had expanded the exploration of the earth; and in that sense, I have spoken of its artists inhabiting a wider and a wilder world. But in some other respects, they inhabited a world which, though certainly wilder, was not so wide. It was very exciting to discover that there were Red Indians or yellow Chinamen; but it did not increase the old Roman and philosophical sense of the broad brotherhood of the *humanum genus*: the human race. Rather it raised new problems about it; problems which produced all sorts of horrible things, from slavery to anthropology. It was very satisfactory to know that you could pay a visit to mountains made of silver or cities made of gold; but humanity was not in fact so much united by the wealth of Ferdinand as by the poverty of Francis. Nothing, indeed, was destined in the long run to produce such bottomless botheration and bewildering intellectual difficulties, as the relation of the precious metals to the older and more practical economics. Those gallant men, who stormed the gates of the sunset to set up the golden banners of Spain, were fortunately unaware that they were fixing on a peak in Darien the enigmatic ensign that we call the Gold Standard.

Chaucer and the Renaissance

What we have to realize, in short (against much of the atmospheric assumptions or allusions of modern literature), is that the older intellectual world was not stupid merely because it was static. Whatever our creed, that is as stupid as calling Confucius stupid because China was static. Chaucer's world was simpler, in the sense that there were fewer unanswered questions. But whether or no we think the questions had been rightly answered, they had certainly been rationally answered. Intelligent men had answered them in an intelligent way; in such a way that an intelligent man like Chaucer could repose in the reasons given. This is simply a fact of history, necessary to the elucidation of biography; it has nothing to do with whether we ourselves accept the theology, or even the philosophy. The point to grasp is that we disagree with it as a philosophy; as we might disagree with the Platonic or the Positivist philosophy; not as we disagree with a wild savage taboo in Africa or a Prohibitionist prejudice in Alabama.

There are inferences from all this which I shall discuss in the last chapter of this book. For the moment, the point to realize is, not merely that there is something to be said for medievalism against the Renaissance (a view which Ruskin and the modern medievalists have sufficiently made clear), but that in some special aspects medievalism could be more rational, or even more rationalistic, than the Renaissance. I am well aware that it is a case not only of complexities, but of contradictions. It is true on the one side that the very reason of medievalism was rooted in religion; it is true on the other side that the very frenzy of the sixteenth century was akin to a thirst for truth. But the distinction I draw is true; and it is of some importance in life and letters. The Renaissance genius was never so much intellectually inspired as when he seemed to be intellectually intoxicated; and his very de-

231

Chaucer and the Renaissance

pression was an exaltation. It would be something to be able even to despair like one of Shakespeare's characters. A dying man might want to live, if he could go on producing such phrases as 'Absent thee from felicity awhile'; he might even continue to absent himself. A murderer might grow cheerful, if he were able to utter his misery in those words about life being a thing 'full of sound and fury, signifying nothing'. But try the experiment of reading a few lines of Aristotle or Aquinas, even as echoed by Chaucer. You will begin to wonder (dare we say it?) whether the great Life of the Renaissance, if it had been a little less full of sound and fury, might not have signified more.

Chapter VIII

THE RELIGION OF CHAUCER

It marks something thin and repetitive, about much of the comment on Chaucer, that we can all remember reading twenty times a comparison between Chaucer and Langland. It commonly adds to a description of *The Canterbury Tales* something like the remark: 'A very different picture is given in *Piers Plowman*.' It is indeed a different picture, because it happens to be a different book, written by a different man. But it would be perfectly easy to make the same contrast concerning two descriptions of the same period written by the same man. It would mark a rather wider contrast to describe the scope and spirit of Pickwick, and then add: 'A very different picture is given in *Hard Times*.' For that matter, it would be almost equally effective to take two of the Dickens novels that come next to each other in his earliest period and say: 'A very different picture is given in Oliver Twist.' And in both cases a reasonable critic will answer, somewhat impatiently, that it is indeed a different picture; for the reason that a good painter does not generally paint two pictures at once. But in the case of the medieval authors, there is always a sort of insinuation that one of the two pictures must be false; and that in any case the happier and more humane picture cannot be true. The suggestion is that Chaucer, being a court poet, was a sort of conservative optimist, while Langland, being supposed to be a popular poet, must necessarily have been a pessimist; and pessimists must necessarily be right.

As a matter of fact, all this view is riddled with inaccuracies, even about the actual comparison between Chaucer and Langland. Supposing there were any particular reason to compare them, a real comparison would be considerably more complex. For instance, though Chaucer is called a courtier, it is Chaucer, much more than Langland, who is always saying that true nobility is not in noble birth but in noble behaviour; that men are to be judged by worth rather than rank; and generally that all men are equal in the sight of God. And similarly, though Langland is treated as a revolutionary, it is Langland much more than Chaucer who is always saying that upstarts have seized power to which their birth does not entitle them; that the claims of family have been disregarded through the insolence of novelty, and that men are bragging and boasting above their station. There is doubtless much to be said for both these views, nor are they really inconsistent with each other. But Chaucer can scarcely have said the first in order to flatter the aristocracy, nor Langland said the second as part of a demand for change. It is also curious that many have missed the point of certain passages in Langland as they have missed the point of so many passages in Chaucer. The author of *Piers Plowman* denounces a vast variety of evils, indeed, an almost universal conspectus of evils; because the very form of his book is an account of something very like a Day of Judgment; and not an account of a casual ride of holiday-makers to Canterbury. But in many places he denounces the fourteenth-century conditions, not so much because certain classes have too little as because they have too much. He denounces the riot and excesses that accompanied the economic overturn of his time; but much of it was a condition of high though perilously precarious wages, and a wealth which was not under adequate or responsible control. He sometimes speaks of beggars as if they were bullies, rather than abject creatures; and while he certainly thinks the poor are in danger, it is not his point merely that they are in destitution. His point is rather that they and everybody else are in chaos; and there is much in that sort of lopsided luck that suggests our own time as well as his.

The point is here, however, that Langland was nothing so simple as a man lamenting over a starving people; and certainly Chaucer was nothing so simple as a smug snob or conservative not knowing or caring whether anybody could starve. They were men of very different temperaments, but they did not after all bear such very different testimony. They were both highly intelligent Christians and Catholics living in an extremely bewildering time of transition; in which some things were certainly breaking free, but a good many things appeared to be breaking down. The rather remarkable ballade which Chaucer addressed to Richard the Second might have been written by Langland himself, in his sternest mood of reproach and responsibility. The burden of it, even in the literal sense of the refrain of it, is a repeated insistence that only Steadfastness can save the nation in such a welter of novelties. It is not difficult to imagine that particular personage called Steadfastness walking about for edification in The Field Full of Folk.

It is doubtless true that while Chaucer could sometimes be as severe as Langland, it is not very likely that Langland would be as jocular as Chaucer. But that in itself hardly shows that Chaucer was lacking in popular sympathies. The English lower classes have been known to make jokes, both then and now. As a matter of fact, I fancy Langland would have been much more harsh to the coarse and common people on the Pilgrimage than Chau-

The Religion of Chaucer

cer. But the whole comparison arises from the initial in-eptitude of not realizing that one kind of man will write one kind of book; and that one kind of book will of its very nature contain one kind of material. We might as well complain that *Everyman* is tragic as complain that *Piers Plowman* is prophetic, in the sense which some call pessimistic. It is by its whole plan and conception a vision of Christ calling all human society to repentance. It is not very likely that Chaucer, considered as an artist, would have attacked that particular literary scheme at all. But if he had attacked it, he would have had exactly the same fundamental ideas about the nature of repentance and the authority of Christ. And, what is perhaps more cogent here, he would have had exactly the same funda-mental belief in the sacramental and ecclesiastical system of the Middle Ages. Those who do not realize that fact simply do not know that system; though it did not, curi-ously enough, disappear with the Middle Ages.

Some critics have vaguely suspected Chaucer of being a Lollard, through a simple ignorance of what is meant by being a Catholic. I am aware that there is a Victorian convention, according to which a literary study should not refer to religion, except when there is an opportunity of a passing sneer at it. But nobody can make head or tail of the fourteenth century without understanding what is meant by being a Catholic; and therefore by being a heretic. A man does not come an inch nearer to being a heretic by being a hundred times a critic. Nor does he do so because his criticisms resemble those of critics who are also heretics. He only becomes a heretic at the precise moment when he prefers his criticism to his Catholicism. That is, at the instant of separation in which he thinks the view peculiar to himself more valuable than the creed that unites him to his fellows. At any given moment the Catholic Church is full of people sympathizing with social

236

movements or moral ideas, which may happen to have representatives outside the Church. For the Church is not a movement or a mood or a direction, but the balance of many movements and moods; and membership of it consists of accepting the ultimate arbitrament which strikes the balance between them, not in refusing to admit any of them into the balance at all. A Catholic does not come any nearer to being a Communist by hating the Capitalist corruptions, any more than he comes any nearer to being a Moslem by hating real idolatry or real excess in wine. He accepts the Church's ruling about the use and abuse of wine and images; and after that it is irrelevant how much he happens to hate the abuse of them. A Catholic did not come any nearer to being a Calvinist by dwelling on the omniscience of God and the power of Grace, any more than he came any nearer to being an atheist by saying that man possessed reason and freewill. What constituted a Calvinist was that he preferred his Calvinism to his Catholicism. And what constituted his Catholicism was that he accepted the ultimate arbitration which reconciled freewill and grace, and did not exclude either. So a Catholic did not come any nearer to being a Lollard because he criticized the ecclesiastical evils of the fourteenth century, as Leo the Thirteenth or Cardinal Manning criticized the economic evils of the nineteenth century. He said many things which Lollards also said, as the Pope and the Cardinal said many things which Socialists also said. But he was no nearer to being a Lollard; and nobody can begin to suggest that Chaucer was a Lollard, unless he can prove either or both of two propositions about him. First, that he held any Lollard doctrine that can be proved to be heretical by exact and authoritative definition: the sort of precise thing not very likely to be found in such poetry. And, second, that if he did hold it as a private opinion, he would in the last resort have preferred that private opinion to membership of the Body of Christ. I need not say that there is not the wildest suggestion of a reason for supposing that Chaucer was a Lollard either in one sense or the other.

To me personally, the Lollard is the most sympathetic of all the heretics. I might say, in a figure of speech, that he was the most Catholic of all the heretics. He was, beyond any possible question, the least Protestant of all the heretics. His whole suggestion, so far as there was any clear suggestion beyond a healthy discontent, was the superiority of the Catholic ideals of holy poverty and brotherhood to the ranks and powers of this world. But 'Dominion founded on Grace' is not tenable; nobody could live in a society in which practical authority and right were only recognized in holy and innocent persons. The experiment of telephoning to a policeman to stop a murder, and being told that he must call on the priest for confession on his way to the scene of the crime, would be enough to settle the legal practicality of Lollardy. It seems to me enormously unlikely that a man of Chaucer's temperament, which was sensible almost to excess, ever thought anything of the kind. It is quite certain that he never said anything of the kind. It is equally certain that he did say something else of a totally different kind, which Lollards said also; that it was disgraceful for priests and men in authority to be base and unworthy; or, as he put it in a picturesque figure, that it was horrible to see a filthy shepherd and a clean sheep. But there is nothing particularly Lollardish about saying that; thousands of Catholics have said it in every age and are saying it now. It is worthy of remark, perhaps, that Chaucer's very strictures on clerics are rather clerical than anti-clerical. That is, they are based on the notion that the priest is not merely bad when he ought to be good, but bad because he ought to be better. In the same passage he uses another figure

The Religion of Chaucer

of speech, which is even more conclusive. 'If gold rust, what shall iron do?' He never doubted that the priest, as a priest, had received something as precious as gold in comparison to iron. But, the ultimate test is even more practical. The question is, even if Chaucer was anticlerical, would he have allowed it to make him anti-Catholic? Would he have left the Church for the love of a grievance? There is not, and never has been, the shadow of a reason to think so.

For the rest, he was unquestionably and even passionately devoted to the particular parts of Catholicism that have been most condemned by Protestantism. He had a devotion to Our Lady perhaps greater than that of Dante; as great as that of St. Bernard in his great oration in Dante. The poem significantly called his A B C, as if it were the first elements of his childlike faith, contains language that goes almost beyond the doctrinal limit in attributing omnipotence and supremacy to Mary. In short, there is no reason for saying that Chaucer was a Lollard; but there is overwhelming reason for saying that he was not a Protestant.

Modern critics have congratulated Chaucer, or congratulated themselves, on the fact that he was so enlightened a reformer as to satirize the Monk and the Friar. Curiously enough, they have neglected to notice what he satirized them for. Rather simple things of this sort do often get overlooked. And the simple truth is that Chaucer satirizes the Monk for not being sufficiently Monastic. He may have been right or wrong; but it is certain that if he was right, the Reformers of the Reformation were wrong; and only on the assumption that they were wrong can we pretend that he was in any sense right. The point is rather practical; because nearly all studies of this period are full of the suggestion that Chaucer, like his contemporary Wycliffe, was a sort of morning star of the Reformation. We can only answer that in that case he was an eccentric star who wanted the sun to move backwards instead of forwards. In the whole of his satirical sketch of the Monk, the point is, not that the Monk is sunk in monkish superstitions, but simply that the Monk is not monkish enough. Protestantism, as it ultimately developed, professed to free monks and nuns from the prison of the cloister. It welcomed runaway monks and nuns to the freedom of the secular world; even when their conduct was rather alarmingly free and somewhat startlingly secular. But all Chaucer's denunciation is directed, not so much at a monk, as at a runaway monk; and that not because he is a monk but because he is a runaway. He jeers at him for coming out of the cloister and partaking of the pleasures of the world. He jeers at him indeed in his own jovial and even genial fashion; making up an imaginary defence for the monk, which is full of a hearty hatred of work and the bother of reading books. Why, he asks, should the jolly fellow do any work at all? Why should he work with his hands, because St. Augustine believed in the Dignity of Labour? Let St. Augustine work, if he wants to. But this breezy outburst certainly cannot be taken seriously as an attack on monasticism, unless it is to be taken seriously as an attack on manual labour, or labour of any sort. There are doubtless modern critics who are capable of taking that or anything else seriously. To those troubled in spirit by the divine disturbance of humour, it will be obvious that Chaucer is simply chaffing a monk for his cheek in not being a monk at all. The whole of this passage, taken in an historical and social sense, is simply a protest against the decline of monastic discipline. It is like a patriotic protest against the decline of military discipline. Such a protest would very probably contain an ironical congratulation, on the lines of 'He who fights and runs away will live to fight another day'. But it is scarcely the sort of congratulation that any soldier would be flattered to receive. The fact is that the man who said this sort of thing was the flat contrary of a modern opponent of asceticism. Neither Chaucer, nor anybody who really counted in Chaucer's day, ever dreamed of complaining that monks were monks. They only complained, as Chaucer did, because the monks were not monks.

Chaucer, of course, took for granted the whole Catholic theory about the normal vocation of Marriage and the exceptional vocation of Virginity. He explains it all, in strictly orthodox theological terms; though in one place he puts it, with a twist of his quaint humour, into the mouth of the Wife of Bath. She is the lady who has buried four husbands and explains that, on the whole, Virginity is not her vocation. Here again, if this were a joke against anything, it would not be a joke against the Virgin but against the Wife; or at any rate against the Wife of Bath. Indeed, anyone superficially acquainted with medieval culture and the Chaucerian origins will know that the latter is the more likely of the two. He will know that while such a satirist was ready to satirize both unmarried and married people, he was rather more ready to satirize the married than the unmarried. The references to Theophrastus and his clerical copyists make that clear enough. But he will also know, what is the most important point of all, that whenever the satirist became a serious writer, he accepted quite as naturally the status of the officially unmarried as that of the officially married. He no more dreamed of suggesting that there ought to be no Monasticism than that there ought to be no Marriage. He was bred in the bone and blood of a whole living society, of which one was as much an organic part as the other. He might, like many another medieval writer, deal rather scandalously with the scandal of monks or nuns who broke their vows. He would never, like a modern writer, think it scandalous that they kept their vows.

As a matter of fact, Chaucer deals even with the former scandal less scandalously than most of his great contemporaries. It is a point of some importance, as marking not only the more genial and less militant temper of the English poet and the English people, but as illustrating the point that England was really less anti-clerical than Europe. The English people were the most remote from heresy, when the English rulers were the most near to schism. But there was also an amiable element, not only national but personal. It is suggested, somewhat plausibly I think, that the extremely abrupt introduction of the Second Nun, followed by her equally abrupt dismissal without any description, and with only the mysterious addition of Three Priests (who never appear again and have no stories to contribute), is really a badly botched excision and join, to cover the fact that Chaucer originally wrote something about the Second Nun which he decided not to publish. Nor, I think, need such an act of prudence have been merely prudential. If Chaucer had ever let his mind run along lines of such licence as did Boccaccio, in suggesting the immorality of nuns, I do honestly believe that Chaucer himself would have been ashamed of it. For that matter, it is true that Boccaccio himself ultimately repented of it. But there was in Chaucer from the first something quite different from the hard scorn and hot repentance of the Italian. It was something which, in the legend of Robin Hood, went along with the same English devotion to the Blessed Virgin; so that it was said that the outlaw 'would never hurt a company that any woman was in'. Chaucer merely as a man (if I understand anything at all of the man) would always have felt that he might say things about monks that he must not say about nuns; in which one other English Catholic may be permitted to agree with him.

Anyhow, whether we take the test of the cult of Mary, or of the code of Monasticism, or of any other recognized mark for modern criticism, it is perfectly obvious that Geoffrey Chaucer was an ordinary orthodox medieval Catholic and never dreamed of being anything else. Nor did he ever dream that he was likely to lose that status (to all who held it the most vital thing in life and death) by making fun of fat friars or monks who went hunting instead of working with their hands. But those who, reading history backwards, look for the later type called the Protestant in a medieval man who was not even a Lollard, may find in every sense a more final answer in the final pages of the great poem. It may be suspected that few of them have read as far as those final pages; still less had the heroic tenacity to read through them. Everybody knows the joke about Lord Macaulay; who said of Spenser that few of his readers were in at the death of the Blatant Beast; thereby proving that Macaulay at least was not one of the few, or he would have found out that the Blatant Beast does not die after all. Something of the same doubt affects the case of those to whom Chaucer's religion seems not only a simple matter, but merely a religion of simplicity.

They are naturally attached to the beautiful description of the Parson, which sounds in many ways very simple, and which occurs at the beginning of *The Tales* and is therefore easily skimmed even by the superficial. They remark very truly that Chaucer, for some reason or other, evidently preferred the parish priests to the monks and friars; though I know not why there should be supposed to be something vaguely Protestant about preferring one set of Catholic priests to another. There is certainly nothing very Protestant about taking it for

The Religion of Chaucer

granted that one medieval Catholic must have been right in his preferences. Nevertheless, those who imagine that Jesus Christ and the Gospels were first discovered by Martin Luther, and are never mentioned among Catholics, have hinted in a hundred ways that the mention of these things in the first description of the Parson shows him to be a good hearty Protestant Parson, with Muscular Christianity and Morning Service at eleven o'clock. May I inflict on such readers the somewhat heavy medieval penance, of reading what is (very deceptively) called 'The Parson's Tale', with which Chaucer deliberately winds up the whole series of tales? It is in fact simply a sermon, and if ever there was a medieval sermon, in the whole range of the Middle Ages, it is that of the simple Parson of Chaucer. It is arranged in the formal and almost decorative scheme of the Seven Deadly Sins, each division having equally formal and doctrinal sub-divisions: and each division and sub-division stating with minute accuracy the exact and distinct Roman Catholic doctrine, as it is to this day. There is the need of Confession to a priest, the distinction between mortal and venial sin, and all the rest. There are a hundred points on which it agrees with itself then and now, and differs from everybody else then and now. It is appallingly long and elaborate, but it does not trip on a single term; and there is written all over it in large letters Nihil Obstat and Imprimatur. For those who believe in the change of morals or the innovations of science, it may be amusing to note that the simple Parson indulges in a ferocious, and somewhat ruthlessly realistic, outburst against Birth Control.

There is one point in this connexion that should be made clear. Nobody understands the nature of man, the nature of medieval man, or above all the nature of the medieval man named Geoffrey Chaucer, who imagines that this sort of long explanation is necessarily a bore. At

The Religion of Chaucer

any rate, it is not necessarily a bore to the writer, even if it is for the reader. All healthy and vigorous minds have great pleasure in explaining anything; and especially in explaining a system. There were so many systems in the Middle Ages, ranging from the gravest to the most trivial matters, from hagiology to heraldry, from the rules of faith to the rules of falconry, from the calculation of planets to the language of colours, that the general effect on the modern mind is that of a complicated and be-wildering pattern. But almost all the men expounding these things took a palpable and even passionate pleasure in the pattern. This was not less, but rather more the case when it was a doctrinal or dogmatic pattern. Chaucer has a huge appetite for theological and ethical explan-ations; he will often turn aside for them in the most casual and incongruous context. It is thoroughly typical of him that he makes the Wife of Bath pour out a torrent of turbulent, gross and egotistical discourse, as coarse as a fishwife's and as personal as a Margate landlady's; and yet feels it perfectly natural that she should pause to explain the correct Catholic doctrine about Virginity and Counsels of Perfection. It was perfectly natural. It would not only have been perfectly natural to Chaucer. It would probably have been perfectly natural to the Wife of Bath. Here and there, even in modern England, we may find the remnants of that ancient relish, when some tavern talker expounds heavily the whole case for atheism or the Anglo-Israelite theory or the proofs from Apocalypse that the Kaiser was the Beast. But if we wish to find the tradition more truly and directly descended from the Middle Ages, and until lately really moving a whole people as it did in the Middle Ages, we must go, strangely enough, to the Puritans of Scotland. There was found the true medieval passion for logic and the long exposition of a system. The Scot in Stevenson's stories, who 'sits

The Religion of Chaucer

with relish' under a thunderous but entirely theoretical theologian—he had preserved one thread, though only a thin black thread, out of the woven tapestry of the Middle Ages. In that sense, so far as this island was concerned, the Calvinists were the last Catholics.

It is the paradox, but the truth of the matter, that what may be called the dullness of medievalism came from the excitement of medievalism. The vigour and vivacious interest required to follow those interminable arguments, or interminable allegories, were the virtues of a young and virile humanity. An eagerness more inexhaustible than that of a child was needed to carry readers breathlessly through the endless decorative forest of *The Romance of the Rose*. It is a truth of psychology that needs a fuller exposition; for no psychologist has yet written a very necessary book called 'A Defence of Bores'. Perhaps it is the bored rather than the bore that needs defence, but it is true that the bored is the weaker of the two. It is the bore who is joyous and triumphant; the true conqueror of the earth. Or, to put the matter less flippantly, it is true that a living and logical gusto for giving long explanations of everything, though it may be an infliction on the sensitive, is itself an attribute of the strong. To anyone who knows what logic is, the sustained lucidity and consistency of the Parson's Tale is itself sufficient proof that writing it was, for Chaucer, not merely a moral toil, but an intellectual joy. A modern man is quite entitled to say that joy in writing is one thing and joy in reading it quite another. But the medieval man may have been the more joyful of the two.

In another sense, of course, the question of Chaucer's religion rises into a region that is far above all this controversy. I have already mentioned certain fragments, from his religious poems, which are like flashes of this more serene and enduring light. But if we are to realize

The Religion of Chaucer

what a man like Chaucer meant by that light, and how and why it differed from daylight (the daylight which he of all men loved as he loved the daisy), we must cast back and consider some more general principles which are the explanations of his attitude; not only because they were universally understood as the basis of medieval thought, but because they are almost universally misunderstood in the outlook of modern thought. The poet never mentioned them because he started with them, and the critics never mentioned them because they have not reached them as yet.

Perhaps the largest fact about the Middle Ages is that two forces worked and to some extent warred in that time. One was that mystical vision, or whatever we call it, which Catholics call The Faith; the other was the prodigious prestige of Pagan Antiquity. Neo-Pagans of the Swinburnian interlude imagined that Paganism stood merely for light and liberty, and Catholicism merely for superstition and slavery. But the case was much more complex, upon any reading. Some superstitions, such as Astrology, still imposed themselves although they were Pagan; or rather *because* they were Pagan. They seemed to be classic, like Aristotle and Virgil. It is amusing to read the medieval Catholics on Astrology, and note how much they resemble the modern Catholics on Evolution. Both feel *first* that no science must be allowed to deny the dignity and liberty of the human soul; but the medievals have the same vague respect for all that is labelled Antiquity that we have for all that is labelled Science. Or again, in the matter of liberty, the mere instinctive growth of a Catholic peasantry had already loosened the old slavery, when lawyers insisting on the old Roman Law tried to revive the definition of the slave. The mystical element had its own crimes and cruelties; but the point is that both elements were mixed and that the conflict was

247

The Religion of Chaucer

very complicated. One truth, however, was fairly constant; that Pagan and Christian conceptions ran parallel; but the Christian *above* the Pagan.

It is wholly typical of our time that the old theologians are commonly blamed for subtle distinctions; because in our time we tend always to superficial resemblances. It is counted the triumph of classification to class everything together; that is, the triumph of classification is to say there are no classes. Imperialism painting the map red and internationalism painting the globe grey are alike in practice; in so far as each will spread the paint very thin, if it can only spread it very far. Almost all forms of popular science shine chiefly by shallow parallels. For instance, the whole business of Comparative Mythology is made up of shallow parallels; that is, of superficial resemblances which cover deep and fundamental divisions. I have legs and a table has legs; if I am large and round, it is also possible for a table to be large and round. Therefore I am the legendary counterpart, or possibly the mythical origin, of the Round Table. But if I modestly advance this claim, it may occur to some that the differences between a man and a table are fundamental; while the resemblances between table-legs and merely human legs are superficial; they are in fact almost metaphorical. A man is alive and walks about; a table seldom does so, save under the moral influence of Sir Arthur Conan Doyle. And the abyss between the organic and the inorganic is too absolute to be bridged by the figure of speech called a wooden leg. So we commonly find in current discussions a pretence of finding things roughly similar when they are radically different; as if a man were accused of splitting hairs because he obstinately distinguished between feathers and ferns.

Thus there are critics so shallow that they cannot see the quite fundamental difference between the Puritanism

248

The Religion of Chaucer

from which England is emerging at the present time and the Asceticism from which England was emerging in the time of Chaucer. The difference, or rather the contrast, is clear and sharp; and has nothing to do with whether we happen to prefer one or the other. It may be maintained that Puritanism is more practical, or even more concerned with the present world. It may be reasonably alleged that ascetic mysticism was too much concerned with the other world. But the roots are utterly distinct; even when there is in both a renunciation of the things of this world in the name of the other world. And the difference is this; that the older ascetic saw heaven as very bright, and this world as dark in comparison. But the later Puritan saw heaven itself as dark, in the sense of stern and rather stormy; and his genuine imagination exulted in the storm. For him the Lord was in the thunder, much more than in the still small voice; and he was thus at the opposite extreme to even the most extreme ascetic, or excessive ascetic, who wished the sound of lutes and viols to cease, so that the still small voice might be heard. The point is, however, that the old ascetic was looking for joy and beauty, whether we think his vision of joy and beauty impossible or merely invisible. But the true Puritan was not primarily looking for joy and beauty, but for strength and even violence. This can be stated, and for a hundred years has been stated, in a form favourable to the Puritan. He has been called the stalwart and virile Puritan; he is always very much gratified to be called the grim and rugged Puritan. The other religious ideal can as easily be stated in an unfavourable form; suggesting a sentimental and childish attraction to bright colours or costly trinkets. I am not at all concerned with the favourable or unfavourable comments here. But, favourable or unfavourable, they point to a clean-cut contrast between the two things. There is such a contrast between those

249

things; which is why so many modern writers describe them as the same.

The contrast instantly appears in black and white, when the two creeds express themselves in externals. When once the ascetic was assured that certain things were dedicated to divine things, he wanted them to be exceptionally brilliant and gorgeous things. He wanted the vestments of the priest to run through all the colours of the rainbow or the marbles of the shrine to mimic all the sunsets of the world. The Puritan insisted that the preacher should wear a black Geneva gown, instead of any coloured vestment, and that the chapel should be a shed or barn and not a temple shining with marbles; and he was consistent with his fundamental conception. He was not merely stern towards other people's religion or irreligion. He was stern towards his own religion; and was most stern where he was most religious. In his religious picture even the high light was a hard light; the sort of harsh and hueless light that can be seen in the black engravings in the old Family Bibles. It was not a question of preferring light to darkness; it was a question of preferring a colourless light to a coloured light. It was not a question of flowers or beautiful raiment, conceived as a vision of heaven rather than of earth; it was a question of being on the side of the storm against the flower or of the stark bones against the garment. As I say, it can be described as a sublime exultation in strength and severity; appealing to sturdy races or to strict family traditions. It can also be described (so far as I am concerned) as a return to heathenism and a howling to the gods of fear. But it is a fact of history, which still plays a part even in politics; that certain people were proud, not of being stern to this or that indulgence; but simply proud of being stern.

Now this note is *never* found in medieval asceticism.

The Religion of Chaucer

Nobody can imagine St. Thomas Aquinas saying, 'I am a grand grim old Dominican, who stands no nonsense; we are a rugged stock, scorning the pleasures of the world.' Nobody can conceive St. Bernard boasting, 'We Burgundians are a harsh, hardy race and like the thunder in our hills more than the pretty flowers of a garden paradise.' These men may have dwelt too much on the supernatural as compared to the natural, according to our own views upon such matters; but they thought the supernatural more beautiful than the natural; not merely more naked or elemental or terrible. M. Reinach, a learned Jew who has an artistic admiration for medievalism certainly quite untinged with Catholicism, has very truly pointed out that the purely medieval artists always represented heavenly beings as gay and happy, and attributed sorrow only to the lost. The insistence even on the Man of Sorrows and the Mater Dolorosa, in artistic expression, belongs to a time after the medieval. It was in the seventeenth century that the two more sombre religious moods appeared in the two religions. In the Catholic world it became in some sense a worship of sorrow; in the Puritan world a worship of severity, and in some cases of savagery. The point here, however, is that we cannot understand medieval men, even the most extreme or extravagant ascetics, unless we understand that to them the contrast was quite clear between the cross and the crown; between the harsh and angular timber of the cross and the coloured jewels of the crown. A man like Fra Angelico might live a very plain life; but he did not imagine paradise as a penny plain, but very decidedly as twopence coloured. A man like John Knox prided himself on being plain even in his religious conceptions; some might say flippantly that he was too much of a Scot to spare the twopence. From him descends a sort of pride of rudeness, growing more self-conscious with later times; but unknown even

251

The Religion of Chaucer

to the rudest people in older times. We may think that the earlier saints tried to be saved by an excess of humility; but nobody tried to be admired for an excess of hardness. They did not even excuse themselves for being hardhearted by calling themselves hard-headed. As a rule, they did not call themselves anything, except miserable sinners.

This is a good example of the subtle contrasts of history; the contrasts which a shallow person will probably see as resemblances. It is much easier to see that Buddhism and Byzantine Christianity both have images or incense or gilded shrines, than to see that their fundamental theories flatly contradict each other. It is much easier to say that Pelagians and Puritans both quarrelled with bishops than to state lucidly their two separate beliefs, which were at opposite extremes of belief. The Lollards of the fifteenth century were in many ways the very reverse of the Lutherans of the sixteenth century. Yet it is found convenient to class them together, because it is now found convenient to class nearly everything and anything together, in a generalization which is obviously sweeping and certainly superficial.

When we have thus firmly grasped that medievalism had a heavenly vision (or illusion) of which the colours were intrinsically beautiful and even gay, we can then follow correctly the curious and interesting process by which the rest of the environment grew somewhat gayer. In other words, the next phase is that in which men like the Troubadours and the Italian poets, and in the present case the English poets, began to give gayer expression to their pleasure in the pagan poets; especially in Ovid. Now this pagan prestige covered, to a great extent, the pranks of the poets; and yet it produced a duality in the medieval mind which often puzzles the modern mind. It is not that the later medieval man is torn, like Tannhäuser, between Venus and the Virgin. He often seems,

252

The Religion of Chaucer

like Chaucer and Petrarch, to be able to turn with comparative lightness and innocence from the subject of Venus to that of the Virgin. But we shall completely misunderstand him, if we think that his levity means that they are too sympathetic or similar to be contrasted. On the contrary, his levity means that they are too unequal to be compared. There still remains the same contrast between this world and the other, even when this world has allowed itself to grow more worldly. There still remains the contrast between the cross and the crown, even when the cross has been moulded in gold, and jewelled more than all royal crowns.

Perhaps it might be pictured somewhat thus; that for a medieval man, his Paganism was like a wall and his Catholicism was like a window. No discussions of degree or relativity can get over the difference between a wall and a window. It is more even than a difference of dimension or of plane; it is very near to one of negative and positive. Anyhow, just as a very white sheet of paper looks black if held up against the sun, so any wall looks dark against any window. It may be a whitewashed wall, but it will not be as white as the dullest daylight. Now in the early days of medievalism, the wall of the world really was rather grey and grim. There was, as Mr. Belloc has said, something stark about the very strength of the first medieval structure of secular society. The wall was, let us say, of the cold colour of earth, and only the window had the colours of heaven. As medieval civilization progressed, and for a time it progressed very rapidly and well, the wall of this world was painted in brighter colours. When men like Petrarch and Chaucer were almost within sight of the Renaissance, they painted the wall with gorgeous designs in gold and scarlet. They did not hesitate to paint with highly Pagan designs of gods and nymphs. Considered as mural illuminations, these things were very illuminating. Contrasted with the dull stone of the Dark Ages, they were very bright. But, contrasted with the window, they were still dark.

It never really crossed the mind of any typical man of the Middle Ages, or for that matter of any typical man of the Renaissance, that the lightness of his mural decoration could approach anywhere near to the light from heaven. They were still divided by that abstract abyss between a window and a wall, which is like the chasm between light and darkness. If the window were curtained, if the wall were considered in itself, by artificial light, he would go almost any lengths in the enjoyment of its glitter or gaiety of colour; not to mention its sometimes rather excessive gaiety of subject. But he did not make it a rival to reality or the daylight. The moment he put the two into competition, he treated the lesser with contempt. For instance, some of the best Chaucerian authorities profoundly doubt, and I as an amateur, ignorant of all but human experience, also profoundly doubt, the authenticity of that queer postscript to *The Canterbury Tales*, expressing regret for all literary vanities except some poems of religion. It seems an unlikely sort of ending to any work; especially to a work that was not in fact ended. But if it were authentic, I could understand it better than men who are better scholars than I. Even if Chaucer wrote it, it would not mean what a modern poet would mean by being ashamed of his poems. It would not mean that they were something specially bad on their own plane: it would mean they were nothing on his ultimate plane: the plane of death and eternity. If this is inconsistent, his admitted works are inconsistent. Venus and Cupid dance in and out of his long love-poems on a principle of unfailing recurrence. They are a burden in the sense of a refrain; before the end, I fear, they are a burden in the sense of a bore. Of the many minor trades

The Religion of Chaucer

that Chaucer seems to be practising before us, perhaps the one he enjoys most is that of an architect of heathen temples. He never used better his beautiful sense of design than when fitting up those shrines with the ivory statue of Venus or the red metal of Mars. Troilus, the heroic lover, is necessarily in perpetual relation to the god and goddess of love, and many might read whole pages of such a poem and suppose it to be a translation from Ovid or Theocritus.

But when Troilus was actually dead and done with, the poet suddenly turned and spat all these things out of his mouth, as the saint spat the cold temples of Laodicea. He treats all his graceful gods and goddesses exactly as 'the damned crew' which the Puritan Milton hurled howling from all their hollow fanes.

> *Lo, here of pagans' cursed olden rites,*
> *Lo, here what all their high gods might avail,*
> *Lo, here this wretched worldës appetites,*
> *Lo, here the end and guerdon of travail,*
> *Of Jove, Apollo, of Mars and such rascaille. . . .*

. . . or (if we may modernize the language further) of all such rascals. That is what the serious Chaucer said of the serious Paganism. That is what he thought of the painted pictures on the wall, when there was talk of their blocking up the window.

To most modern people, with their notions drawn from the nineteenth century rather than the twentieth, this will seem an inconsistency, and in a sense it is indeed a complexity. But it is a complexity essential to the understanding of what they would call the simplicity of the Middle Ages, and especially the simplicity of 'Dan Chaucer'. There are perhaps three elements in it; one concerned with his time, one with his creed, and a third very specially with himself. The first was a general char-

acter of medieval philosophy, especially Thomist philosophy, if we compare it with the real rival philosophies of
the world; with the Buddhist philosophy or the Calvinist
philosophy or the Positivist philosophy. It is the main
mark of St. Thomas Aquinas, for instance, as compared
with the few sages who are as great. He does lift Faith
above Reason; but does not lower Reason. He does put
the supernatural higher than the natural; but does not
lower the natural. He says that the lower thing is in
every sense worthy; except that compared with the higher
it is worthless. This led to a habit of thinking on two
levels, or even on three. It was like the medieval theatres
which sometimes had three stages, one above the other;
so, in the poetry influenced by this philosophy, there was
the lower stage in which the heathen gods were high, and
the higher stage in which they were low. Secondly it was
connected with a character in Catholic morality as distinct from Protestant morality. I do not wish to state the
contrast controversially, for it is easy to state it favour-
ably or unfavourably to either side. But the point of
Protestantism was that it wiped out *all* a man's sins at
once, as if they were all equally sinful. *All* Christian's
burden fell from him before the Cross. He did not have
to unpack his own luggage in the confessional-box. But
Catholicism always tended more to a table of sins, as of
different weights and measures, and a real sense that
while all are positively heavy, some are relatively light.
This accounts for the very varying laxity of medieval
and other writers about lighter things. Even when they
thought the lover was a sinner, they never thought he
was so great a sinner as the traitor. They might have
thought Lancelot infinitely inferior to Galahad; but they
also thought Modred infinitely inferior to Lancelot. We
see these shifting and conflicting crosslights shining or
darkening continually on the figure of Troilus. These

The Religion of Chaucer

matters of medieval philosophy and morality made up much of the paradox; but there was a third part of it that was not entirely of any period or system, but came out of the character of Geoffrey Chaucer.

If there is one feature that stands out, we might say sticks out, from the literary personality of Chaucer, it is a curious sort of hilarious half-ironical welcome to people more cynical than himself. He has an impulsive movement to applaud what he does not approve. It is as if their impudence gave him so much pleasure, that he could not withhold a sort of affection based on gratitude. We all remember the extraordinary virtues attributed to the Summoner:

> *He was a gentle harlot and a kind,*
> *A better fellow could men nowhere find:*
> *For he would suffer for a quart of wine*
> *A good fellow to have his concubine*
> *A twelve-month, and excuse him at the full.*

Fastidious readers have formed the impression that Chaucer's Summoner must have been about as objectionable a person to go on a pilgrimage with as anybody in the world, even the Miller; yet Chaucer cannot contain himself for gladness at the thought of such sociable eccentricities. His attitude towards the Shipman is more sympathetic than that of Stevenson towards a pirate. And indeed, so far as I can make out, the Shipman was, among other things, a pirate. But Chaucer is not to be shaken out of his geniality by trifles like that.

> *And certainly he was a good felawe*
> *Full many a draught of wine would he draw*
> *From Bordeaux Ward, while the chapmen sleep;*
> *Of nice conscience took he no keep.*
> *If that he fought, and had the higher hand,*
> *By water he sent them home to every land.*

The Religion of Chaucer

which is said to be a polite way of saying that he made them walk the plank. But while Chaucer is on this level of artistic amusement, a little murder does not trouble him. Yet there were some murders that troubled him very much indeed. When he was once on the higher level, of considering the sufferings of the murdered, and facing the serious question of whether murder is morally advisable, he was rather specially a pathetic, rather than a stoic moralist. It would be hard to count the number of times he repeats the piteousness of the death of this or that person unjustly slain, as in the piercing lines about the boy martyr in the Tale of the Prioress. But he had set up, as part of the structure of his own mind, a sort of lower and larger stage, for all mankind, in which anything could happen without seriously hurting anybody; and an upper stage which he kept almost deliberately separate, on which walked the angels of the justice and the mercy and the omniscience of God. This was a sort of cosmic complexity, which was supported by the dual standpoint of his morality and philosophy, but which belonged in any case to his individual temperament. It was a temperament especially English; but it is not quite fair to infer, in the usual fashion, that it was therefore merely illogical. At bottom, it was no more illogical than the three dimensions are illogical. It depended on whether he was thinking along one line; or in the flat, as in broad farce; or of the solid images of virtue.

Chaucer did not hate the world; he did not undervalue it or despise it; he only distrusted it, as a mellowed and matured old gentleman might distrust a bridge made by larky little boys. His sense of the vanity of earthly fortune and success was the recognition of a fact; not the insurgent rise of a feeling. He did not particularly dislike fate or dislike fortune, any more than he disliked the Shipman or the Wife of Bath; he was simply aware of

what they were really made of. In this unruffled and
radiant receptivity, he is rather unique among poets, and
even among great men. Perhaps it would be true to say
that he had the power of liking people whom he did not
respect; and that he extended this sentiment to the Goddess of Fortune and even to the Three Fates. His Christianity warmed and deepened whatever in this was Stoic,
nay, whatever in this was Epicurean; but it is the whole
point that his creed and culture had digested the dead
philosophies; that is, brought them to life in a living
organism. But his spiritual sanity showed itself most in
this variety of emphasis or pressure; in being able to take
at once his heathenism so lightly and his Christianity so
weightily; in treating the gods and the grim fates as trifles,
and the little relics and holy tokens as if they were larger
things.

Thus the personal humour of Chaucer is an indirect,
and perhaps distorted, derivative of the moral mood of
his age and creed. It had bad by-products and good by-
products; and Chaucer's wit was one of the best. But
they ramified back to that double root in the rationalism
and super-rationalism of the medieval moral philosophy.
In short, Geoffrey Chaucer was exactly what 'the gentle
Pardoner' was not—he was a gentle Pardoner. But we
shall misunderstand all the men of that curious and rather
complex society, if we do not realize that in a sense their
eccentricities were connected with the same centre. The
official venality of the bad Pardoner, and the very unofficial amiability of the good Pardoner, both came from
the peculiar temptations and difficult diplomacies of the
same religious system. They came because it was not, in
the Puritan sense, a simple system. It was accustomed
even in minds much more serious than Chaucer's, to seeing (so to speak) two sides of a sin; to seeing it, now as
awful and appalling merely because it was a sin; now as a

venial sin utterly and unutterably different in its ultimate direction from a mortal sin. It was out of the abuse of distinctions of that kind that the distortions and corruptions appeared, which are made vivid in the flagrant figure of the Pardoner; the practice of Indulgences which had degenerated from the theory of Indulgences. But it was out of the use of distinctions of that kind that a man like Chaucer had originally reached the sort of balanced and delicate habit of mind, the habit of looking at all sides of the same thing; the power to realize that even an evil has a right to its own place in the hierarchy of evils, to realize, at least, that in the abysmal relativities of Hell and Purgatory, there are even things more unpardonable than the Pardoner.

In any case, this attitude is directly connected with the reality of his religion. Chaucer was more unmistakably orthodox than Langland; not because Chaucer was more superficial, but because he was more fundamental. Langland was troubled about many things, though most of them were worthy things; social order and moral discipline and the economics and ethics sharply needed in his time. But Chaucer had the one thing needful; he had the frame of mind that is the ultimate result of right reason and a universal philosophy; the temper that is the flower and fruit of all the tillage and the toil of moralists and theologians. He had Charity; that is the heart and not merely the mind of our ancient Christendom; and between the black robes of Gower and the grey gown of Langland, he stands clothed in scarlet like all the household of love; and emblazoned with the Sacred Heart.

Chapter IX

THE MORAL OF THE STORY

Those strangely fanatical historians, who would darken the whole medieval landscape, have to give up Chaucer in despair; because he is obviously not despairing. His mere voice hailing us from a distance has the abruptness of a startling whistle or halloo; a blast blowing away all their artificially concocted atmosphere of gas and gloom. It is as if we opened the door of an ogre's oven, in which we were told that everybody was being roasted alive, and heard a clear, cheery but educated voice remarking that it was a fine day. It is manifestly and mortally impossible that anybody should write or think as Geoffrey Chaucer wrote and thought, in a world so narrow and insane as that which the anti-medievalists laboriously describe. They have no chance, on their own theory and argument, of answering that Chaucer was cheerful because he happened to be lucky in some ways, though unlucky in others; and certainly lived among the rich, though himself, at certain periods, decidedly poor. The whole point of Chaucer is in the fact that he does not retire with lords and ladies, like Boccaccio, to tell his tales. He is enjoying not the walled garden but the world. The world he is enjoying is just as much the world of the Ploughman and the Cook as of the Prioress and the Squire. Moreover, it is vital to the hostile contention that even emperors and princes could be crushed under superstitions that paralysed them like nightmares;

The Moral of the Story

and that to all men even the promise of heaven was only the threat of hell. And it is a stark staring fact, of everyday psychology, that a man like Chaucer could not have lived in a world like that. We are placed in a dilemma; but the horns are hardly of equal length. We know that Chaucer did live in the fourteenth century; we cannot be so certain of estimates formed in the twentieth century—or (as a matter of fact) surviving out of the nineteenth century. We know that Chaucer did live; and we are by no means so certain that the modern historians are alive.

In this chapter I would advance a certain general proposition, which I know will be called a paradox. We know the thousand things in Chaucer that converge to make it inconceivable that he should have walked about alive in a merely barbarous or bigoted or benighted epoch. We know, to mention one thing out of the thousand, the gentleness of his controversial manner; the way in which he feels confident that a light touch will tell; his assumption that his companions, gentle and simple, will understand each other. We knòw that men do not write like that, in an age when nobody could understand them. We know his bottomless bonhomie and good temper; as of one who had certainly never been tortured to exasperation by an alien world. We know his levity; the way in which he can flit from flower to flower even in the garden of heathenism; obviously without any pressing panic about the possibilities of heresy. We know his soaring hilarity and high spirits; never stronger than in his old age and comparative poverty, when he began to sing of the April day when men took the road of Kent to Canterbury. We know that this did not come out of a dark and twisted superstition or a debased social slavery; and it only remains for us to ask what it did come from.

Now I will here advance the thesis that this cheerfulness or sanity came from theology. I say deliberately, not religion, but theology. It was not *his* theology: it was the theology at the back of the philosophy at the back of his mind. So far as a general religious sentiment goes, that might indeed have given him moods of thankfulness; but it would also have given him moods of melancholy. In so far as he was romantic (and he was); in so far as he was sometimes sentimental (and he was) he would often have become that sick and smitten lover so common in medieval romances. In all that medieval province there was something of Botticelli; even something of Burne-Jones. Nothing is more typical of that time than the fact that its very real valour and virility were nevertheless covered with a veil of merely poetical sentiment, which strikes us as rather affected and lackadaisical; like the iron armour of a knight covered by some embroidered vestment with figured patterns of broken lilies or heart-broken ladies. All the literature of that time is loud with Complaints of Lovers and Confessions of Love; and there is a sense in which men like Chaucer did make of it a religion as well as a romance. For instance, we have seen that Chaucer, with very Chaucerian freshness (almost in the slang sense of impudence), calls his collection of Pagan ladies, like Dido or Cleopatra, by the title of 'Cupid's Lives of the Saints', or 'The *Acta Sanctorum* of Cupid'. Romance was a religion; certainly it was all that the modern Romantics mean by a religion. It was even rather more respectable than some of the modern developments that owe their inspiration to Byron or George Sand. It demanded very real virtues; fidelity to the death; patience even in despair; courtesy even in combat. Now if Love had really been a religion to Chaucer and Petrarch, even in the sense in which it was to some extent a religion to Keats or Rossetti, it might well have been in many cases a rather sad religion. Chaucer, however romantic, is quite sufficiently realistic to realize that Cupid can be a tyrant or that

263

The Moral of the Story

jealousy is cruel as the grave. If this sort of poetic sense of beauty is what we mean by religion (and it is what many moderns mean by religion), *that* alone would not have kept Chaucer cheerful. It was his real religion that kept him cheerful. Perhaps it will seem less paradoxical, if I point out that it is exactly parallel to the example of the greatest of Chaucer's contemporaries. You will find precisely that religion of lovers in Dante's *Vita Nuova*; and in *that*, therefore, Beatrice fades away like a fancy and leaves the poet sad. It is only when Beatrice reappears as a Theological Virtue in the *Paradiso*, that things begin to brighten up a bit. They were so paradoxical that they thought brightness came from the sky.

The real trouble of the Middle Ages lay in their rudimentary and relatively bad communications for the handing on of their good things; not in the least in their not having the good things to communicate. We are in a position to appreciate the distinction at the present moment; when we have very good communications and nothing to communicate. The comparative importance of medievalism to carry out its own plans, whether evil or good, can indeed be best tested by comparing their processes with a practical thing like a large modern newspaper; that loud and regular organ by which our civilization daily proclaims that it has nothing to say. Had it existed in the Middle Ages, it might conceivably have 'made the philosophers more popular; it would certainly have made the tyrants more tyrannical. No man in the Middle Ages was so rich that he could have sent a herald to every man's house every morning, to challenge with trumpet and tabard any other view than that which this particular rich man wished to promulgate; yet that is exactly the power now possessed by several rich men, much less dignified than any rich man in the fourteenth century. No man was rich enough to nail a proclamation

The Moral of the Story

upon every man's door at dawn, as some are now rich enough to place a newspaper upon every man's table at breakfast; in both cases to be taken as unanswerable because it is unanswered. It is amusing to speculate what would have happened if Caxton had come a century earlier and developed all the powers of a few centuries later; and that an engine like the Press had been (as of course it would have been, and indeed still is) in the hands of the governing class of the day. If the King could have made the same statement suddenly and simultaneously to all his subjects, it would doubtless have averted many revolutions founded on rumours; nor would this be the less effective because the rumours were true and the royal explanation was false. Richard the Second could probably have prevented the Peasants' Rising, if he could have posted his promise of reform and offer to be a popular leader, made in the famous speech at Blackheath, to every cottage and hovel in the whole feudal countryside. After that the promise could be broken in due course, as it was then and probably would be now; possibly through the same agency, the pressure of the plutocrats in Parliament. Similarly, if Bolingbroke had been able to send horsemen so swiftly all over England that every squire, yeoman or vassal could hear his side of the case and no other, if he could have done all that in one day on the very day when he deposed Richard the Second, there would probably have been no rising in the North, no Battle of Shrewsbury or legend of the return of Richard. It would certainly have hugely solidified the position of the usurper; and whether that would have been a good thing the reader must be left, on his own general principles, to judge. It is enough to note, as one aspect of the rudeness and delay of medieval communications, that revolutions could occur in one part of the country without the most powerful persons, in another

The Moral of the Story

part of the country, having even the power to parley with them. And if, on the other hand, something happened about which any parley was undesirable, there was then no really efficient machinery for keeping the public misinformed on the matter.

But whatever we may think about the halting of political information, there is no doubt that the halting of general information was a defect of the ruder conditions of medieval life. The information existed, and was in many matters very varied and full. Nor was it necessarily regarded as privileged information; it was never impossible for a poor man to obtain instruction in medieval England as it was impossible for a Negro to obtain it in a great part of nineteenth-century America. It was not so much that he was forbidden to get it, as that it was physically difficult to get. All books had to be laboriously transcribed by hand; the possession of a mass of such manuscripts was rare; and they were handed about cautiously, by comparison with all modern caution in the lending of books. Even a cultivated man like Chaucer, with a comfortable salary, seems frequently to get glimpses of the most important books indirectly, or even accidentally. Often he seems never to have seen the very books that we should chiefly expect him to see. After having been long regarded almost as a mere copyist of the Decameron, he is now supposed, by the most recent scholars, never to have seen the Decameron at all. But he did see one story out of the Decameron; not as it was written in Italian by Boccaccio, but as it was translated into Latin by Petrarch. It is possible that he owed even this to the accident of meeting Petrarch. Similarly, while he had certainly read Ovid and Virgil, it is thought improbable that he had ever seen a manuscript of Livy: though he invokes Livy and praises Livy and actually tells a tale out of Livy. Probably he took it from somebody who took it from

The Moral of the Story

Livy. There is any amount of this indirect, distorted and scrappy element in the culture; education by haphazard and hearsay. In this sense the opportunities of culture were limited; the communications for conveying culture were limited; the machinery for popularizing culture was limited.

But the culture was not limited. The education that was imparted, the education that was interrupted, was not limited. The books, that were borrowed or copied or translated or mistranslated, were not narrow or limited books. They were books which often conveyed, more completely than the fashionable books of any other epoch, the idea of an enlarged and enlightened philosophy of life; the consideration of both sides of a question; the balancing of one consideration against another; the conception of the whole sublunary world under the light of reason. Consider only one ordinary possibility, which in the case of Chaucer amounts to a probability. Suppose at some time some medieval man had only three medieval books. And suppose those three were first, some version of the works 'of Aristotle and his philosophy'; second, the Divine Comedy of Dante; and third, the Summa of St. Thomas Aquinas. This is not to possess books but to possess worlds. They are three universes of thoughts and things; or rather three aspects of the same universe; the one positive and rationalist; the other imaginative and pictorial; the third moral and mystical, but still inherently logical. A man might own a whole Circulating Library of modern novels and minor poets, without having anything like such a cosmic conspectus, or complete consideration of all sides of the real world. But the vital point to seize, in connexion with the particular case of Chaucer, is that the philosophy considered as a philosophy, and even the theology considered as a theology, was one which aimed at a certain equilibrium, achieved by

The Moral of the Story

giving so much weight to one thing and so much less or more to another. I know all about the harsher side of it, and especially the harsher defence of it, as it affects the humanitarians of our own time; that it believed in devils; that it defended itself by inquisitors. But that has nothing whatever to do with the present point, about the nature of the thing defended. That thing was a poised and proportioned thing; thought out and thrashed out by the comparison of many thoughts; not a single thing or a simple thing, in the sense of the isolation of one thought. And though even a man like Chaucer, through the limits of the medieval machinery, received this culture in a rather fragmentary way, he received enough of its fragments to be filled with its fulness. He was full enough of that fulness not to let his own thought be merely fragmentary; in the sense of thinking one fragment of truth as good as the whole. Still less did he think, as does the true heretic, that the fragment of truth is better than the whole.

External ecclesiasticism had indeed so far degenerated in Chaucer's day that many good and simple people then, like many good and simple people now, had begun to cry out for a simpler religion; for a simplified Christianity. They had that natural yearning, which always begins with a prayer for a single eye and always ends (with painfully exact fulfilment) in winking the other eye, in a one-eyed concentration on a single object. Modern historians often accept it, even now, as the purest form of idealism; but it always means being a man of one idea. It means very precisely fulfilling the proverbial phrase about the man 'who has not two ideas in his head'.

Now the Schoolman always had two ideas in his head; if they were only the Yes and No of his own proposition. The Schoolman was not only the schoolmaster but also the schoolboy; he examined himself; he cross-examined

The Moral of the Story

himself; he may be said to have heckled himself for hundreds of pages. Nobody can read St. Thomas's theology without hearing all the arguments against St. Thomas's theology. Therefore, even when that sort of faith produced what many would call ferocity, it always produced what I mean here by fairness; the almost involuntary intellectual fairness of one who cannot help knowing that the universe is a many-sided thing. That is precisely the temper of Chaucer; and that is what I mean when I say that he got his broad-mindedness from his theology; though it was not what is now generally meant by a broad theology. The essential point is that it was not a simple theology. As I have said, many medieval heretics, admired by modern historians, were even then beginning to cry out for a simpler theology. In the time of the Lollards, and in their particular and painful circumstances, it was often pardonable, and certainly ought more often to have been pardoned. In the time of Mr. G. M. Trevelyan, which is somewhat later in history, it is more mystifying. One would suppose that an able and cultivated man, who has lived to see the subdivision and suicide of all the sects, would have had enough of such simplifications. But in his interesting book, on the Age of Wycliffe, he makes a comparison equally suicidal. He says that his hero proposed, in the most sweepingly Protestant manner, to free the parish clergy of all control by Popes or Bishops or anybody else; until every parson should be as independent as a Presbyterian minister in Scotland. The example is somewhat unfortunate. Certainly the creed of Calvinism, which all Scottish ministers were forced to teach for two hundred years, was a simple creed. Nothing could be simpler than saying that men go to Hell because God made them on purpose to send them to Hell. But even of that childlike innocence and simplicity a good many people seem to have grown tired at

The Moral of the Story

last. Nothing could be simpler than the stark negation of the Scottish Sabbath; for nothing can be simpler than nothing. Yet even of the childlike Scottish Sabbath, it is sometimes said that the children grew a little restless towards the end of the day. Their modern descendants certainly grew as restless towards the end of the nineteenth century as ever the Lollards did towards the end of the fourteenth century. And when among *these* eighteenth-century Presbyterians there arose a Poet, that unfortunate bard was not quite so calm or so contented or so cheerful as Chaucer.

Matthew Arnold coupled Chaucer with Burns, as two fine poets who fell short of 'seriousness'. It is queer that he does not see the very contrast he suggests. Chaucer may or may not be serious, but he is not seriously in revolt against seriousness. He does not resent the Parson or the Clerk of Oxford being wholly serious. He leans back easily against the hundred books of Aristotle; like a man in his own home. Chaucer may be too much at ease in Zion. But Burns is not at all at ease in his Zion. The attitude of Burns to the local and national theology is one of revolt and nothing else. It was simply a dingy provincialism that could only narrow the mind. But for Chaucer his theology was a thing that broadened his mind. It brought him into contact with great minds like Dante and Aquinas; it linked up his country with all Europe; it even referred him backwards to the greatest sages of pagan antiquity. That is the fact that must in fairness be balanced against the slow progress and patchy incompleteness of medieval education. Chaucer, though a courtier and diplomatist, might have only one or two books; little trifles tossed off by Aristotle or Dante. Robert Burns, though a peasant and a poor man, might have a chance of buying a whole load of books of Scottish theology; a small library of Calvinistic sermons. Only he did not want to. He did

270

The Moral of the Story

not like them. He was never moved to say of them, 'On bokës for to rede I me delyte.' Poor Burns never got out of the Puritan fog for one breath of that fresh air and daylight, of quite spontaneous spiritual joy and gratitude, with which the medieval poet stretches out his hands to saints and sages as to his best benefactors and friends. In that larger enlightenment of theological theory, Chaucer could afford to be relatively cheerful and charitable even about the degradations of ecclesiastical practice. Chaucer had more tolerance for the corruptions of Catholicism than Burns had even for the decencies of Calvinism. And it is not hard to see why; because, while Chaucer's mind had been irritated or distressed by the incidental evils of a corrupted Christianity, at least his soul had not been poisoned and blackened and blasted by the monomaniac horrors of a Simple Christianity.

He had not seen all theology shrivel to a single thought; its very thunders of indignation all on one note; or the whole great Christian philosophy hardened into one harsh doctrine. It is that flat featureless inhumanity, that repetition of pattern, that absence of ornament, that made Puritanism to a man like Burns, not a castle of enchantment, not even a false enchantment, but merely a prison. It is that which gives that indescribable irrationality and violence to the cry of Burns; an irrationality that was perhaps the beginning of Romanticism. But Chaucer is never irrational; however much he may be irritated. He feels in a vast if vague fashion that he has Reason behind him; as he has Aristotle and Aquinas and a whole civilization behind him. It was in many ways a decaying civilization; it was (for the time being) even a dying civilization. But it was a dying civilization by which a man might live; and even live merrily. He did not suffer the particular kind of suffocation that comes in the *cul-de-sac* of a single idea, which is called a simple creed. He had the breadth and

271

the blessings of a complicated creed. Its corruptions, as distinct from its complications, often took the form of the most abominable abuses; because the corruption of the best is the worst. But the corruption of the worst is nothing at all; it simply ceases; it does not even continue to corrupt.

As I have already emphasized, I have very considerable sympathy with the Lollards; the particular heretics of the Chaucerian epoch. They were often infamously treated; they were sometimes intuitively right. In so far as they originally set out to reform the practical Catholicism of their day, there were few reputable Catholics then, and there are no reasonable Catholics now, who would deny that Catholicism very much needed it. In so far as they had a desire to purify Catholicism, they may often have been spiritually right even when they were intellectually wrong; and in that sense, may have been better Catholics than the Catholics. But in so far as they had a desire to *simplify* Catholicism, the Catholic Church was ten thousand times right in its desire to defeat and crush them. That notion, in its essence a very negative notion, has never wrought anything but ill to Christendom; and is always returning with a plausibility and a false simplicity to tempt and to betray Christians. Mahomet, centuries before, had tried to create a simplified Christianity, and had created a world of fatalism and stagnation. Calvin, centuries afterwards, tried to create a simplified Christianity, and created a world of pessimism and devilworship. It was of the very life of the ancient civilization, Pagan as well as Christian, from which medievalism drew its deep and strange type of strength, that it was rooted in very varied realities; that it had made a cosmos out of a chaos of experiences; that it knew what was positive and could yet allow for what was really relative; that its Christ was shared by God and Man; that its government was

The Moral of the Story

shared by God and Caesar: that its philosophers made a bridge between faith and reason, between freedom and fatalism; and that its moralists warned men alike against presumption and despair. Only by understanding all that ten times complicated sort of complication, can we see how Geoffrey Chaucer could find life so simple.

The meaning of Aquinas is that medievalism was always seeking a centre of gravity. The meaning of Chaucer is that, when found, it was always a centre of gaiety. For very many modern people, even of those who are sympathetic with, or even reverential towards, the religion that prevailed before the Reformation, quite honestly believe that it is solely a mystical ecstasy; and that sincere believers in it must be saints or nothing. In fact, it is exactly the other way round. It was Protestantism that was a mystical ecstasy; especially Protestantism in its pure form of Puritanism. It was the really good and sincere Protestants who were saints or nothing. The political period, that was actually named The Reign of the Saints, meant the Commonwealth that was The Reign of the Puritans. A frivolous Puritan was not a Puritan at all. But it is not true, in the same sense, that a frivolous Catholic is not a Catholic at all. A Catholic may be like (or indeed may actually be) a dancer whose whole business is dancing, a clown who has to be continually thinking about clowning; but may feel all the time that there is solid ground to dance on, in the sort of solid world that his soul inhabits. And this has a way of happening, especially at moments when the world is becoming much less solid, for people who are more serious. When corruption and chaos are disturbing ordinary minds, and many good men are only worried and serious, it has often happened that a great man could apparently be frivolous; and appear in history almost as a great buffoon. One of the sonnets of Mr. Maurice Baring has a haunting line about the souls of

lovers blown upon a wind: 'to rest for ever on the unresting air.' In a very different connexion, it can be said
that these rare and sane spirits did rest on the unresting
air of a revolutionary epoch or a dissolving civilization.
And there is always something about them puzzling to
those who see their frivolity from the outside and not
their faith from the inside. It is not realized that their
faith is not a stagnation but an equilibrium. If we take
three men as types; Chaucer and Thomas More and
Cervantes, we shall note that they were three Catholics
whose lives cover the whole story of the breakdown of
Catholicism; the first appearing in the earliest disturb-
ances at the end of medievalism; the second at the very
crisis of the crash; the third just after the division of
Christendom was practically complete. And our first impression will be that they were all three of them humorists,
who took things very easily, considering the dreadful days
of destruction and transition in which they lived. The
only legend left by Sir Thomas More was that he actually
died laughing. It is quite true that he died joking, though
there was already the beginnings of the Puritan stiffness
that would not unbend to jokes; just as his fellow-martyr
Kimball died smoking, in spite of the fury which faddists
like James the First were to fulminate against tobacco.
There is something almost irresponsible in the intellectual
ease with which Cervantes feels himself free to chaff
chivalry out of existence; when so many greater things,
that went with it, had largely ceased to exist. The greatest
of all satires on mere medievalism came out of the man
and the country most full of what is called the medieval
creed. But Catholicism is not medievalism. It is only
something that could make medievalism tolerable to a
man like Chaucer; just as it could make something more
like modernism tolerable to men of the Renaissance like
More and Cervantes. The whole story will make no sense,

unless we realize that the Catholic philosophy can content a man; rather specially if the man is a philosopher; and not least if he is a laughing philosopher.

In this sense we are quite ready to admit that Chaucer was only a lucky and lonely elf, who found a sunbeam and danced in it. But sunbeams only come from the sun, and the sun is the centre of a solar system. At any rate, his sun was the centre of his solar system. If we are to understand it, we must go back to a very ancient sunrise; nay, to many repeated sunsets. It is *not* true that his daylight spirit belongs only to the day that had not yet dawned; the day of the Renaissance. If we want to trace that light, we must trace it backward through the ages; and, by way of a beginning, as was here recorded at the start, we must go back to Boethius. It does not matter for the moment whether we call that culture Catholicism or the continuity of an ancient Humanism. We must go back to that 'long evening by the Mediterranean', as it has been finely called, when all that was best in a Christian Empire, in the person of Boethius, remembered the Stoics and defied a tyrant and died. There were not two men who died, a Christian and a Stoic; but one man who was already both. That is the heritage that had been handed down to Christian men; and it was not lopsided or bigoted. Why did Alfred throw himself at once upon the translation of Boethius? There were any number of dreary hagiographical legends for him to translate. Why did St. Thomas, at the very top of the Middle Ages, think also of Boethius? Why did he resist the short-sighted panic that condemned Aristotle? Because against a thousand wild and wanton accidents, in the confusion following on the barbarian invasions and the failure of the Roman scheme, the spirit of all that society was making for a balance; a balance like that of the two eyes of a man; or that which gives two scales even to Justice blind. It was holding hard on to civilization and an equal law, and that hold did not fail, even when the civilization failed.

The ancient central civilization from which the Lollards and Lutherans and later Puritans broke away was, or looked like, a dying civilization. So the central civilization from which Mahomet and the Moslems broke away was, or looked like, a dying civilization. Byzantium appeared in the eyes of Mahomet, as Babylon in the visions of Petrarch, as a thing stiff with gold but stiff also with fossilization; a thing visibly sinking under the weight of its own wickedness and wealth. It is not specially surprising that many in the Dark Ages preferred Bagdad to Byzantium, and even called it the superiority of Islam to Christendom. But it has not in the long run meant the superiority of Asia to Europe; or even the absorption of Christendom by the advance of Islam. Similarly, the setting up of sects in the sixteenth and seventeenth centuries has not meant in the long run the absorption of Catholicism by the advance of Puritanism. What Mahomet and Calvin and all those thus breaking away from the dying civilization did not realize, is the curious fact that it is a dying civilization that never dies. It does decline, and has done so any number of times; it does decay; it is always at it. But it does not disappear; and, at the end of more or less debased periods, has a way of managing to reappear, when its enemies have in their turn decayed. The moral is, I will venture to think, that it is unwise to desert this perpetually sinking ship, or betray this everlastingly dying creed and culture. It has had another period of final extinction; even since its final extinction at the end of the Middle Ages. It has suffered eclipse in the Enlightenment of the Age of Reason and Revolution; which in their turn begin to look as if they had seen better days. And to-day it stands erect and resurrected; and to right and left of it the Moslems have stagnated

The Moral of the Story

and the Puritans starved; starved not only for the art and symbolism normal to men, but now for the faith and conviction once special to themselves. No; it was not wise to leave it, even for the Republic; it will not be wise to leave it, even for the Soviet.

The moral is that no man should desert that civilization. It can cure itself; but those who leave it cannot cure it. Not Nestorius nor Mahomet nor Calvin nor Lenin have cured, nor will cure, the real evils of Christendom; for the severed hand does not heal the whole body. Those outside the body will endure only centuries of separation and then death. Where are the Nestorians? Meanwhile, within the body of the Christian world, there was a perpetual and centripetal tendency towards the discovery of a just balance of all these ideas. All those who broke away were centrifugal and not centripetal; they went away into deserts to develop a solitary doctrine. But medieval philosophy and culture, with all the crimes and errors of its exponents, was always *seeking* equilibrium. It can be seen in every line of its rhythmic and balanced art; in every sentence of its carefully qualified and self-questioning philosophy. It was everywhere in the air, though it affected various people in various degrees now impossible to distinguish. But it was everywhere a movement towards civilization; towards the centre of ideas; whatever might be the wild decentralization of events. And, while there are many proofs of this, there could be no more full or unanswerable proof than the shout that showed that normality had been found. For a great voice was given by God, and a great volume of singing, not to his saints who deserved it much better; not to any of those heroes who had made that clearing in the ancient forest; but only suddenly, and for a season, to the most human of human beings.

277

other people think merely sportive; and they must be
made the rites of a religion of patriotism. With this went
all the kindred things: the pride in evading emotion; the
contented confession of a certain ignorance of music or
foreign refinements; the hazy identification of the vices of
industrialism with the virtue of industry. This Englishman did exist; at any rate he did try to exist. And there
is a sense in which the ideal is more important than the
real. The real is only useful to realistic novelists. It is
the ideal, or in a better language the god, who really
leads the masses of men and turns the corners of history.

When we have firmly and clearly modelled the image
of what the whole modern world has meant by an Englishman, we must instantly and utterly destroy it. When
we have once vividly understood what was really meant
by the national ideal in the nineteenth century, we must
utterly sweep it away from the whole field of the fourteenth century. Nothing whatever resembling that conscious ideal of common sense, or cold virility, existed for
Chaucer and his contemporary countrymen. Indeed, so
far as there was a general atmosphere and attitude, it was
all the other way. If the Victorians could have actually
had a vision of Chaucerian England, they would have
thought the Englishman was a Frenchman. All the jokes
against the Frenchman would be jokes against the fourteenth-century Englishman. All the emotions and expressions of emotions were there, especially those considered most un-English. If Jules and Jacques kissed
each other, it would seem altogether absurd to Thackeray.
If Palamon and Arcite kissed each other, it would not
seem in the least absurd to Chaucer. That men should on
occasion weep, and even weep in public, seemed no more
unnatural to the writers of the older England than it did
to the writers of the Old Testament or the Iliad. But the
contrast is even plainer in the gesture of joy than the

INDEX

279

Index

Index

Index

Index

Index

Index

Index